Advance Praise for *T*

"A murder mystery wrapped like a de ial love story. *The End of Her* is the story of a journalist attempting to solve the long-ago puzzle of who shot his great-grandmother in her bed in small-town Winnipeg in 1913. But the why of it is at the heart of this beautiful book. Wayne Hoffman throws himself into this old-fashioned shoe-leather reporting (a true education for budding journalists) because he wants to give his mother the gift of her history before he loses her completely to dementia. The book's portrayal of Alzheimer's is horrible and hilarious; Wayne's voice is warm, deeply loving, drily funny, and thankfully unsentimental."
    —Marjorie Ingall, author of *Mamaleh Knows Best*

"This is one of those rare, fine books that gives you two of the dearest gifts in literature: a story so consuming you forget time, and an author with the gift to spin, from these supposedly ordinary lives, a profound chronicle of identity, family, memory, and love—and suspense, too."
    —Boris Fishman, author of *Savage Feast*

"Wayne Hoffman has produced a fascinating and compelling story of his family history. Meticulously researched and skillfully written, he brilliantly weaves together the mystery of his great-grandmother's murder long ago in Winnipeg, his nearly decade-long search to find the truth about this tragic event, and his joyous and poignant relationship with his ailing mother that inspires him and propels his quest. In particular, his recreation of Winnipeg's impoverished immigrant quarter during the first decades of the twentieth century and the various complexities that shaped the lives of his great-grandparents and relatives is an absorbing tale rich with detail and vivid personalities."
    —Allan Levine, Winnipeg historian and author of *Seeking the Fabled City: The Canadian Jewish Experience*

THE END OF HER

WAYNE HOFFMAN

THE END OF HER

RACING AGAINST ALZHEIMER'S TO SOLVE A MURDER

Heliotrope Books

NEW YORK

Other Books by Wayne Hoffman

Hard: A Novel
Sweet Like Sugar
An Older Man

Heliotrope Books LLC
heliotropebooks@gmail.com

ISBN 978-1-942762-90-4
ISBN 978-1-942762-91-1 eBook

Cover design by Alexandre Venancio
Typeset by Naomi Rosenblatt

For my mother
and her mother
and her mother

SARAH

my great-grandmother

ETHEL

my grandmother

SUSAN

my mother

WAYNE

CONTENTS

PART 3

PART 4

PART 5

PROLOGUE: THE FAVORITE

I was always my mother's favorite.

When we were growing up in suburban Maryland, my brother and sister used to complain any time they felt that I, the baby of the family, was getting special treatment. My mother would only feebly deny it; I was her *zisa* boy, as she called me in Yiddish—her sweet boy. And I embraced my role: "Of course I'm her favorite," I'd boast, "because I'm the best."

My ranking solidified further after my siblings left for college. My mother and I never fought, rarely even had a cross moment, during what are usually a teenager's "difficult years." She'd spent so long stressing about my brother and sister, she'd joke, that by the time she got to me, she had "given up" and become a more mellow parent. True enough, I'd think—but then again, I'd never done anything to cause her stress.

That changed during my senior year of high school in 1987.

During my last semester, I missed my curfew for the first and last time, and she was furious. I had a good explanation: I was taking my first, tentative, awkward steps into a season of sexual experimentation with Heather, one of my best friends. But I didn't dare tell my mother. I apologized for being late, but didn't explain why. I suspect that—missed curfew aside—she was mad because she knew I was hiding something.

I was hiding more than she guessed.

I had started coming out to my friends the previous year, one by one, and as my senior year started to wind down, I came out to

13

the rest of them—including Heather. But I kept being gay a secret from my parents. That spring, I withdrew every evening into my bedroom, where I could make long phone calls to my friends and talk in private about what I was going through.

As a graduation present to myself, I placed a personal ad in an alternative weekly newspaper, and met a guy named Larry, an undergrad from Louisiana—blond, Catholic, with a soft New Orleans accent—who was spending the summer working in Washington. I had my first date with him, and my first kiss—once he showed me how to do it properly. Larry was the first person I told, "I love you." While I didn't tell my parents any of the intimate details, I didn't hide him completely. I told them I was spending time with someone named Larry, but said that he was a friend from the Jewish Community Center, where I was working at a day camp for the summer.

Of course, I couldn't tell them when I had sex for the first time, with Larry, a couple of weeks later. When I subsequently had a full-blown panic attack about AIDS—this was 1987, a scary time for a gay man to be having sex for the first time—and took Larry to a clinic to be tested for HIV, we had to wait a full two weeks for his results.

During those two weeks, I started to feel the weight of everything I'd been through in the span of a few months. I'd changed my appearance: I had a nose job over spring break, got rid of my glasses, and started growing out my (surprisingly curly) hair. I'd graduated high school, learned to drive, come out to my friends, met my first boyfriend, fallen in love, and had sex for the first time. The coming months would bring more turmoil, as I got ready to move hundreds of miles away for college, leaving my friends behind. And now, while I waited for Larry's test results, I was forced to face the grim reality I thought awaited me as a gay man, based on what I had read about AIDS in the newspapers and seen on television: that I'd probably die long before I reached thirty.

Of course, I couldn't explain to my parents why I was so anxious and edgy as I awaited the results of Larry's HIV test, but I was acting strangely; my mother surmised it had something to do with my new friend. "I don't want you seeing this Larry character anymore," she said. "We haven't even met him." I protested, something I'd rarely done, and told her I'd see anyone I wanted to see. My mother started to cry.

"Stop upsetting your mother," my father interjected. At which point, I said three words to my father I wish I could take back more than any three I've ever uttered: "Go fuck yourself."

This was not the behavior my mother had come to expect from her "favorite child."

The rest of that night involved a lot of screaming and crying and slamming doors. Still, what followed was worse: weeks of awkward silences and cold stares. My mother didn't know what was turning her normally upbeat and compliant *zisa* boy into this angry adolescent, and I wasn't ready to tell her the truth. I was too busy worrying about my own future and my health—even after Larry tested negative—to think about her. But my mother was clearly alarmed by me. Once, she was so rattled that she forgot where she parked the car at the mall and had to call a friend to pick her up. She waited outside on a bench in tears.

After I left for college that fall, our time apart helped to heal the relationship. I was five hundred miles away at Tufts outside Boston, growing my curls even longer, playing my music too loud, and wearing clothes she wouldn't have liked. ("You're wearing shoes off a dead person," she once quipped about a pair of old shoes I'd bought at a thrift shop.)

I was also busy coming out. By the end of my first year at school, I had become an activist, speaking about gay life in classes, helping to run the campus gay group, and peer counseling. I also had a second boyfriend, and a third, briefly, and got more educated about AIDS and safer sex.

I came home for the summer of 1988 to work at the JCC again. On my way out the door to the annual orientation session, my mother stopped me. "If you're trying to make an announcement, camp isn't the place to make it," she said.

"What are you talking about?" I asked.

She pointed at the silver ear cuff on my right ear, which I'd been wearing since I left home. "You are trying to make an announcement, aren't you?" Apparently she knew the saying, "Left is right and right is wrong"—an earring in your right ear means you're gay.

"I do have an announcement to make," I told her as I walked quickly out the door, "but this isn't how I make it."

When I got home that evening, she had already told my father that I was gay. He stayed upstairs in their bedroom while my mother and I had "the talk" downstairs. She had figured out that I was gay when I'd come home that spring for Passover with the cuff on my right ear. "This doesn't change anything," she told me. "And you can believe me because I've already known for months, and you didn't realize it."

She cried. Not because I was gay per se, but because she was scared about AIDS, and anti-gay violence.

"So am I," I said.

"And I'm sad," she said, "because I'll never look around the Seder table and see all my grandchildren."

"I could still have children," I told her. She was not ready to hear this.

She asked me not to "tell everyone" yet. I told her I was already out on campus, had been leading classes and writing about gay issues for the school newspaper, and had already appeared on a local television talk show in Boston. She was not ready to hear this, either.

Nevertheless, the summer of 1988 went more smoothly than the previous one, and by the end of it, we could talk about gay life a little bit—mostly broader, less personal things like politics and movies. The week before I went back to school, the *Washington Post* ran a particularly homophobic op-ed piece by conservative columnist James J. Kilpatrick, and I typed up a response. I left the letter on my parents' bed before I took the train back to Boston, with a note telling them to mail it to the editor if they were ready.

I didn't have a problem coming out in print, but my parents' friends didn't know about me yet, and I wasn't sure this was how they wanted to make that kind of announcement for themselves; this would surely qualify as "telling everyone." When I got back to my dorm, I called to tell my mother I'd arrived safely, and she told me she'd read the letter and decided not to send it. "I'm not ready yet," she said. "But I will be."

By the summer of 1989, she was much more comfortable having a gay son. I started dating Mark. He was blond, Catholic, and had a hint of a Southern accent. He also had a sense of humor "so dry it could blow away," according to his (accurate) newspaper personal ad, which I'd answered. He lived on Capitol Hill, but we spent most weekends at my family's house in the suburbs. I took that fall semester off from school to stay longer in Maryland and intern with what was then called the Human Rights Campaign Fund, the largest gay political organization in America.

It was my mother's idea.

Dancing with my mother at my brother's wedding in the summer of 1989

PART I

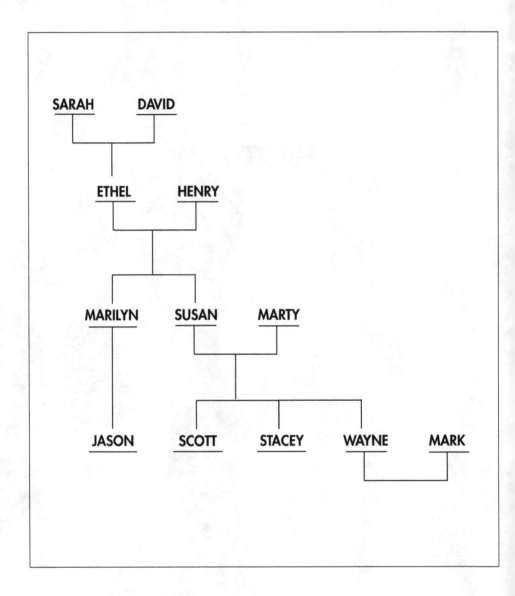

1: I CALL BULLSHIT

My mother's decline started with a laugh.

On Fourth of July weekend in 2009, I had just put a platter of lemon-pepper chicken on the dining room table. Out of deference to my observant parents—and my brother, who's a rabbi—I had bought kosher meat. On a religious level, the difference between kosher and non-kosher poultry is a matter of how the bird is slaughtered and prepared. But on a practical level, the difference is that kosher chicken costs twice as much, tastes twice as delicious, and is twice as big.

"One time, your aunt Marilyn had some kosher chicken thawing in the kitchen," my mother began, launching into a story I'd heard years before. "She had a plumber working on the sink, and while she was in the next room, she heard him say, 'I've never seen such gigantic breasts!' She was flattered—you know, it's not like either of us has what anyone would call gigantic breasts. So she called into the kitchen, 'Thank you!' And then she realized he was talking about the chicken on the counter."

Everyone laughed. Mark and I, who were hosting at our weekend house in the Catskills, had seats at the heads of our long, rectangular table while everyone else—my parents, my brother the rabbi, and his three sons—sat on the sides. What made us laugh wasn't just the story itself, or even the surprise of hearing a grandmother talking about gigantic breasts in front of her adolescent grandsons. My mother knew how to deliver a punch line, stressing the right words, getting to the laugh quickly, using exaggerated facial expressions and gestures—in this case, mimicking my aunt looking down in disbelief at her modest cleavage.

I kept bringing food out of the kitchen—crusty bread from the local bakery, corn on the cob, a salad filled with vegetables from the farmers market. And as my mother picked up the platter of chicken to pass it around, she launched into another story.

"One time, your Aunt Marilyn had some kosher chicken thawing in the kitchen," she began. "She had a plumber working on the sink—"

One of my nephews interrupted her. "Grandma, you already told that story."

My mother stopped. "I did? When?"

"About thirty seconds ago."

She looked around to make sure we weren't teasing her, and then, when it was clear we weren't, she fell conspicuously silent. Nobody commented as the conversation shifted gears and moved on to other subjects; my family is good at filling in the silence. But the look on my mother's face—embarrassed and confused—troubled me through the rest of the meal.

After dinner, when my parents were sitting on our wraparound porch, I talked about it in the kitchen with Mark, who'd been an admiring member of her audience for twenty years.

"She's forgotten things before," I said.

"This seems different," he said. And I had to agree.

That evening, after my mother went to bed, I talked to my father alone. "Has anything like this happened before?" I asked.

"She's had a few 'senior moments,'" he said—misplacing her glasses, or forgetting the name of a movie she'd seen. Normally in those instances, he said, there was an "of course" to follow, when her memory would recover after a momentary lapse: "*Of course* this is where I left my glasses! Now I remember." Not this time.

Mom was sixty-nine.

When my parents took the bus home to Maryland, they talked about what had happened. My mother was anxious about what might be wrong, while my father was calmer and more focused on finding out the facts before jumping to any conclusions—these were their typical roles in most situations. (I inherited a little of my mother's free-floating anxiety, but most often adopted my father's level-headed, wait-and-see approach.)

A few weeks later, my mother went to see a neurologist, who diagnosed her with "mild cognitive impairment." Although he couldn't give her a definitive prognosis, the doctor told her that there was nothing to worry about at this point: It was unclear if her memory lapses would continue, or get worse. He'd keep an eye on her and see how things went.

Throughout my life, my mother's memories tended to be keen and detailed—particularly memories from her youth. Each detail came with a story, usually a funny one. Because if there's one thing everyone who met my mother could agree on, it was this: Susan Hoffman knew how to tell a story. She had a greatest-hits list of funny tales, most of which revolved around money (or the lack of it), food, and her mother.

When my brother, sister, and I were growing up, she would entertain us by reminiscing about her childhood in Jersey City. In the narrow brownstone, two windows wide, where she grew up on York Street—her paternal grandparents owned it, and lived upstairs— not only did she not have her own bedroom, she didn't even have a proper bed. Susan and her little sister slept in the front room. Marilyn slept in a crib—until she was six years old. "But at least she had a crib," my mother would tell us, knowing that the person who had it toughest always got the biggest laugh. "I slept on a cot, and every morning my mother would fold it up and put it away in the closet. If anybody ever came to visit, they'd never even know that a little girl named Susan lived there."

These hard-luck stories were always the funniest.

"In the summer, my mother would send me to the movies with Marilyn," she'd start. "We'd see a double-feature, with a newsreel and cartoons—it was a whole-day affair. And my mother would give us a nickel to buy candy."

"A nickel?" we'd ask, incredulous.

"Back then, for a nickel, you could get a Milky Way that was so big, it took two of us to carry it," she'd say, holding her hands three feet apart.

But it wasn't as much fun as it sounded. (It never was.) Their mother Ethel had filled them with fear about diseases lurking around every corner, so they were forbidden to drink from the water fountain ("trench mouth," my mother would say, imitating Ethel's finger-wagging warning), sit on the toilet ("polio"), or even put their heads back on their seats ("ringworm"), so they'd come home from a supposedly relaxing day at the movies dehydrated, with neck cramps, and bathroom anxieties that would last a lifetime.

My mother's childhood stories were told with great skill and a knack for getting right to the funny part. But one tale wasn't so funny. It was the strangest set piece in her repertoire.

"When I was growing up in Jersey City," she'd begin, "I found a photograph in my parents' drawer." At just seven or eight years old, she recognized the man in the black-and-white picture—unsmiling, seated in a chair, with a trim mustache and neatly parted hair, wearing a stiff-collared shirt under a jacket and tie—as her maternal grandfather, whom she called Zayde Dovid, the Yiddish version of Grandpa David. She had met him once on a family trip to Winnipeg, the Canadian city where Ethel had grown up. But the woman next to him in the picture—also stern-faced, but tall and narrow-waisted with her hair swept upward, standing straight with one elbow resting on the back of the man's chair—didn't look familiar.

"Who's this woman with Zayde Dovid?" my mother asked.

"That's my mother," came Ethel's reply.

"No, it's not," said my mother, who had met Bubbe Bayla—Yiddish for Grandma Bella—on that same trip to Winnipeg. "Bubbe Bayla is short and fat."

"Bubbe Bayla isn't really my mother; she's my stepmother," Ethel replied. "This was my mother." She turned the photo over, and on the back, in pencil, was written a name my mother had never heard before: Sarah Brooks.

My mother, surprised to learn that her grandmother wasn't her grandmother after all, asked what had happened to Sarah Brooks. This is what her mother told her: "One winter morning when I was very young, my mother was nursing her new baby—your aunt Anne—on our front porch in Winnipeg, when a sniper drove by and shot her dead."

Ethel continued to briefly explain the rest of her family history: David, now a widower with four young children, went on to marry Bella—herself a widow with one child—and together they had three more children. While Sarah was Ethel's biological mother, Bella had been the only mother she had known for most of her life.

It had long irked my mother that she had been given the Hebrew name Shifra, a lowly handmaiden from the Torah—especially when her little sister Marilyn got the Hebrew name Malka, meaning queen—but now she learned the reason: Shifra had been Sarah's Hebrew name, and in keeping with the Ashkenazi Jewish tradition of naming children after deceased relatives—choosing the identical Hebrew name and, most often, an English name beginning with the same letter—my mother Susan had been named after Sarah, whose Hebrew name had also been Shifra.

Ethel wasn't the kind of person who took kindly to being interrogated, so my mother—who was never one to talk back to authority figures anyway—simply accepted this story as fact. Marilyn heard the same story as a child, and despite being the sibling more likely to ask questions or rebel in any way, she, too, took it as truth.

The story became one of my mother's favorites. She told it to my brother, my sister, and me many times as we were growing up.

I inherited many things from my mother: her sweet tooth, a (probably not unrelated) lifelong struggle with my weight, the webbed toes that she'd gotten from her father. But most importantly, from a young age, I wanted to be a storyteller just like her. I loved the way she could hold people's interest, create memorable characters, and above all, make people laugh. My father called her "the funniest broad I ever met."

My mother was so adept at telling stories that people didn't usually complain when she told stories they'd heard before. Quite the opposite. People—not just her own family, but pretty much anyone who'd met her more than once—would specifically ask her to "tell the story about..." again. If you're skillful enough at delivering the goods, I learned, people will want to hear your stories again and again, the way they listen to their favorite records or watch old movies or repeats of classic sitcoms.

When I was little, I didn't have much life experience to draw upon, so I simply fabricated stories. (At the time, this was known as lying; now I refer to it as writing fiction.) After I wet my pants in nursery school one day, I told my mother with utter conviction an elaborate tale about how a different boy, named Avignon, had done it—when an innocent game of "I'll-show-you-mine" ended with him peeing down my leg. (She didn't believe this, of course, but I like to think she was impressed at my creativity.)

A few years later, I had become a geography buff, taking atlases and even a globe to bed to study them every night. My knowledge of maps was so exhaustive and my manner so authoritative that when I told one of my mother's friends in synagogue a made-up tale about the Purple Sea off the coast of Japan, I had her so thoroughly convinced it was real that she had to go home and check her encyclopedia.

By the time I was a teenager, I had some real-life experience to draw upon. I learned how to turn "what happened today" into concise nuggets with punch lines to deliver at the dinner table, which was where I essentially workshopped my material.

A few of my stories included my mother as a character, which she never objected to.

My mother, my sister, and I all share a craving for chocolate. (My father and brother do not share this trait.) Knowing that we could not be trusted with bags of chocolate bars in the house before Halloween, my mother usually bought things for trick-or-treaters that none of us liked: Almond Joys (only my father liked coconut, and he had will power), candy corn, or other sweets we could easily pass up. But one fall, as my sister and I sat in the family room watching television, my mother walked past us into the laundry room—without any laundry—and closed the door behind her. We heard wrappers tearing, and loud moans of satisfaction: "Mmmmm! Mmmmmmm! Mmmmmmmmmm!" We opened the door and caught my mother in the act: She had stashed a bag of miniature Milky Ways in the cabinet with the detergent.

"But how did you catch me?" she asked.

"Well, you didn't have any laundry," I said. "And then you closed the door behind you and started making all those 'yummy' noises." She shared the candy, and got better at hiding such things in the future; when she'd visit her mother, she hid bite-size Milky Ways in her box of tampons, where Ethel—who would surely criticize her for eating junk food—never looked.

Eventually, I'd turn storytelling into a career—as a journalist and later as a novelist. But for me the real joy of telling stories remains more intimate: I get pleasure by bringing a group of people together, and entertaining them. That's the most important thing I inherited from my mother.

During Passover in 2010—the first family gathering after that fateful Fourth of July in the Catskills when we feared my mother's memory was starting to fail—I drove to Maryland a day before the rest of the family arrived, armed with a miniature video camera so I could record her tracing her family tree and telling stories before her memory deteriorated further.

She was already getting somewhat reticent to launch into impromptu stories, worried that she'd get lost in the retelling. Instead, she let me steer the conversation, asking basic factual questions about her family history.

She first got confused just thirty seconds into the video, trying to remember the year her sister Marilyn got married to my uncle Hal.

"They got married in...um...I was married already," she said, struggling to remember. "I would say '70, maybe 1970."

I didn't know the right answer, but I knew this was the wrong answer, because I knew how old my cousin Jason was.

"No, she must have married Hal earlier than that," I said, "because Jason was born in 1968."

"Okay," she said, trying hard to concentrate for several seconds, reasoning out the answer aloud. "Um...Jason is forty-one. I would say...forty-four years..."

"So around 1966?"

And then the light bulb went off—the "of course" moment when the right answer suddenly appeared. She sat upright, and her forehead unfurrowed.

"Oh, I'll tell you when," she said, happy to get the date right with certainty. "I was very pregnant with Scott, so it was '64."

It took her some time to arrive at several other answers. But with prompting from me behind the camera and my father calling out from off-screen, she told stories about her childhood, and her relatives.

The camera captured not only her memories but also her emergent mental struggles: gaps in her narratives, key details and punch lines missing from familiar tales, and a few moments of true forgetfulness when she'd stare into the camera with total blankness. She was already becoming unsure about facts she had once known by rote: which synagogue she attended as a child, or her cousins' names.

I asked what she was told about her mother's mother, Sarah. "My mother's parents are Sarah Brooks and Dovid Fainstein," she began—one Shifra talking about the other—as we started going through the maternal side of her family tree. She was already shaky about the birth order of her mother's siblings. But she remembered "the drive-by shooting" when "a truck went whizzing by" and shot Sarah, even if she wasn't sure anymore whether it was her father or her mother who first told her about it. "Sometimes the story changes just a little bit," she said, meaning that the exact details she'd heard sometimes changed over the years. Maybe "she was sitting by the window, not necessarily on the porch," for instance. But the basic plot was always the same: Sarah Brooks with a baby at her breast, shot by a drive-by sniper.

The story about the Winnipeg sniper was a fixture, typically hauled out by my mother at family gatherings. I never truly believed it when I was growing up; there's simply too much about it that's plainly impossible. But just as my mother never directly confronted me about how Avignon could possibly have peed in my pants in nursery school, I had never openly confronted her with my doubts about the Winnipeg story, even though I suspected she had doubts about the details, too.

My goal in making the video in 2010 wasn't to question her, but to listen while I still could. Nonetheless, I could barely contain my good-humored skepticism as I prodded my mother to tell this tale of "this drive-by shooting in Winnipeg that somehow the family believes happened." And my giddiness rubbed off on my mother: She smirked as she told the story on camera. But neither of us ever said flat-out that this legend was a lie. This was the story my mother grew up with, and she was sticking with it no matter how unlikely it sounded. ("Why would someone make up such an awful story?" she'd ask.)

My mother didn't have a great deal of time to sit and reminisce after we made the video. She still had to prepare for the Passover Seder. I ran the service around the table, but she had to make the dinner for more than twenty people—matzo ball soup, brisket and a turkey (and a spare turkey because my mother was always needlessly worried there wouldn't be enough food), stuffing and mashed potatoes and sweet potatoes—and wrap presents for all the kids.

The Seder went off without a hitch, as it always did.

The night after the Seder, Susan and Marilyn were sitting on the living room couch, going through a plastic shopping bag filled with old photos. These had been their mother's photos, which she'd never properly labeled or put in an album. After Ethel died in 1983, they ended up in the back of my parents' linen closet, largely unexamined and in no particular order. Eventually my mother and my aunt came across the photo of Zayde Dovid and Sarah Brooks, a sepia-toned four-by-six-inch print mounted in a cardboard frame.

As they looked at the photograph—the same one my mother had found more than sixty years earlier, the only photo of the two of them in existence—they started to tell the story again. Passover is a holiday that specifically instructs us to tell stories about the ancient Israelites' exodus from Egypt again and again, so that the future generations of listeners will make them part of their own histories; at our Seders, we also shared stories about our childhoods, our families, and Passovers past, so that these, too, would become part of a history shared by everyone around the table.

I'd held my tongue, more or less, while I made the video a couple days earlier, but now I stopped my mother and Aunt Marilyn in the middle of the story.

"I call bullshit," I said. "You know this story isn't true, right?"

Their eyes opened wide. Not, I think, because they truly believed it. But because nobody had ever dared to question its veracity.

"It doesn't make any sense," I said. "First of all, who breastfeeds outside in the middle of winter—in Winnipeg? Second of all, back in—what was this, the nineteen-teens?—how many cars were there in Winnipeg? A dozen? And why on earth would a drive-by sniper, if there even was such a thing back then, shoot a nursing mother in broad daylight? And how could he have good enough aim with an old shotgun to kill her but leave the baby at her breast unharmed, all while making a getaway in a Model T?"

"But that's the story we were told," my mother said. "Why would we question it?"

"Because it's so obviously not true," I said.

My mother let this sink in. I wasn't just teasing anymore. I was calling her bluff.

"But if it isn't true," she said, "then what really happened?"

Now she was calling mine: Okay, smarty-pants, you tell the story.

I was silent for a moment. Even though I'd suspected since I was a child that this story was a fabrication, I'd never taken the time to think of what the true story might be. I believed that my grandma Ethel's mother had died when Ethel was a little girl, and that her father had remarried. But murder? My mother's question—"Why would someone make up such an awful story?"—played in my mind. I didn't have an answer.

But I also had a measure of confidence that after twenty years as a journalist, I could get one. I thought to myself, how hard could it be? I told my mother that I'd try to find out the truth about Sarah Brooks—to solve this mystery that had hung over the family for nearly a century.

2: GETTING LOST

For years, the first words out of my mouth every morning were "Hi, Ma." A lot of people call their mothers out of a sense of obligation or duty; I did it because I genuinely loved talking to my mother. I looked forward to our talks every day. I'd call her on my cell phone as I walked to work across Greenwich Village. She'd either be in the kitchen, having her morning coffee, or at the desk in the upstairs office that had once been my brother's bedroom. That's where she typed reports and correspondence for my father, an intellectual property attorney who ran a small law firm, on the increasingly frequent days when he worked from home.

Our morning phone calls didn't change much during the first year after her diagnosis: I'd tell her about what was happening at my job, or what movies and plays I'd seen in New York, and she'd catch me up on what was happening at home, or with my brother and sister, and we'd usually talk about the news—the latest outrage we shared over Republicans, most often. (Faced with the havoc the party was wreaking on the country, she'd conclude our political discussions the same half-joking, half-maudlin way: "I'm glad I'm old," meaning, I'm glad I won't be around when our economy/environment/democracy falls apart.) The rest of her daily routine was similarly unchanged. She still met friends for lunch, went to synagogue on Friday night, watched *The Good Wife*, read the *Washington Post* in the morning, cooked dinner every night,

and bought herself new outfits at Chico's or—if there was a sale—
Lord and Taylor.

Our daily phone calls gave me a regular window into how her
"mild cognitive impairment" was progressing. Her memory faltered
more often, I noticed, but not in any way that would indicate something other than "normal" aging-related forgetfulness. Details that
were once immediately certain now took a moment to recall. It was
her short-term memory that went first.

"Your father and I went to the movies last night," she said.

"What did you see?" I asked.

She paused. "I don't remember."

Maybe, I thought, she just doesn't remember the title. "Do you
remember what it was about?"

"No."

"Well...did you like it?"

"Oh, yes, it was good," she said. "That, I remember."

Or she'd tell me about a book she was reading: "I put it down
for a couple of days, and I had to start over, because I forgot what
happened."

Once or twice, she told me—with a laugh—that she had a funny experience when she went shopping: "When I came outside, I
couldn't remember where I parked the car."

I made mental notes about all these things, but never made a big
deal of them—to her or to myself.

Her neurologist started her on Namenda, which was meant to
slow the progress of the memory loss, but not stop or reverse it. A
few months later, he added Aricept, which was supposed to aug-
ment the Namenda, but the new drug made her congested and
sometimes violently nauseated—it had a negative interaction with
the Prozac she had taken for more than twenty-five years to fight
depression—and she had to stop taking it after a couple of months.

Soon after she stopped taking Aricept, her physical health
seemed to rebound. When my parents came to the Catskills for
the Fourth of July in 2010, my mother was in good spirits: She
remembered our next-door neighbors, whom she'd met on previous
visits. A lifelong animal lover, she spent a long time playing with
Pearl, our friend David's Bedlington terrier. She was talkative and
funny, and still knew how to dominate a conversation with her
stories. People who'd met her before didn't notice any difference,

and people who met her for the first time didn't realize anything was amiss.

Don and Doris Herman also stayed with us that weekend; Don and my father had been fraternity brothers in college, and my mother and Doris had been best friends for fifty years. They lived near my parents in suburban Maryland, and my mother and Doris were each other's confidants, talking on the phone in the afternoons and meeting frequently for lunch. ("It always felt more like family," Doris told me recently. "She's like a sister to me.") Over that Fourth of July weekend, we all went to see the New York Philharmonic at the new outdoor amphitheater at Bethel Woods, the site of the legendary Woodstock music festival. We searched for the hotel where, more than fifty years earlier, Don had worked as a waiter one summer just up the road from our house. We sang old show tunes, mostly Rodgers and Hammerstein, while Mark played the piano in our foyer. *Oklahoma. Carousel.* My mother still remembered all the words.

I drove my parents half an hour down the highway to the Nevele, the recently closed Borscht Belt resort where they had honeymooned back in 1962. A security guard in a golf cart wouldn't let us past the front gate, but being there for the first time since they were married brought back plenty of memories for my parents, about both their wedding at the Essex House in Newark, and the few days afterward they'd spent at the Nevele. This time, however, my father—who'd spent decades playing Ed McMahon to my mother's Johnny Carson, always by her side but rarely getting the chance to speak when she was "on" ("Nobody knows what his voice sounds like," my mother would tease, "because nobody's ever heard him talk")—sometimes had to get the stories started, or pick up the thread when my mother forgot where those stories were going.

There was one story she still remembered on her own, though. It was their origin story, about how they met—or, more accurately, about what happened soon after they met.

"When I was in college, I was sitting in the library with my friend Honey," my mother said. "She was telling me about a terrible double-date she had over the summer, with a couple of creeps who'd taken her and her girlfriend to the beach at Atlantic City. I was telling her about a boy from Newark I'd met on a blind date—who was coming to meet me at the library. Honey looked up whispered to me, 'Don't look now; here comes one of the creeps from the beach.' I turned around and there he was. And I said, 'Honey, this is the boy I was telling you about.'"

The friendship with Honey didn't last long. But three years later, my mother married my father, "the creep." They had their first funny story as a couple, a story my mother would repeat for decades to come.

The erasures in my mother's memory were beginning to reach back further than before: where her kids were living, what jobs we had, exactly how old we were. She still had those "of course" moments.

I'd end our morning phone call by telling her I had to get to the office.

"Where are you working?" she'd ask.

"At Tablet," I'd say.

"Right! Tablet!" she'd say. "I remember." And then to prove she really did remember things (once she'd been prompted about the basics), she'd ask about my editor, whom she'd met and adored: "And how's Alana?"

The week after the Hermans' visit to the Catskills, Doris went with my mother to the neurologist. Doris took a leather-bound notebook to write down what the doctor said, so my mother wouldn't forget. In addition to the slow progress of my mother's memory loss, Doris felt that other longstanding issues were also coming into play: "There is a huge depression component to your mom's wellbeing," she told me in an email. My father's law firm, which he had opened almost forty years earlier, was splitting up, and suddenly his professional future was unsure: He couldn't run the office alone but also didn't want to work for someone else, and although he was seventy-one, he wasn't prepared to retire. Even though a resolution was eventually found—my father would be "of counsel" to a firm that provided him with office space and administrative support—the summer of uncertainty had been stressful at home.

Doris urged my mother to see her psychiatrist to talk about all of this, and enlisted my help to persuade her, although she was concerned that my mother would try to cover up her problems in an effort to be an entertaining patient. "If I know my friend Susan, she will waste time with him by joking around," Doris wrote to me. "She will present her happy/peppy side to him." I brought up the psychiatrist every morning during our phone calls until my mother finally scheduled an appointment, and as that date arrived, I reminded her that she had to be honest with him about what she was going through. I didn't like being in the position of nudging my mother—much less telling her what to tell her doctor—but I wanted her to get help.

The psychiatrist recognized that she was out of sorts. He put her on anti-anxiety medication, but the pills knocked her out and she quickly stopped taking them. So he started her on a different pill, and this one seemed to do the trick.

"Susan sounds like her old chipper self after having an emotionally draining but productive session," Doris emailed me after my mother had seen her psychiatrist.

Encouraged by my mother's lifted spirits, I tried to encourage her to keep seeing the psychiatrist after this initial turnaround.

"I feel much better," she told me. "And he says I can call him anytime to set up a session."

"Great," I said. "So why don't we set up a regular appointment?"

"No need," she said. "Because I can call him anytime."

"How about if we make a regular weekly appointment, so you won't have to wait until there's a crisis next time?"

"No need," she repeated. "Because I can call him anytime."

I was not going to win this battle. But by the end of the summer, she did seem, on an emotional level, to be back to her old self. Or at least back to the new version of her old self.

But her mental decline continued. If losing track of things (her keys, her glasses) or forgetting bits of information was occasionally embarrassing, she could always laugh and chalk it up to "senior moments." It became much harder to deal with lapses about people: A fellow congregant at synagogue might not take offense if my mother forgot his name, but if she didn't realize that she knew him at all—had seen him every week, talked to him every week, sometimes for years—that was mortifying for both of them. She could either pretend she already knew everyone (which made it awkward if the person was actually a stranger) or pretend that she was meeting everyone for the first time (which was embarrassing if they'd already met). For a woman accustomed to schmoozing and telling stories, a people person with a wide array of friends and acquaintances, this led to bouts of acute social anxiety.

It's a cruel irony: Socializing is beneficial to people with memory issues; it helps ground them with a sense of time and place, and can provide a sense of emotional support and continuity. But those very memory issues make socializing a minefield of embarrassment and humiliation. For my mother, her anxiety was winning the battle.

When my parents were invited to the bat mitzvah of an old friend's granddaughter that fall, my mother said she couldn't handle it: unfamiliar surroundings, lots of strangers, and no way for her to be sure she could recognize the few people in the crowd whom she actually knew. "It's too much!" she told my father. The next spring, when it was time for an annual convention my father attended where his associates from around the world got together, my mother—who had long loved these gatherings—begged off for the same reasons. Her world of socializing was beginning to shrink.

Since my father had a secretary in his new office, he no longer needed my mother's help typing letters and reports. And since she wasn't on the computer every day, she stopped checking email. Within a few months, she had forgotten how to use the computer at all.

Talking on the phone got more challenging, too. I still spoke with her every morning as I walked to work, but our conversations had changed: We had once talked about everything from politics to movies, and I'd frequently stand outside my office after completing my fifteen-minute walk and continue talking to her for another fifteen minutes. Now, I had to prod the conversation along, and it rarely included news—she couldn't follow the headlines anymore from one day to the next. Ten minutes was usually enough for us to exhaust our conversation, and often she'd pepper me with questions about things we had just discussed, or get confused over the details of what we were talking about.

This was difficult for me. Since we lived two hundred miles apart, phone calls were our main connection. When we'd have a particularly tough conversation, I'd tell myself that everybody has bad mornings, when we're forgetful, or overtired, or cranky. But I couldn't ignore the trends; where once I'd need to linger outside my office door to finish a conversation we didn't want to end, now I found myself saying goodbye long before I finished my brief walk. It was becoming a lousy way to start the day, a daily reminder of my mother's worsening condition.

By 2011, she started having mood swings, sometimes getting unusually angry or upset at something my father had said or done—or something she believed he had said or done, which was not necessarily the same thing. Even the smallest thing, like him not putting his teacup in the sink, could set her on edge. It wasn't just family: "I didn't like the way the butcher talked to me this morning," she said, recounting a perceived slight whose details she couldn't exactly recall, "so I'm going to take my business somewhere else." Or I'd ask her about a friend of hers: "Last time I talked to her, she told me I was repeating myself," she'd tell me. "So now she's on my shit list." Small incidents became magnified in her mind, and she held onto these grudges for days; she could remember who was on her list long after the original offense had been forgotten. And there were other signs of her deterioration: She got confused occasionally when she was driving, getting turned around going to otherwise familiar places, or misjudging a parking space as she backed out. She grew unsteady on her feet. She started having panic attacks.

She told me about some of these things; others I discussed with my father, often by email—he was now in charge of all things computer-related—so she wouldn't overhear him talking about her. But while he saw her panic attacks or memory lapses as discrete incidents, I began to spot a pattern.

My father took her back to her psychiatrist. When I called later that day to see how the appointment went, my mother said she couldn't remember, and she handed the phone to my father. He told me that the doctor had given her a prescription for Aricept.

"And what did you say when he mentioned Aricept?" I asked.

Silence.

"You know Mom can't take Aricept," I said. "We had to take her off Aricept because it had a bad reaction with her Prozac, remember?"

My father did not remember.

"I'll call the doctor and clear it up," my father said. He handed the phone back to my mother.

"So the doctor wants you to take Aricept?" I asked her.

"No, I can't take Aricept!" she said. "Don't you remember how sick it made me?"

"But Dad said you got a prescription for Aricept."

"It's for Abilify," she said. "I know I can't take Aricept."

At least my mother is still on the ball at least a little bit, I thought, relieved. It made sense: My father had simply misheard the doctor.

I went to visit the following week, and on the refrigerator, held in place by a magnet, was the psychiatrist's prescription—for Aricept. I threw it away.

I had two parents going to appointments together, but neither of them was a consistently reliable narrator. Sometimes she was right, sometimes he was right, sometimes neither of them was right. But I never knew exactly what was happening two hundred miles away. I felt powerless. I had a full-time job, and I couldn't run to Maryland to drive her to doctor's appointments. I had to put my trust in my father. The most I could do was call her, email him, and try to piece together the facts from what they both told me.

A few months later, her psychiatrist ultimately did put her on Abilify, an anti-psychotic, to help with her newly developing fits of rage, most often directed at my father. The mood swings weren't unusual, the psychiatrist told my father over the phone: People with dementia are often quick to anger, commonly triggered by confusion or frustration—forgetting how to do something, not understanding what's happening, feeling barraged by questions and corrections. So it would be best not to provoke or prolong arguments.

"Dementia" was the word the psychiatrist used. Her "cognitive impairment" now had a name, although that name was not "Alzheimer's"—a distinction we'd asked about. "It might get there, it might not," he told my father, "and there's no way to judge how quickly or slowly." But he told my father to watch out for signs of further decline, like getting lost.

When my parents came to the Catskills with my aunt Marilyn for the Fourth of July in 2011, my mother's decline was becoming apparent—particularly to our friends and neighbors who hadn't seen her since the previous summer. She still put on a good face for company, but she forgot that she'd met our next-door neighbors Mary and Barry a half-dozen times. "It's nice to meet you," she said with a smile. "Where do you live?" Some of our friends seemed vaguely familiar to her, but she couldn't recall their names. She still adored David's dog Pearl, but kept asking David a short series of questions again and again: How old is she? Does she sleep in the bed with you? What kind of dog is she? How old is she? Does she sleep in the bed with you? What kind of dog is she? When it came time for funny stories, she could still follow someone else's anecdote and understand the humor; many of our friends are accomplished storytellers in their own right. But she didn't tell many stories of her own, either because she couldn't remember any, or because she was unsure of her own ability to tell them from beginning to end. She was still a good audience, with a bright laugh that carried across the house, but she was no longer the star of every room she entered.

My second novel was published that fall. A section of it was set in Jersey City in the forties—when my mother had grown up there. While I'd been doing research for the book three years earlier, when my mother was still at her sharpest, I'd taken the PATH train across the Hudson and called her on my cell phone from her old street, so she could describe things she remembered about the area—things I'd heard about but could never properly picture.

"The boys in the neighborhood used to play stickball in the middle of York Street," she told me. Up the block was Van Vorst Park, "the only place we ever got to see grass," she said—although posted signs reminded neighborhood kids not to actually walk on it, and cops reprimanded any who dared to play on it; Van Vorst Park was a "sitting park," with benches and paved paths, and a gazebo in the middle where a band would play on weekends. Two blocks past the park, on Grove Street, was Sons of Israel, the Orthodox synagogue where her father Henry prayed every week. Built in 1920, it was the biggest synagogue in downtown Jersey City, and the most ornate: Its four-story tan façade was decorated with Stars of David and stained-glass windows, its foyer covered in real marble. Nearby was P.S. 3, the grade school my mother attended, coming home every day at lunchtime for a tuna sandwich.

I found her old brownstone, with ten steps, painted white, leading up to the glass-paned wooden double doors at the entrance. In front of the basement window, next to the steps, was the section of sidewalk that my mother generously referred to as the "yard," a fenced-in area of just a few square feet where she and her little sister once played hopscotch. "We'd mark lines on the pavement with stray bits of coal we found in the street after the coal man made his deliveries," she told me. Just above the yard was the front window where Ethel would keep watch over the kids, and yell for them to come inside, while Henry hunched over a sewing machine in the back room making girls' underwear he called Baby Susan Snuggies—"the only thing anyone ever named after me," my mother said.

Henry's used 1937 Chrysler taxi cab—which he'd painted black, "not shiny black like a normal car," my mother said, "but flat black"—sat for many years on York Street directly in front of the brownstone, on blocks, waiting in vain to be repaired, before he finally upgraded to a 1953 Dodge. This was the car my mother learned to drive as a teenager, but after she had her first accident at age seventeen, she told me, she handed her father the keys. It would be years before she'd get behind the wheel again.

My mother had opted not to read my first novel; it was a sexually explicit, semi-autobiographical book that my father had read and recommended she not read—too much information for a parent to know. I didn't take it personally. But I had written this new book with my parents in mind: It was a story about a young man wrestling with his Judaism in suburban Maryland, not far from where they lived, and a piece of it was set in my mother's old neighborhood. Although this one was far less autobiographical, I knew it would resonate more with my parents. My father became my best publicist, talking about the book to everyone he met, pushing business associates, members of his synagogue, and even the guy who sold him bagels every Sunday to buy it. My mother read the book—although she'd forgotten about my research trip to Jersey City and our phone conversation from three years earlier—and proudly attended my reading in September 2011 at a Barnes and Noble in Bethesda.

It may have been one of the last books she read. Her attention span was dwindling, and she couldn't follow a long narrative anymore; she could still handle short stories on occasion, but for the most part, the only book she picked up was a collection of word finds, which her doctors had prescribed as a brain exercise. Before long, she couldn't remember the title of my novel, or what it was about. Eventually, as I continued my book tour, we got to conversations like this:

"I did a reading last night," I said.

"What did you read?"

"A chapter from my book."

"You wrote a book?" she asked.

My mother forgetting I was a writer was a particularly unhappy milestone for me. Over the years, she had routinely and consistently suggested ideas for books to me. She'd bring up a crazy relative, and say, "There's a whole book right there." Or she'd launch into a funny story by saying, "Here's an idea for your next book." Or, if something was especially nutty: "You could write a book about that—but nobody would believe it." She was never serious about it; these were usually funny anecdotes or quirky characters, but they weren't sufficient material for a novel, or I'd have a thousand books half-written by now. Nonetheless, I was sad to know that she'd never call me up with an idea for "a guaranteed bestseller" again.

As my book tour started to wind down a few months later, I decided to delve, at last, into an idea we had long ago agreed would make a great book: the Winnipeg murder mystery. But before I had a chance to get started, my literary agent came to me with a different project that had already attracted a publisher's tentative interest. I immediately got excited about it, but it had a short deadline—so I put off my investigation into what really happened to my great-grandmother, and started working on a new novel instead. It was another sexually explicit book, but this time I wasn't worried about my mother reading it; her days of reading books were over.

Right around this time, she started getting lost in the car—one of the signs her psychiatrist had warned us about.

"There's all this construction on Rockville Pike," she told me one day after getting turned around, "and nothing looks familiar."

I was dubious until I went to visit: I drove to Rockville Pike and realized she was right; they'd rerouted streets and changed traffic patterns, and it was indeed hard to know where to go. So even though, as her psychiatrist had suggested, getting lost and failing to recognize familiar landmarks are hallmarks of Alzheimer's, my mother had a good excuse this time, and I stopped worrying about her driving—until she got lost coming home from lunch with her friend Doris a few months later. This time, there was no excuse about landmarks or traffic patterns; she got lost in her own development, where she'd lived for forty years, since I was an infant.

Flustered, when she finally found the house, she told my father that she couldn't drive anymore, and she handed him the keys— much as she'd handed the keys to her own father after her first accident as a teenager. Only this time, she would never get behind the wheel again.

My parents' wedding at the Essex House in Newark, 1962

3:

CAUSE OF DEATH: 'HOMICIDAL'

During a staff meeting in the summer of 2012 at Tablet, the Jewish online magazine where I work as an editor, my co-workers were discussing an article we had recently published about bootleggers in Montreal. This true crime story set in Canada prompted me to share a similar Canadian crime story: the unlikely tale of my great-grandmother's murder a century earlier in Winnipeg. "When my mother was a little girl," I began, as I always did, "she found a photograph of her grandfather with a strange woman." In less than a minute, I recounted my now well-rehearsed tale of the outdoor wintertime breastfeeding, and the drive-by sniper with impeccable aim. This story had, by this point, become part of my own repertoire of entertaining anecdotes, passed down from my mother—although I told it with a more obviously skeptical tone and raised eyebrows.

In the past, when I'd told this story to friends, they usually laughed, either at the improbability of the whole scenario, or at my delivery. But this time, telling the story to a roomful of journalists, I was met with questions rather than laughter.

"Is this true?"

I said I doubted it, but didn't honestly know.

"So what happened to her?"

Again, I didn't know. And then came the question that any decent journalist would have asked me: "Why haven't you tried to find out?"

With this challenge from my colleagues, I thought, the time had finally come to look for answers, regardless of what other projects I was working on.

My mother still remembered the story of the sniper, but it was becoming increasingly clear that her memories wouldn't last forever. (I had spoken to her neurologist in the spring of 2012, and he said her "mild dementia" would continue a "slow decline" for some time.) I wanted to solve this mystery for her—the mystery of what happened to the woman she was named after. I was the one who had introduced uncertainty into this piece of my mother's personal history when I expressed my doubts about its veracity two years earlier; now I could be the one to resolve it once and for all.

Besides, I thought, the truth probably wouldn't take much time to figure out. I'd been a journalist for more than two decades, and I was feeling a bit cocky. I thought that after a little internet research and a few days of digging around, all the questions would be answered.

I started searching online after work that same day. I Googled Shifra Fainstein, Sarah Brooks, Dovid Fainstein, Winnipeg, murder—and various combinations of English and Yiddish names. Nothing. Then I put on my reporter's hat and tried to think who might have more information. After a few minutes, I found an email address for the province of Manitoba's Vital Statistics Agency, and sent them a note asking if they had any ideas where I might search. I got a response almost immediately, pointing me to a database where I could enter a name and see if there were any official documents—birth certificates, marriage certificates, death certificates—on file about that person. I typed in every combination of names I could think of. Again, nothing.

Before I gave up, I tried searching official Canadian records on a different site, and here I had my big break: There were still no records for Fainstein—the way my grandmother Ethel had spelled her maiden name—but there was something for Feinstein: A 1911 census report showed a David and Shifra Feinstein living in Winnipeg with two children named Etta and Aaron. The names didn't quite match, but they were close enough, and the children's birth years matched my grandmother Ethel and her older brother Harry. Under "occupation," it said David was a cattle dealer, a detail I knew to be correct. It seemed I had found them.

I checked Vital Statistics again, this time spelling the last name Feinstein rather than Fainstein, and I found what I was looking for: a single record for Sarah Feinstein. All the database would tell me was that there was a death certificate for her on file, dated 1913—when she would still have been a young woman with small children. I sent away for it, hoping it would reveal how my great-grandmother had actually died.

I waited more than a month for the document.

When Sarah's death certificate finally arrived in the mail at my apartment in New York City, the cause of death was listed concisely as "bullet wound through brain—homicidal."

Those few words stopped me cold. My great-grandmother had indeed been murdered. I wondered whether my initial skepticism was misplaced: What if the outlandish story my mother grew up believing was actually true?

I knew that Sarah's death certificate was not the end of the search for answers, but merely the beginning. If a young mother was murdered, shot through the head, it would have been in the newspapers. I searched the archives of Winnipeg's daily papers, and found an article about my great-grandmother, accompanied by the same photo my mother had found decades earlier.

My parents marked their fiftieth wedding anniversary in July 2012. Instead of the usual small Fourth of July gathering, Mark and I filled our house in the Catskills with visitors to celebrate a few weeks later. Our family reunion comprised a dozen people, including my sister Stacey and her partner Victor, and my brother Scott, his wife Phyllis, and their sons David, Reuven, and Ethan, as well as my aunt Marilyn.

By the time the family gathered for the reunion, I could tell them what had actually happened to Sarah, and how she had died.

My mother had forgotten a lot of things by that summer, but the story of the drive-by sniper was still fresh in her mind. When I showed her the death certificate that had come in the mail from Manitoba, she grasped its significance. Aside from the photograph she'd found as a child, this was the first physical reminder she had about the woman in whose memory she'd been named.

When I shared the first newspaper story I'd found about Sarah's murder, she understood that, too, and it touched off a whole round of discussion while the family was together. The death certificate and newspaper clipping hadn't solved the mystery, as I'd initially hoped they would; they had answered a few questions but brought up many more.

Now I wanted to dig deeper into the story.

The death certificate would propel me into a long period of research, trying to find out all I could about my great-grandmother— her death and her life. I would eventually find more than two dozen newspaper stories about the murder; these articles helped me recreate the crime and its aftermath. I'd spend years poring over official documents, reading historical accounts, searching online databases, and interviewing people, trying to learn more about my great-grandmother than I could know from a single photograph, a death certificate, and newspaper reports.

Along the way, I'd learn much more about my great-grandmother than I'd originally anticipated. It wasn't just about how she died, but also about how she lived. And it wasn't the story of what happened one day in Winnipeg, but the story of what happened to an entire family over the course of decades.

David and Sarah's wedding photo

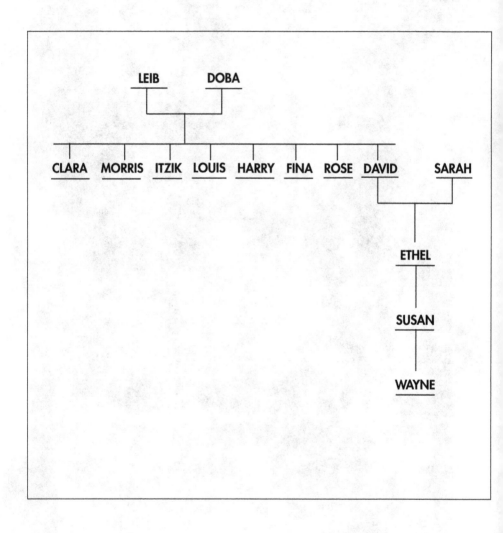

4: SARAH AND DAVID

Sarah was born into a Jewish family in Russia in May 1887. She was the oldest of four children born to her parents Aharon Michael and Beila. It's difficult to be certain what her family name was, since there are differing accounts and inconsistencies with translations and spellings, and women's maiden names quickly vanished from official records, but it was most likely Auerbrook or Averboock or Awerbruch or Averbuch.

As a teenager, after her mother died, Sarah was pursued by a young man from a wealthy and powerful family in her hometown, the Ukrainian village of Dobrovoda. After he spent considerable time trying to woo her, she finally rebuffed him. Furious, he swore revenge, "even if it takes me a lifetime." Perhaps fearing what the spurned suitor might do—or perhaps more broadly concerned about a wave of pogroms starting in 1903 and lasting three years, taking thousands of Jewish lives across Russia and driving a massive wave of Jewish emigration—Sarah left for North America in 1906.

It's difficult to pinpoint the date of her arrival, since Canada had open borders at the time and didn't create records of immigration until 1908, and without an exact last name for Sarah, it's not possible to find her name on a ship manifest with absolute certainty. But it seems likely that she was the Russian Jewish immigrant whose name was recorded on a manifest as Sara Freida Awerbruch, who sailed out of Liverpool, England, into Quebec City on the South-wark, a four-masted, four-hundred-eighty-foot long steamship built in 1893, which at the time of her journey was servicing the Dominion Line across the Atlantic. She arrived on May 7, 1906, with twenty-five dollars to her name. Her original plan, according to the manifest, was to visit her cousin David Nemerovsky—who had immigrated from Russia more than a decade earlier and ran a second-hand furniture store with his wife in Portland, Oregon—and find work as a domestic. Instead, she ended up staying with an uncle in Winnipeg, either due to an unexpected change of plans, or as part of a pre-arranged temporary stop on her way across the continent that turned into something more permanent when an opportunity arose that sounded better than domestic work.

Within a few months of her arrival in Winnipeg, Sarah married David Feinstein on October 27, 1906. Their marriage certificate doesn't name a synagogue or even a specific address as the location of their wedding ceremony; it simply says they were married at the corner of Manitoba and Powers Streets in the city's North End. They had their wedding photo taken by William A. Martel, the manager of the Winnipeg College of Photography (advertised as the "original and only" college of photography in Western Canada) who also produced postcards and operated a small shop in the neighborhood, at the corner of Main Street and Euclid.

David was twenty-six at the time of the wedding, with black hair and brown eyes; at five-foot-seven, he was the tallest person in his family. He was one of eight surviving children (another three girls and one boy had died very young) born to Louis and Dorothy (Applebaum) Feinstein—known primarily by their Yiddish names, Leib and Doba—in Chudnov, a mostly Jewish shtetl of several thousand on the Teperovka River thirty miles southwest of the Ukrainian city of Zhitomir.

David had set out across Europe on foot with his oldest brother Morris. The two were separated in France, however, so David made his way to England alone, and sailed from Liverpool into Halifax in January 1904 in steerage class on the Laurentian—a four-hundred-foot-long Allan Line ship built in 1872 that had been nicknamed "Rolling Poly," because of its reputation for rough rides.

David became a naturalized Canadian citizen in 1906. By the time his parents Leib, a bricklayer, and Doba sailed to Canada on the Dominion in June 1908, their entire family—five sons and three daughters—had made the crossing. With the exception of David's sister Rose, who ended up in Portsmouth, New Hampshire, they would all settle in Winnipeg.

After initially working as a bricklayer like his father, David bought a horse and wagon and went into business with his brother Harry. They bought cattle and other livestock from small farms and sold animals wholesale in the city, racking up commissions in the process. Their three other brothers would soon join them in this endeavor, setting up operations in Canora, Saskatchewan, a newly established hamlet where the government was giving away free farmland. The brothers went back and forth between Canora and Winnipeg; at any given time, most of them lived in Winnipeg but at least one of them—Harry was the first—was living primarily in Saskatchewan so the rest had a place to stay when they went there on business.

As newlyweds, David and Sarah lived at 633 Manitoba Avenue, a few blocks from where they were married, in Winnipeg's North End.

Jews had been living in the North End since the early 1880s, when Russian refugees—fleeing an earlier wave of pogroms that arose in the wake of the 1881 assassination of Czar Alexander II—were first welcomed to Canada in modest numbers, lured by the promise of free land, to set up what Prime Minister John A. Macdonald called "a Jew colony." A few hundred had then settled in Winnipeg, which prior to the arrival of this wave of Russian immigrants had just one hundred Jews, mostly of English and German heritage, scattered across various parts of the city.

Over the next three decades, the Jewish population of Canada would climb from thirteen hundred to more than seventy-five thousand; the majority of these newcomers were from towns and cities in Russia—Marxist-leaning, Yiddish-speaking workers who fled growing anti-Semitic attacks following political unrest and the abortive revolution of 1905. Ten thousand of these Russian Jews *would eventually settle in Manitoba, nearly all of them in Winnipeg. Newcomers initially lived in immigrant sheds, crowded wooden barracks housing hundreds of people along the Red River in the part of town known as "The Forks," or in shanties in "the flats" nearby. Nearly all of the Russian Jews eventually settled in Winnipeg's North End, giving it the nickname "New Jerusalem" or, to those less fond of the newcomers, "Jew Town."*

When David and Sarah were married in 1906, the North End was a run-down, working-class immigrant neighborhood. Most of Winnipeg's Jews—four thousand by that point—lived there, the majority having arrived within the previous five years.

But it was not an exclusively Jewish area; in fact, the vast majority of residents were gentiles. Recently arrived Jews lived alongside other Eastern European newcomers—Serbians, Croatians, Ukrainians, and ethnic Poles from Galicia, then an autonomous region of Austria-Hungary—in tiny houses built close together along black muddy roads lined with wooden sidewalks. In many cases, the immigrants separated from one another along national and religious lines: One block might be all Polish Catholics, while another block would be entirely Russian Jews. But there were exceptions: Some blocks were more mixed, sometimes including the odd English Anglican, German Lutheran, or Scottish Presbyterian family.

Taken as a whole, the neighborhood included a wide array of immigrants, and an equally varied assortment of houses of worship. The area already had five synagogues in 1906: Rosh Pina—which David's brother Harry helped to found—as well as Beth Abraham, B'nai Zion, Chevra Mishnayes, and the more liberal Shaarey Zedek. New congregations were opening every year to accommodate the swelling population of Jewish immigrants.

Less than a mile from downtown Winnipeg, the North End was literally on the wrong side of the tracks, separated from the rest of the city by the sprawling Canadian Pacific Railway yards—where many of the recently arrived men, particularly the non-Jews, found work, making perhaps twenty dollars a week. (Others made less; paving roads or hauling lumber might earn a man two dollars a day.) When David and Sarah lived on Manitoba Avenue in 1906, an underpass had opened just two years earlier beneath the expansive train tracks, which had space for twelve-thousand rail cars. Since new immigrants couldn't typically afford cars or even bicycles or horses, the only way for most people to get out of the neighborhood—women, for instance, going downtown to work as maids and garment workers, making a small fraction of the men's wages—was via streetcars that ran through the new underpass. Even with this new connection to the rest of the city, however, the North End remained a relatively isolated enclave.

Most of Winnipeg was booming: In 1906, the city was in the middle of a decade that saw its population triple to more than one-hundred-thirty thousand. And as the population grew, so did the city's economy, as was evident from the daily newspapers: Downtown department stores like Hudson's Bay Company and the newly opened Eaton's advertised furniture and fabric, alongside ads for patent-leather shoes, oil heaters, and second-hand bicycles, as well as elixirs for every ailment, from Dodd's kidney pills to "fruit liver tablets" to Sozodont cream ("for the teeth"). Shops hawking grand pianos and "unshrinkable" wool underwear competed for space with train companies offering deals on round-trip vacations to Port Arthur, Ontario, or Minneapolis, Minnesota. But the hottest item in Winnipeg at the time was land: from five-acre plots across the Red River in St. Boniface, to more modest twenty-five-foot-wide lots along the Main Street streetcar line.

While most of the city was thriving, in the North End, living conditions were generally poor: Some houses had electricity, but others did not, their walls covered in soot from wood stoves and the air inside heavy with the smell of kerosene lamps. Those who couldn't afford the city's steep fees for sewer connections made do with privies in their backyards, next to their chicken coops, and bathed in basins in the kitchen. Drinking water was filthy. An epidemic of typhoid, called "Red River fever," swept the neighborhood in 1905, one year before David and Sarah moved into their new home.

Crime was also part of daily life in the North End: Anti-Semitic violence was common from some of the Christian immigrants; Jewish children were routinely taunted and bullied at school. Robberies plagued the residential areas, and drunken brawls were common along Main Street, where bars were concentrated on the eastern edge of the neighborhood. Bootlegging was commonplace. Prostitution was openly tolerated in the whorehouses along Rachel Street in nearby Point Douglas, on the other side of Main Street.

The streets closest to the rail yards were the poorest and the roughest, and the most likely to be covered in smoky black dust and rattled by noise from the nearby trains; moving farther north, away from the tracks, was an indication of success. David and Sarah's home on Manitoba Avenue, six blocks north of the tracks, quickly got crowded: David's teenage brother Louis, his youngest sibling—twenty-three years younger than Morris, the oldest—emigrated from Russia in 1907 and moved in with them. That same year, David and Sarah had their first child, Harry. They moved to 475 Flora Avenue, three blocks south, closer to the train tracks—a move in the wrong direction.

Flora Avenue was a relatively poor street. But it was only one block below Selkirk Avenue, the commercial heart of the North End, filled with delicatessens, cobblers, and small wooden shops selling everything from hardware to kosher meat. Shop-owners typically lived above or behind their stores, conducting business in a number of Eastern European languages. Although most Jews in the North End strived to learn English as soon as they could—David and Sarah both spoke English by the time the national census was taken in 1911—it was possible for new immigrants to do all their business speaking only Yiddish. In 1907, when David and Sarah moved to Flora Avenue, Queen's Theatre opened on Selkirk, offering major stage productions in Yiddish.

While the family—including David's brother Louis—was living on Flora Avenue, Ethel was born in 1909. Fanny followed in 1911, by which time David and Sarah had hired a live-in domestic, a Catholic immigrant from Austria named Mary Bulka who (officially) worked seventy hours a week for the family.

After a few years in Winnipeg, the Feinsteins' cattle business—which David ran with his brothers Louis, Harry, Morris, and Isidor—was going well, and things were looking far better for the family financially. They could even afford a bit of travel; around 1911, David and Sarah crossed the American border to visit his sister Rose and her husband Harry Cohen—a real estate agent—in New Hampshire. (David's brother Harry's visit to Rose was more eventful, however: He accidentally knocked on the wrong door in Portsmouth, and a young college student named Pauline Katz answered. They were later married.)

David and Sarah, by all accounts, were considered prominent members of the North End's Jewish community, refined and well-to-do. In 1912, around the same time as their fourth child, Anne, was born in the fall, David and Sarah moved to a bigger house—a white cottage with green trim, and a neatly graveled backyard—at 520 Magnus Avenue, the same street where David's brothers Harry and Morris and his sister Fina were already living. Although it was still crowded and unpaved, Magnus Avenue was four blocks north of Flora Avenue—four streets farther away from the railroad tracks, and four steps up the economic ladder. They were indeed doing well financially; by this point, Sarah could enjoy some of the finer things in life, such as jewelry and fur coats.

The future must have seemed full of promise. But it would not last.

On Thursday night, July 31, 1913, David's sister Fina came to visit, penning a couple of letters for Sarah, who could not write well. She wrote one to Sarah's sister Gertrude, who had immigrated to Canada in 1908 with their younger brother Ben. And she wrote another to David, who had been away buying cattle in Canora with his brother Harry since July 20. After Fina left, Sarah's neighbor Lucy Kesler stopped by around eleven to sit on the porch for a spell. When Sarah retired for the night before midnight, Lucy went home, not realizing she would be the last person ever to speak to Sarah.

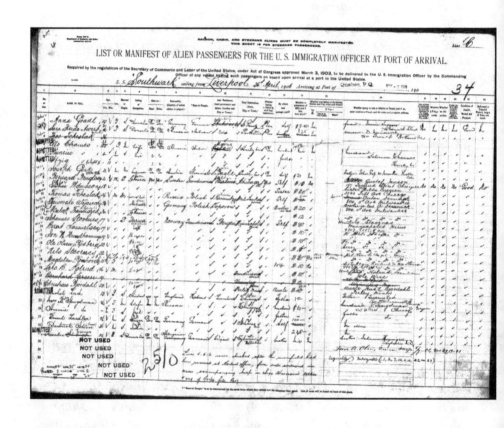

The ship manifest from the *Southwark*, arriving in Canada on May 7, 1906

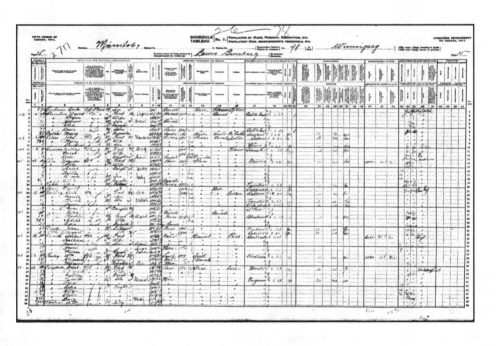

The 1911 Census

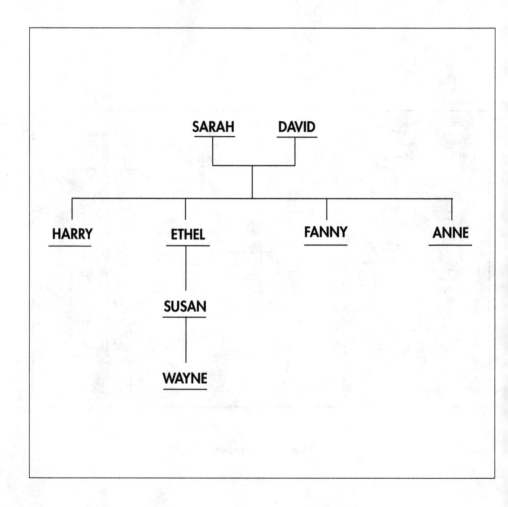

5: THE WOMAN IS SHOT!

Nobody in the house heard the intruder fire a gun at Sarah Feinstein's right temple as she slept, in the early hours of Friday, August 1, 1913. Even two-year-old Fanny, curled up at her mother's breast, continued to sleep as the blood seeped into the sheets and dampened her nightgown.

It was Anne, the infant in the crib next to Sarah's bed, who made the first noise shortly after two-forty-five in the morning. She started crying, perhaps because she had witnessed a stranger in the house, or sensed that someone had hurt her mother—although there had been no confrontation or struggle—or possibly simply because she was hungry and wanted to be fed.

It wasn't unusual for Anne to wake up crying in the middle of the night, but it was rare for the crying to continue without Sarah tending to the baby's needs. Harry, the oldest child, two weeks shy of his sixth birthday, sensed that Anne's continued crying was an indication that something was wrong. He got up from the room where he was sleeping alongside his little sister Ethel and the family's current hired girl, a Ukrainian immigrant named Victoria Komanowska, and walked into his mother's bedroom in the rear of the house to wake her. When he could not, he told Victoria, who tried to rouse Sarah—without success. The small red light that Sarah typically left on during the night had been extinguished, so she turned it on. Then she saw the blood.

Frightened and unsure what to do without Sarah's husband David at home, Victoria shouted to the Feinsteins' neighbor, Lucy Kesler, through the window: "I have been calling my mistress and she did not wake up." Then Victoria ran out the front door, which was closed but unlocked—something she noticed because she had locked all the doors before going to bed, and Sarah had checked them as well. Victoria woke the Kasners, next door at 516 Magnus Avenue. "I can't wake the missus," she told them through her tears. "I don't know what is the matter with the missus."

Lucy arrived first and accompanied Victoria to the back bedroom. While Sarah lay motionless with Fanny still asleep by her side, baby Anne was crying in the crib; Lucy picked her up to comfort her. Robert Kasner came in next, with a young man named Abram Schurman. Robert saw the bullet hole in Sarah's right temple, and Abram shouted at Victoria: "You are crazy! The woman is shot!"

Abram ran back next door to call the police—the Feinstein house, like most in the North End, didn't yet have a telephone—although a sleepy telephone operator initially had a difficult time understanding him because of the language barrier and his agitated state. He then called two local doctors, Dr. George Hirsh Kalichmann and Dr. Abram Bercovitch, a native of Montreal who'd opened a family practice on Selkirk Avenue in 1908—and who had delivered Ethel when she was born in 1909. Kalichmann, a Romanian-born Jewish immigrant who had come to Winnipeg and opened his First Old Country Clinic on Selkirk Avenue in 1912, arrived first on the scene just after three o'clock. He found Sarah in bed, facing the wall, with blood and bits of brain tissue on her pillow. He pronounced her dead. Sarah's body was still warm, indicating to him that she'd been shot within the previous half-hour.

Eventually, two police officers—Sergeant Rice and Patrol Sergeant Livingston—showed up from North Winnipeg station to find Sarah in a peaceful pose, her cheek resting against her hands on the blood-soaked pillow, while her children lay on a cot at the foot of her bed, crying. They found all the doors locked except for the front door, and all the windows closed except one in Sarah's bedroom that Victoria had left open a few inches to let in the cool night air—temperatures had dipped into the mid-fifties. They searched for other possible points of entry, crawling out a small dormer window on to the roof of the back shed.

The coroner, Charles A. Ritchie, arrived to do a preliminary investigation: He surmised that Sarah had been shot at very close range—not through the open window, but closer to point-blank, close enough to leave powder burns near the bullet hole. The house was cordoned off, pending a full coroner's jury that he called for five o'clock that afternoon. Other than police—there were now more than twenty officers on the scene—the only person allowed inside the Feinsteins' front gate was a representative of the local chevra kadisha, the Jewish burial society, which would ensure that someone would sit with the body until burial, in accordance with Jewish law.

After several unsuccessful efforts to reach David in Canora by telephone, Abram ultimately contacted him by telegraph shortly after noon. Informed of his wife's death, David set out for Winnipeg by train as quickly as he could, but there was only one direct train on that route each day, leaving at four-fifty-five in the afternoon. Canora was three hundred miles northwest of Winnipeg on the Canadian Northern Railway, whose acronym gave the recently incorporated town of several hundred people its name. David would not make it back until the following morning, so his brother Harry's wife Pauline took in David and Sarah's children at her house down the block on Magnus Avenue. Pauline was devastated, crying from grief and fainting several times; David's sister Fina and his brother Morris's wife Pearl, both of whom also lived on Magnus, came to help her with the children.

As temperatures climbed into the eighties that afternoon, people gathered in the heat outside 520 Magnus Avenue, talking in Yiddish about what had happened and who might be responsible. Most of the fingers—including that of Abram Schurman, who said he lived next door—pointed at a woman named Mary Manastaka and her boyfriend, Stefan Kushowsky.

The previous Friday, neighbors said, Sarah had dismissed Mary, a Galician girl she'd recently hired. Sarah reportedly didn't approve of Mary's relationship with Stefan, a twenty-four-year-old brakeman for the railroad who lived in a boarding house on Selkirk Avenue. After she was fired, the story went, Mary tried to convince seventeen-year-old Victoria, who had worked for Sarah since she arrived in Canada less than four months earlier, to follow her out the door: When Victoria was scrubbing the veranda, Mary stopped on the sidewalk to admonish her: "Why do you work for the Jews?" she asked. When she could not goad Victoria into responding, she stepped up onto the veranda to continue her tirade: The Jews were cast out of Russia, Mary told her, using expletives, and "so they should be in Canada." Sarah came out of the house at this point and shoved Mary off the veranda; according to neighbors who claimed to have witnessed the exchange, Mary left vowing revenge—the kind of threat that Sarah knew quite well from her spurned teenage lover back in Russia: "You'll hear from me again," Mary threatened.

Lucy Kesler said that when she'd been visiting with Sarah the previous night, a few hours before the murder, Mary and Stefan had walked by the Feinsteins' house while Sarah was sitting on the front porch. After they passed, Sarah told Lucy that Mary had looked at her funny, "as if she'd never seen me before." A young woman returning from her job at a downtown café around midnight that evening said she saw Mary behaving amorously with a man in front of a house at 426 Magnus Avenue, down the street from the Feinsteins' home. Harry Exelrod, who lived across the street from the Feinsteins, said that he'd heard a woman shout the name "Stefan!" at three in the morning, while another neighbor, Mrs. Harry Shane, claimed to have heard the gunshot—the only person to make such a claim. C.D. Polson, who had been walking by Magnus Avenue at around the same time, claimed to have seen a man rush across the street from the Feinsteins' house into a vacant lot and then run out of sight.

As the news of the murder spread through the North End, a crowd gathered outside the Feinsteins' home. There were never fewer than three hundred people on the street that day, barred from entering by a local constable who blocked the doorway. Several tried to get in the back entrance by sneaking up the alley behind the house, *where the previous day's laundry still hung on clotheslines in the backyard; police had secured this door as well. Some people had walked as much as a mile, bringing their children, to witness the scene. Others were neighbors, friends, or relatives: Sarah's sisters-in-law were inconsolable, shrieking with grief. Journalists from Winnipeg's rival daily newspapers—the* Manitoba Free Press *and* Winnipeg Telegram, *both of which came out in the mornings, and the afternoon* Winnipeg Tribune—*spoke with the onlookers, digging for information; but like the police, who were talking to neighborhood residents in hopes of finding clues, they were faced with a language barrier, since the locals tended to speak Yiddish or Polish or Ukrainian.*

By four o'clock that afternoon, the Tribune *had splashed news of the murder across the top of its front page: "Prominent Member of Hebrew Colony Shot to Death As She Slept," read the headline, four columns wide, above a large photograph—identified as their wedding portrait—featuring a neatly dressed David seated in a chair with Sarah standing tall next to him, pendants hanging from the necklaces that rested on her shiny blouse. Anti-Semitism was cited as a possible motive in the story: "One well defined rumor, and the one on which it is believed the police department is working, points to the tragedy as being the culmination of certain anti-Semitic feeling," the* Tribune *reported.*

But it was clear from the very first day that the reporting had its limitations. Beyond rampant typos and minor inconsistencies with exact dates, times, ages, and names—Feinstein sometimes became Finestein, Komanowska became Kamanowsky, Schurman became Scherman—there were some larger discrepancies. Many problems likely arose because the non-Jewish reporters had to rely on interpreters to translate their questions into Yiddish and other languages, and then translate the answers back to English; confusion was inevitable. For instance, Abram Schurman initially told the Tribune *reporter, incorrectly, that it was Mary who had awakened him, when it had actually been Victoria. Police were undoubtedly having similar difficulties. Details were hard to nail down, with so many conflicting stories and so few English speakers in the crowd—*

something that would soon come back to haunt the investigation.

When the coroner's jury of a dozen men adjourned after five o'clock, the body was brought out of the house in a wicker casket. After the men carrying the body pushed through the throngs in the street, it was taken in a wagon to Thomson's undertaking rooms, where Dr. Gordon Bell, a bacteriologist working for the city, performed a post-mortem examination. He found the bullet that killed Sarah lodged inside her skull, and determined that it had traveled a straight course from her right temple to the opposite side of her brain, indicating it had been fired from directly above her.

Chief of Detectives Eli Stodgill was reluctant to give many specifics to reporters that afternoon, but he assured them that he was on the right track with the investigation, and would be in pursuit of the murderer by that evening. Both hired girls, Victoria Komanowska and Mary Manastaka, were taken to the central police station and held as material witnesses. When police had asked Mary about her boyfriend Stefan Kushowsky, she'd shown them a photograph of the two of them together; he was dressed in cowboy gear, as a gag— it was a costume he'd found in the photographer's gallery. When police tried to take the picture from her, she tore it in half, which police reportedly viewed as suspicious.

Stefan had not yet been arrested, but he had been spotted: After allegedly skipping work at the rail yards, he had appeared just before nine o'clock at Feinman's confectionery store at 192 Andrews Street, around the block from the Feinsteins' house. He bought a bottle of aerated water and sat on a box to drink it. He casually asked the proprietress what had happened on Magnus Avenue to attract such a crowd. "Don't you read the papers?" she replied. "Mrs. Feinstein was shot at three o'clock this morning." Stefan told her that he hadn't read about the crime, since he couldn't read English, and then he asked if anyone had been arrested. "Oh yes," said the storekeeper, who recognized him as a frequent customer. "Mrs. Feinstein's girl, and the one that used to come here with you." Stefan knew she meant Mary, whom Stefan had brought in more than once to buy a pop. His lip started to quiver. He dropped the bottle on the floor, where it smashed into shards, and fled through the doorway.

As the sun set around ten past eight on Friday night, the Jewish Sabbath began. The police investigation was temporarily put on hold, since witnesses would be unable to provide testimony until the Sabbath was over. The coroner's jury, which included several Jewish members, paused its inquest as well. The funeral was also put off for a day, since Jewish burials cannot take place on Saturday. But that evening, in synagogues across the North End—by now there were a dozen of them—all the talk was of the young mother who'd been murdered early that morning.

The next day, Saturday, August 2, David's train arrived in Winnipeg at seven-twenty in the morning. The story of his wife's murder appeared in all three daily newspapers' Saturday editions: In the morning, the Telegram—which consistently spelled the family name "Finestein"—ran the front-page headline "Mrs. D. Finestein Murdered While Asleep With Baby," while the Free Press ran the same photo of David and Sarah that the Tribune had run the previous day, announcing: "Little New Light on Feinstein Murder Mystery in North End." In the afternoon, the Tribune declared on its front page: "Murder of Mrs. D. Feinstein Still Wrapt in Mystery." Journalists tried to interview David but, as the Tribune explained, "He appears to have suffered terribly since the news was broken to him and was altogether too much under stress of grief to speak very much to the reporters."

Coroner Ritchie filed his Medical Certificate of Death (incorrectly listing the victim's name in one instance as Mary Finestein) that Saturday. The cause of death was listed as "bullet wound through brain—homicidal."

On the same day, synagogues across Winnipeg were reading the week's Torah portion, Masei, the final section from the book of Numbers. Preparing the Children of Israel to enter the Promised Land, God tells Moses in Masei to instruct his people to set up cities of refuge when they enter Canaan. But anyone who intentionally kills another person—with a stone, or wooden tool, or iron object—will not be allowed sanctuary there. That person is a murderer, the Torah makes plain, and that person must be put to death.

4 O'CLOCK EDITION — **The Winnipeg Tribune.**

PROMINENT MEMBER OF HEBREW COLONY SHOT TO DEATH AS SHE SLEPT

Mrs. David Feinstein, of 520 Magnus Street, the Victim of a Mysterious Murder

PERPETRATOR OF DEED UNKNOWN

VICTIM OF MURDER AND HER HUSBAND

CASTRO AGAIN CAUSES REVOLT IN VENEZUELA

OTHER NATIONS MAY FOLLOW THE LEAD OF BRITAIN

ALLEGED PLOTS TO DYNAMITE MINES AROUND CALUMET

EXPLOSIVE FOUND ON A PRISONER

THREE CANADIAN JUDGMENTS BY PRIVY COUNCIL

TRIBUNE TRUMPS

DISAGREEABLE FLAG INCIDENT OCCURS AT SASKATOON, SASK.

Ten-Line Talks

GEN. BRAMWELL BOOTH TO PAY WINNIPEG A VISIT

JULY PERMITS NUMBERED 441

CANADA GRANARY OF ALL BRITAIN'S OTHER DOMINIONS

The Tribune Continues to Lead in the Local Display Field

WINNIPEG, SATURD...

MRS. D. FINESTEIN MURDERED WHILE ASLEEP WITH BABY

Home at 520 Magnus Avenue Is Scene of Brutal and Mysterious Crime

POLICE PUZZLED OVER DIFFERENT THEORIES

Two Girls Held as Witnesses, While Suspected Man Is Searched for

Husband of Victim On Way to Winnipeg

The police were successful yesterday afternoon in obtaining telephone communication with David Finestein, the husband of the murdered woman. The police state that the husband left Canora, Saskatchewan, at 4:55 yesterday afternoon, and will arrive in Winnipeg at 7:20 this morning. Finestein has been in the vicinity of Canora for the past week buying cattle.

An assassin's bullet, yesterday, ended the life of Mrs. David Finestein, of 520 Magnus avenue. Someone, as yet unknown, gained entrance to the pretty little home, about 2:30 in the morning, shot Mrs. Finestein while she was quietly sleeping with her baby daughter and escaped from the neighborhood, evidently without awakening anyone in the vicinity. In police circles it is considered one of the most brutal murders in the history of the city. Beyond a possibility that it was for revenge, there seems to have been no motive for the crime. All day yesterday the police were working on the case, but up to a late hour had made little progress. There are many clues, but little in the way of direct evidence that points to the murderer.

Many Theories Presented

The difficulty of getting anything like a connected story from any of the highly excitable residents of the district, is almost insurmountable, until they have had an opportunity of calming down. There are rumors of every description afloat, involving almost everyone who has ever had any connection with the Finestein family, but few of them have any evidence of authenticity. A neighbor is responsible for a story that Mrs. Finestein, several days ago, noticed a man hanging about the place, who, at different times, attempted to gain an entrance. In consequence, she had kept all doors and windows tightly fastened at night.

Girls are Held by Police

So far, two girls, who are being held by the police as material witnesses, have furnished the strongest clues for a solution of the mystery. They are Mary Monastaka and Victoria Komanowska, the first a former servant in the employ of Mrs. Finestein, and the latter employed in the house at the time of the shooting. Along with one

(Continued on Page 13, Col. 5)

Above: *Winnipeg Tribune*, August 1, 1913

Right: *Winnipeg Telegram*, August 2, 1913

Little New Light on Feinstein Murder Mystery in North End

Husband Has Been Located in Saskatchewan and Will Be in Winnipeg This Morning—Police Searching for Young Railwayman—Coroner's Jury Views Remains and Will Re-assemble Tuesday Night—Wild Rumors Circulate Among Residents of Vicinity.

Shot through the right temple with a .38 calibre bullet, fired by an assassin as yet unknown, Mrs. David Feinstein was found by her hired girl, Victoria Kosanowska, at 3 o'clock yesterday morning in bed at her home, 520 Magnus avenue, lying beside her two year old daughter, Fanny, her blood soaking the childs nightgown. The "hired girl and Mary Manasiska, who worked at the place until last Friday are being held as material witnesses by the police.

A thorough investigation of the affair by the police lasting all day yesterday and late into the night brought little to light apparently, although Chief of Detectives Eli Stodgill states that he feels he is on the right track and in case he is he will make it hot for the murderer by tonight.

Acting Coroner Ritchie took charge of the case immediately after being notified and gave orders to allow no one to enter the place with the exception of the police and a member of the Jewish society, who is allowed to stay with the body in accordance with the customs of that people. At 9 o'clock last night the coroner's jury viewed the remains as they lay in the bed and were then adjourned until next Tuesday night at 8 o'clock when it is hoped more evidence than is now at hand will be in shape to be presented to them. The body was removed to Thomson's undertaking rooms immediately after the jury had left and several hundred residents of north Winnipeg who had been attracted to the spot by morbid curiosity crowded to get glimpses of the wicker basket in which the body was removed to the undertaker's waggon.

At 3 o'clock yesterday morning Vic-

located and will arrive on the first train in this morning.

Robbery Not Motive.

Robbery was not the motive for the crime as a watch and other articles of value were left lying on the bureau in the room in which the crime was committed. Nothing in the house was touched as far as can be learned.

Very few clues of any importance were found by the police and they are working at a disadvantage as they have to work with the Jews and Galicians, whose language they are unable to speak. It is practically certain that the shot was fired from directly over the woman's head into her temple, and apparently from close range, as powder marks are to be seen about the wound. It could not have been fired from the window, and struck as it did. The window could hardly have been raised without awakening the woman. It is in all probability likely that the murderer entered the house by way of a door to which he had a key and left by the same way. Death was instantaneous as was shown by the position of the woman's hands which were resting on the left side of her face as though in prayer.

Death Instantaneous.

As soon as Abraham Scherman had notified the police, he called Doctor G. Kalichnikin and Dr. Borovitch, the former being the first to arrive. He pronounced the woman dead, the bullet having plowed through from the right temple, through the brain and out on the left side. Death was instantaneous. It is thought the shot was fired from near the door, because of the location of the wound. The two year old baby lying beside her, with her head on the dead bosom, was spattered with blood and brains, but was not wakened by the shot. This fact arouses the suspicion that the weapon used was of the latest Pat-

G. Gagnon, W. Cameron and Alfred G. Carter. After being sworn, the jury proceeded to the room where the murder had been committed and viewed the remains. An adjournment was then made until Tuesday evening next at 8 o'clock when the evidence will be taken at the police court room.

A post mortem examination has been ordered and this will be held tomorrow by Dr. Gordon Bell, to which the coroner ordered the removal of the body this morning. Arrangements are being made to hold the funeral tomorrow.

MAGNUS STREET TRAGEDY

The Above Photograph of Mrs. Feinstein and Her Husband Was Taken When They Were Married Eight Years Ago.

News For Touring Real Estate Men

REALTY DELEGATES VISIT SASKATOON

100 years equally pleased, and perhaps within that period we may find the means of providing for the federation of the English speaking people throughout the world, when the great and free nation to which most of you belong, will be brought into more intimate relations with the greatest real estate enterprise that the world has

FIGHT IS OPENED ON DETROIT FARES

Mayor Introduces Resolution for Three Cent Charge—Purchase of Lines Probable.

Detroit, Mich., Aug. 1.—The engagement of Burns Henry to Miss Josephine Irvine, daughter of Mrs. R. J. C. Irvine, is announced.

Below: *Winnipeg Tribune*, August 2, 1913

Above: *Manitoba Free Press*, August 2, 1913

MURDER OF MRS. D. FEINSTEIN STILL WRAPT IN MYSTERY

NOW MEMBERS OF ROYAL COLLEGE OF PHYSICIANS & SURGEONS

London, Aug. 2.—(C.A.P.)—The following have passed the final examination of the Royal College of Physicians: E. C. Hanna, Jessie McDonald, H. A. Williams, of Toronto; and W. J. McKay, of Manitoba.

Many Stories as to Possible Perpetrator of the Crime

AN ECHO OF HER LIFE IN RUSSIA

Woman, Claiming to be Relative, Says She Discarded Sweetheart, Who Vowed He Would Some Day be Avenged

PART 2

6: TRAVELS WITH MY MOTHER

Even when I was a kid, travel was in my blood. I used to study maps in my bedroom, staying up late—waiting until my parents were asleep and then turning my light back on—and imagining places I might see someday, places I couldn't reach by car. I was past the point of making up imaginary places, like the Purple Sea I'd so convincingly described to a woman at synagogue years before. I wanted to go to new places and see interesting things.

After I finished college, I spent weekends hopping around the country, from Atlanta to San Francisco, Chicago to Miami, New Orleans to Seattle. And in the course of seven or eight years, I broke in my new passport and my new backpack: I went with my sister to Australia and New Zealand, the U.K. and Ireland, France and the Netherlands. I went with Mark—who would eventually become a travel writer—to Ecuador, Venezuela, and Guatemala. I went with other friends to Costa Rica, Portugal, Mexico, Turkey.

My parents seemed to enjoy my travel tales, but they hadn't done much travel themselves: a week in London and Amsterdam in the seventies, a Caribbean cruise two decades later after all the kids had left for college, a legal conference in Budapest. In the fall of 1999, my brother, sister, and I pooled our money and got them a trip to Paris to mark their sixtieth birthdays—his a few months earlier, hers coming several months later. I thought they'd be thrilled when we told them. But when I spoke to my mother on the telephone, she didn't seem very excited.

"We're nervous," she confessed.

"About what?" I asked.

"We're worried that we'll get lost," she said—and, knowing my parents, this was an entirely justified fear. Neither of them was great with a map.

"So you get lost," I said. "What's the worst that could happen?"

"Since we don't speak French," she said, "we won't be able to ask anyone for help so we can get un-lost."

She asked if I'd go with them: "It'd make me feel better." I knew I wouldn't be much help. I'd been to Paris exactly once, and I spoke "vacation French": I could order off a menu, buy a ticket to a museum, and read street signs, but that was about it. I scrambled and made a plan—including connecting with a friend of mine from Montreal, a native French speaker named Laurent, who'd happen to be in Paris on business at the same time. My parents were set to arrive on a Tuesday, and I wouldn't arrive until the next day, but I made it as easy as possible for them: I booked them in an English-speaking hotel near the Louvre.

"When you arrive," I told them, "you can walk to the Musee d'Orsay, where you'll recognize all the Impressionist paintings. Then, that afternoon, right by your hotel, you can get on a boat tour in English along the Seine. Ask your English-speaking concierge for a restaurant recommendation for dinner. Then, the next morning, walk to Notre Dame Cathedral; they have an English tour every Wednesday at noon. When you get back to the hotel, I'll be there."

My mother seemed relieved. She was excited to travel, but planning the details overwhelmed her. With me playing tour guide, and my friend Laurent helping to navigate the language, my parents could relax and enjoy their birthday present. All they had to do was get through the first day.

They found the museum, they took the boat tour, and they got a restaurant recommendation from their hotel's front desk clerk—a small bistro across the river in the Latin Quarter. Then everything went wrong. After crossing one bridge to get to the Latin Quarter, they took a stroll down the Left Bank of the Seine. Then they walked across a different bridge, thinking it would take them back to the Right Bank. What they didn't realize is that they were now on an island—Ile St. Louis—in the middle of the Seine; they'd have to walk across the small island and then take a second bridge to get back to the Right Bank, where their hotel was located. But without a map, they couldn't figure out where they were, or why they kept seeing more bridges. Without knowing even a few words of French, their worst anxieties had come true: They were lost, and couldn't ask for help. They eventually happened across a café where another guest from their hotel was having dessert in the window seat. She waved them inside. "Won't you join me?" she asked. "We will," my mother said, "if you'll get us back to the hotel afterward."

The next morning, they set out for Notre Dame—located on a different island: Ile de la Cite. They followed my instructions, arriving just before the weekly English tour at noon. They saw a sign that said "Tour," and followed the arrow; strange that the tour would start at the top of a staircase, they thought, and through a side entrance. (Not knowing the language, they didn't realize that the sign was not in English, meaning "tour," but in French, meaning "tower.") They waited idly at the top of one of the cathedral's massive towers, my mother's fear of heights preventing her from standing too close to the edge, but the English tour never materialized. By the time they realized their error and got back downstairs and around to the front, the group had already departed.

Once I arrived, they could breathe easier, and we enjoyed several days visiting the Champs Elysees, Sacre-Coeur basilica, and the cemetery at Montmartre. With Laurent's help, we navigated subways and taxis and ate at restaurants off the beaten path. And we spent a day in Le Marais, the old Jewish district, visiting the Museum of Jewish Art and History and sampling the chopped liver at Finkelsztajn's kosher deli. We took a walk through the Louvre, when my mother—who admired art, but was never one to spend her free weekends at galleries or museums—was suddenly captivated by the Mona Lisa. "It's so much smaller than I thought," she said when we first stopped to look. Then, minutes later, after we'd moved to a different room, she said she wanted to go back and look at it again. "I never understood what the fuss was about," she said, "but now that I've seen it, I can't stop looking at it."

After their early misadventures, my parents had relaxed. They were even more romantic than I'd ever seen them, holding hands on the street, my mother taking my father's arm on the Metro. Paris, I thought, was working its magic on them.

It was only after we returned to the States that my mother told me that she had been having dizzy spells ever since she mistakenly climbed the tower at Notre Dame. That's why she'd been holding on to my father in Paris. Her doctor diagnosed her with Meniere's Disease, a chronic condition that would give her periodic episodes of vertigo and balance problems for years.

But my mother was determined that Meniere's would not stop her from taking more trips. By this point, my parents had caught a bit of the travel bug, too—especially now that we'd found the formula for minimizing their stress: I made the schedules, got the tickets, found the hotels, and planned the itineraries. Over the next decade, I went on a string of trips with them.

To focus on things of interest to my parents—traditionally observant Jews and committed animal lovers—most of our trips centered on "Jews and zoos." In Mexico City, we took a guided tour of the city's Jewish history, had lunch at a kosher steakhouse, and then spent an afternoon at the zoo in Chapultepec Park. In Antwerp, we ate at a kosher restaurant in the largely Hasidic diamond district, and then walked through the zoo behind the main railway station, a historic park known as much for its nineteenth-century architecture as for its animals. In Prague, we spent one day exploring the city's Jewish history—the cemeteries, the restored synagogues, the concentration camp nearby at Theresienstadt—and spent the next day taking an overpriced cab to the zoo outside the city.

While I saw travel as a way to see new places, my mother also thought of travel as a way to see family. The few trips she took as a child were all to see relatives—grandparents, aunts and uncles, cousins—and once she had kids of her own, most of the travel she planned was focused more on family time than on sightseeing.

Now that I was an adult, I continued to think of travel with my parents as family time, as well as adventure. Some of our trips became larger family affairs, involving six of us: my parents, my sister Stacey and her partner Victor, and Mark and me; together we went to Costa Rica and Argentina.

Traveling with my parents had become something I treasured. I liked knowing that I could help take care of the details and leave them with just the trip itself to focus on. I particularly relished the knowledge that I knew my parents well enough to plan trips they would truly enjoy. And since I had usually been to these places before,

I already knew where I wanted to take them: I was sure they'd love a certain store in Berlin, or a specific ice cream shop in Mexico City.

When my mother was diagnosed with dementia, I didn't think it would have any immediate effect on the travel we were now doing every year. But it did, sooner than I thought.

In the fall of 2009, just months after the Catskills weekend where her memory loss became noticeable, we were making plans for the trip we had all dreamed about: an African safari. The Costa Rica trip had convinced me that my parents loved seeing animals in the wild even more than they loved seeing them in zoos. We started researching our options. We started talking about dates and destinations, and looking for plane tickets.

Then my mother got cold feet.

Unlike her Meniere's, her cognitive impairment had shaken her confidence, more than it had affected her memory at that point. She was unsure if she'd be able to handle such a long plane ride, or if sleeping in a tent, even a luxuriously furnished one, would be uncomfortable. She was anxious—in general, more than about these specific details. This was not like Paris, where I could think of a simple solution; this time, there was nothing I could say to put her at ease. We called off the trip.

But I knew that if we didn't come up with an alternative plan quickly, we'd never get my mother to travel again. And I wasn't ready to stop. Travel had become my favorite way to spend time with my mother. Unlike my trips home, where I slept in my childhood bedroom and she made dinner and did the laundry, or our Fourth of July weekends in the Catskills, where I spent much of my time cooking and cleaning, our trips together gave us a unique opportunity to all be on vacation at the same time. We'd gotten into an enjoyable rhythm with our annual trips, and I wanted to keep it going as long as I could—for her and for me.

I proposed a different trip—with a shorter plane ride, and more familiar accommodations, and food she already loved. Not much wildlife, but it made up for it with a lot of Jewish history: Spain. She liked this plan, and even sounded excited.

In early 2010, the six of us rented a gorgeous apartment in Seville and spent several days eating tapas, marveling at the palace at the Alcazar, and catching a cheesy flamenco show. We took a side trip to Cordoba, where we visited a medieval synagogue, as well as the Mezquita, a spectacular mosque-turned-cathedral.

Then we got to Granada, where we explored the Alhambra. My mother was a bit confused at times, and had trouble remembering what we'd seen, but she was taken by the Alhambra on a visceral level, much as she had been with the Mona Lisa in Paris years before. "How long were we in there?" she asked when we got back to our hotel. It had been more than four hours, I told her. "I lost all track of time," she said. Mark and Victor took video footage of our trip, and in the Alhambra my mother spent most of her time looking up at the architecture in awe.

Her memory issues were noticeable but still fairly minor. Her physical ailments, however, were becoming a major concern on the trip to Spain, something we hadn't anticipated. Her medications—this was when she was trying Aricept—were giving her horrible side effects: vomiting, coughing, and difficulty sleeping, which jet lag only exacerbated. She was too weak to carry her own bags, too tired to climb many stairs, and too unsteady to handle cobblestone streets without steadying herself on someone's arm. She enjoyed the trip, but by the end, she was exhausted.

When she got back home, her doctors took her off Aricept, and she was soon feeling better. But she told me that her traveling days were over—she wasn't in good enough physical condition to keep going. "It's too much," she said. "I can't do it anymore."

Travel was my gift to my parents; I wanted to show them the world, to share with them the joy I felt in going somewhere new. I wasn't ready to give up yet. My sister and I knew that if we wanted to convince her to take one more trip, it had to be soon—and it had to be about family. We settled on a return visit to Israel.

Israel was the first—and only—trip we took overseas as a family when I was growing up, in 1979. We rode camels, swam in the Dead Sea, visited the Western Wall. At the ancient mountain fortress of Masada, we skipped the steep "snake path" ("The walk is too much for the kids," my mother said) and took the cable car instead, but my mother was afraid of heights—a phobia I inherited from her—so instead of enjoying the spectacular views on the way up, we stared at the floor of the cable car, gripping the handrails. Toward the end of our trip, we spent a few days outside Tel Aviv with family: My mother's uncle Leo, her father Henry's baby brother (a plastic surgeon and one of the founders of Tel Aviv's Tel Hashomer

Hospital) had lived in Israel for decades with his wife (a brilliant, beautiful, and feisty Holocaust survivor named Vicky) and their three Israeli-born sons, all young adults at the time, handsome and aloof in their army uniforms.

By 2010, Vicky—now a widow—was in her eighties, and she'd been ill. "This might be our last chance to see her," I told my mother, and that clinched the deal. Just months after returning from Spain, I rented us an apartment in Tel Aviv, and lined up the same tour guide we'd had back in 1979, an old family friend named Bonnie.

Even though part of me knew this might be our last trip with my mother, part of me held out hope that she'd have such a wonderful experience that she'd agree to keep going. Maybe we'd take that African safari after all, or sail through the Galapagos Islands, or fly to Australia. And I knew that if my mother was able to keep traveling, she would—for my sake, if not her own. If the gift I gave her was to show her the world, the gift she gave me was to let me.

It was clear from the very first night in Israel, however, that my mother was not in good enough physical condition to handle even this trip. Our apartment was only a couple blocks off one of Tel Aviv's main squares, but it was up a hill—and then, once we got to the building, there were three more flights of steps. My mother tired easily, but didn't seem to know—or be able to communicate—when she needed to rest. The more tired she got, the faster she walked; the more difficulty she had going up a hill or steps, the more she leaned forward and stubbornly sped up.

On our first night in Tel Aviv, we strolled to the beach, maybe twenty minutes from our apartment. On the way back, I could see that she was exhausted; she didn't typically walk this much at home.

"We can get a cab," I suggested.

"No, no, I'm fine," she said.

"Here's a bench," I said. "Let's stop and catch our breath."

She waved me off, and walked farther ahead of the group.

She picked up her pace, racing up the hill toward our apartment even while she was running out of breath, dashing up the steps so fast she was almost tripping over her own feet. She couldn't get inside until I unlocked the front door, but as soon as I did, she rushed into the living room only to stumble and collapse on the tile floor, face first. She couldn't get up on her own, so we lifted her by the arms and sat her on the sofa. We gave her a glass of water and waited for her to calm down before sending her to bed. (In a rare instance of her condition's mercy, she forgot this incident almost immediately, asking me a few days later why she had bruises on her legs and hips. "You fell on the floor," I told her; "I did?" she asked. "When?")

We were all concerned, but we chalked it up to overexertion—the long flight, the jet lag, the overambitious walk. But when Bonnie took us to the City of David archeological site in Jerusalem, another physical challenge faced us: a walk through ancient water tunnels carved through a mountain. The floors were wet and uneven, the winding passages narrow and dark, the walls jagged and irregular. My mother couldn't hold anyone's arm, or steady herself against a smooth wall. She started taking half-steps, slumping into a half-sitting position with each step but unable to fully straighten her legs and stand upright. She was shaking, and weak, and embarrassed, but there was really no way out except to continue. When we finally got out of the tunnel, she was in worse shape than that night in Tel Aviv.

We all knew what this meant without saying it: A decade after we all started traveling the world together, there would be no more big trips for us with Mom. This would be the last one.

In the video that Mark and Victor shot in Israel, what was most apparent about my mother was that she was constantly looking for something to hold on to—my father's hand, my elbow, a banister, anything to keep her steady. It's possible this was the Meniere's rearing its head again; it might have been a problem with her looking down through her bifocals and misjudging where the ground was; or it might have been an occasional numbness in her feet preventing her from stepping with confidence. Whatever the cause, I felt guilty that I'd overestimated what she could still do, wondering if I pushed too hard for this trip, afraid to see our travel together come to an end. Maybe, I thought, I shouldn't have insisted on one more vacation.

We were all more attentive to her energy level after the trip through the tunnels. We cut back on walking, taking cabs around the city. In the afternoons, we'd come home to watch Israeli television and take naps; in the evenings, we'd stay at home, eating carry-out shawarma and reading in our bedrooms.

She was well-rested by the time we went to Aunt Vicky's apartment in Ramat Aviv for dinner with our cousins and their families. Back in the States, it was Thanksgiving, so Vicky made a traditional dinner for her American relatives. She roasted a turkey—something that's hard to find in Israel, where turkey is popular but people rarely cook a whole bird at home—and sweet potatoes, and found perhaps the only can of cranberry sauce in the Middle East.

My mother had trouble following the conversation; there were too many voices talking about too many things, from news and politics to our plans for the week. She wasn't silent, though; she still remembered a few anecdotes about her relatives from decades before—about the first time she met Vicky when she was growing up in Jersey City and Uncle Leo brought her to York Street to meet the family ("Finally, we've got a normal one in the family," my mother recalled thinking), or what she remembered about her cousins from the fifties, when they were babies. She repeated these stories several times at the table. She still knew how to deliver a funny line. But the stories got less funny—in their own right, and because of what they represented—by the fourth or fifth telling.

I reminded her about our first visit with Leo and Vicky more than thirty years earlier: the turtle I'd found (and briefly adopted) in the orange grove near their house, or the *khamsin*—a hot desert wind—that had blown in from the Sinai with such force that it pushed insects right through the patio's screen doors and onto the dinner table. (As I swatted the bugs, Uncle Leo teased me about the futility of my efforts: "The trouble is that every time you kill one," he joked, "a hundred come to its funeral.") But even though my mother could recall the fifties, 1979 had already vanished from her memory.

At the end of our trip, we went back to Masada. At the base of the mountain, we faced the same decision we'd faced decades earlier: walking up the snake path, or taking the cable car. "The walk is too much for them," I said to my sister. On our ride to the top, the view was the same as it had been in 1979: everyone else looking out the window, while my mother and I gripped the railing until our knuckles went white.

7: JOINING THE CLUB

During my senior year of high school—in 1987, around the same time our relationship was starting to strain—my mother went back to work for the first time in twenty-three years. She had worked before, in a dress shop in Bayonne when she was a college student, and then as an elementary school teacher. With my high school graduation—and college tuition bills—looming, my mother took a job working for a nutrition program run by the county's Division of Elder Affairs. She helped monitor county-subsidized meal programs for senior citizens, which were operated by a variety of organizations, including the Jewish Council for the Aging.

My mother would visit sites that provided senior lunches, where she got to know the clients as well as the people overseeing the programs. The job gave my mother material for some new stories. Once, for instance, she was helping to prepare food for a particularly large lunch, which wasn't generally part of her duties.

"We put out all the food, and when I was washing my hands, I noticed that the diamond was missing from my engagement ring," she told me that evening. "It could have been anywhere—maybe it had fallen out, or maybe it was in the food! I'd been making tuna salad for a hundred people, mixing it up with my hands. We didn't know what to do. If we told people there might be a diamond in the tuna, would they all start searching for it, like the prize in a box of Cracker Jacks? But what if we didn't say anything and someone swallowed it, or worse, choked on it? One of the women I work with is Catholic, and she started praying to Saint Anthony, who's in charge of finding lost things. Sure enough, right after she started praying, someone found the diamond—on the floor—thinking it looked like a piece of Saran Wrap. The woman who'd been praying came up to me and said, 'Thank God you found it. I was ready to start praying to Saint Jude.' I said, 'What's he the saint of?' And she said: 'Hopeless causes.'"

My mother didn't believe in saints, but once her ring was reset, she made a donation to Catholic Charities. "Just to be on the safe side," she said. Still, she had limits, as she mentioned in a speech at my father's sixty-fifth birthday party: "I'll give money, but when they started writing me letters that they needed a priest? I said, 'I gave a rabbi, I cannot give a priest.'"

She enjoyed her new job—not just the work itself, but her co-workers, most notably a woman named Helen Abrahams, who'd urged her to apply for the position and put in a good word for her. My parents had known Helen, and her husband Howie, for many years; they were close friends of my parents' friends Doris and Don. They'd see each other if Doris hosted a big gathering—for a holiday or a family affair, like a bar mitzvah—but they hadn't developed an independent friendship. Now that Helen and my mother were working side by side, however, they grew closer. "We were under the same roof," Helen told me recently, "so we saw each other on a daily basis, and we had our own connection." Such a friendship seemed only natural: They were both upbeat and empathetic, but above all, they were both expert storytellers with a flair for comic timing.

Helen told me that my mother had "the right personality" for the job: "She could schmooze with the best of them. She was quite good at dealing with people who could be a li-i-ittle difficult."

My mother quit her job after just a couple of years, when she was passed up for a promotion by a supervisor who reportedly wanted "the Jews out of middle management." (I mailed my mother a "congratulations" card after she quit, with a brief personal note inside: "Put your feet up and relax after two years of stress. Remember— it's their loss, so fuck 'em.") But my mother and Helen's friendship continued. For several years after my mother stopped working for the county, a group of six women—my mother and her sister

Marilyn, Doris and her sister, Helen and her sister—would take an annual trip to a spa together. The "spa ladies" would typically take a few simple treatments—a massage, perhaps—but mostly they'd spend a few days eating well and cracking each other up, creating more stories to share with their families when they got home.

When my mother started suffering from dementia, Helen was the one who found a place for her to go, just as she had done twenty-five years earlier when my mother went back to work.

Kensington Club was a "social day program" that had launched a few years earlier for people dealing with dementia. Helen knew about it—not only because she had continued to work in elder affairs for many years after my mother quit, and still frequently worked with the Jewish Council for the Aging, which oversaw the program, but because her husband Howie was now a client, dealing with his own dementia.

Although "dementia" was still my mother's official-yet-vague diagnosis, by 2012 she'd started saying—sometimes—that she had Alzheimer's, and I'd done the same. I read medical literature about the stages of the disease, and her progress seemed to track almost perfectly, from the early stages of "normal" memory loss to the more recent stages of "mild" impairment where she'd repeat herself, suffer from social anxiety and more frequent mood swings, and lose track of what day it was. (My father resisted this change in terminology, probably because his own mother had died of the disease after a prolonged and awful decline, and he feared what it would mean to call my mother's condition "Alzheimer's": It would mean acknowledging that we knew what lay ahead—the horrors it would bring, and how many years they would last.)

Toward the end of 2012, soon after I'd shared with her the basic information about the Winnipeg murder mystery, my mother started going to Kensington Club. My father hired a driver to take her to these half-day sessions, where she joined a dozen or so people in the early stages of dementia. Sometimes the organizers would bring in a speaker to talk about current events or books, or they'd listen to music, or take a trip to a museum. A kosher lunch was provided as well, before everyone went home in the early afternoon.

My mother enjoyed Kensington Club: It got her out of the house, independent of my father, which had become a challenge since she stopped driving. She got to socialize with other people, including Howie, who wouldn't judge her if she repeated herself. ("It's okay," people would say to each other, "here, you don't have to remember.") She started going two days a week, and eventually bumped up to three, and then four. Kensington Club became a place she looked forward to going.

It was good for my father, too. It gave him time away from her—which had also been tough for him to wrangle since she'd stopped driving. And Kensington Club included a series of evening meetings for clients and their caregivers: The caregivers would have a support group meeting, where my father could talk to other people in his situation—including Helen—about everything from emotional difficulties to logistical questions, and plan for what was to come; this was the first time my father and Helen spent time together without their spouses. Meanwhile, my mother would be down the hall having her own meeting, talking about her own concerns and doing what she had always done: tell stories and keep people entertained. ("Her stories were wonderful and everyone enjoyed them," the support group facilitator later told me. "She was able to re-tell them each week to the group, who did not remember them from week to week, and I was delighted each and every time!") One of the things she worried about most was how my father could possibly run the house when she grew unable to do it. "For goodness sake," she told the group, "the man can't even find the butter in the fridge. How is he going to manage the household?"

In 2013, the Jewish Council for the Aging held a meeting for its program directors and funders to discuss Kensington Club. Five years after the group's launch, they wanted to see what kind of impact it was having. Some of the organizers remembered my mother from twenty-five years before, when she had worked with them through the Division of Elder Affairs. So when they were looking for one of Kensington Club's clients to speak at the meeting, talking about how the program functioned from an insider's perspective, they asked her if she'd be interested. Never one to shy away from a public presentation, she said yes.

What the program directors didn't know is that the speaking engagement caused my mother some deal of confusion. Preparing to speak at a professional meeting alongside the organizers—some of whom were her former colleagues—my mother began to think she was one of Kensington Club's directors herself, delivering a speech about how her program was serving others. For weeks before the presentation, she would tell me about how she was overseeing this program, not participating in it. She slipped back in time twenty-five years, to the time when she worked with the Jewish Council for the Aging.

When the day came, she got dressed up for the event. And when the car came to drive her to the meeting while we were on the phone, she told me, "I have to go to work now."

Her dementia was evident to the people in the room; she repeated herself several times. But everyone at the meeting agreed that she did a great job, presenting an articulate and moving speech without written notes. She spoke about how accepting people were at Kensington Club, and how supportive the clients were of one another. The program included elements of humor and camaraderie, she explained, which made it a fun place to spend her days. She recalled her time volunteering at the Jewish Council for the Aging's Senior HelpLine—this was right after her job with Elder Affairs—and told the group, "Now it's my time to need help, not give help."

One woman, who had worked with my mother many years earlier, sent my father an email telling him that her presentation was "charming, articulate, humorous." ("I was totally impressed," she wrote. "She is my hero!") Even though she was attending a group for people with dementia, my mother was still lucid enough to write and deliver a speech, and still enough her old self to come across just as she always had. Years later, the program director said that people were still talking about my mother's speech, telling me, "She stole the show."

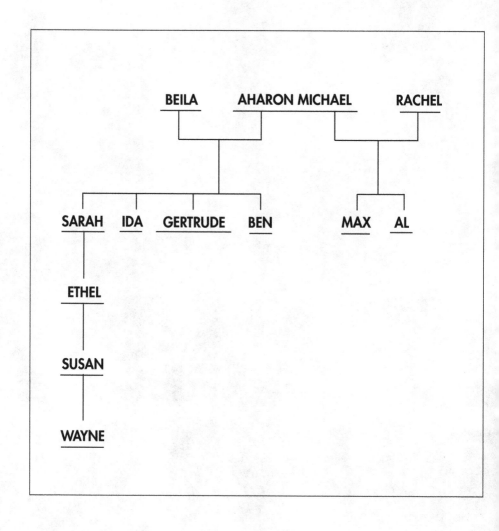

8: WHAT'S IN A NAME?

A generation after my mother found a photograph of her grandfather David with a strange woman, that same photograph sparked a different question from me. It wasn't the image itself that I found curious, but the name written on the reverse: Sarah Brooks.

To me, that sounded more like a refined English actress than an immigrant from some Eastern European shtetl.

It's hard to know for certain how my great-grandmother referred to herself because my relatives, like most recent immigrants at that time, probably used their English names only on official documents. Even then, they typically weren't filling out the forms themselves—they were saying their names aloud to an English-speaking interpreter or clerk, who would then write down the information.

Among themselves, my relatives used their Yiddish names. David and Sarah were known as Dovid and Shifra, for instance; David's brothers Morris and Isidor were Moishe and Itzik, and his sisters Clara and Fina were Kreintzi and Freydl; Sarah's sister Gertrude was called Greena. This undoubtedly made it very confusing for the clerks who came to take census reports. Children's names in particular seem to shift wildly from form to form, but it's unclear whether this was due to clerks who didn't understand what they were hearing, or Yiddish-speaking parents who couldn't remember exactly what each child's rarely used and unfamiliar English name was.

Although they had only been used for the occasional official document, English names made it easier for me to track my relatives through Canadian censuses, immigration forms and transit manifests, birth and marriage and death certificates, cemetery listings, and newspaper reports—even if many of my relatives wouldn't have answered to their own English names. These names were for the outside world; they didn't carry meaning and family history the way their Yiddish and Hebrew names did.

My great-grandmother's first name—Sarah—is fairly consistent in English-language records. (Her son Harry's death certificate is the lone exception; it lists his mother's first name as Shifra.) But figuring out her last name, her maiden name, would take much more investigation. Official documents, I soon discovered, only reveal so much, and they aren't always reliable.

Official documents helped me trace when people were born, when they got married, when they died, as well as where they lived. But when I was searching for information about my great-grandmother's murder, they weren't much help. The death certificate told me that she'd been murdered, but offered no details beyond "bullet wound through brain—homicidal."

Fortunately, Winnipeg's three daily newspapers followed the case closely. These became the backbone of my research.

The first paper whose archives proved useful was the *Manitoba Free Press*, which was founded in 1872, just two years after the province was established, and a year before Winnipeg was incorporated. The oldest newspaper in western Canada, it became the *Winnipeg Free Press* in 1931, and is today the most widely read newspaper in the province, with a daily circulation of over one hundred thousand. Since it's still being published, its archives were easy for me to find and search online. The *Free Press* covered the murder in a string of eight stories, one of them on the front page, starting on August 2, 1913.

For quite a while, the *Free Press* was my only major source of news about the murder. The *Winnipeg Tribune*, the city's afternoon broadsheet, which was founded in 1890, folded in 1980. I assumed its archives were lost, but I was happy to eventually learn that the University of Manitoba has placed its entire run online. The *Tribune* was the first paper to cover the shooting, mere hours after it occurred on August 1, 1913, and published an additional dozen articles about the case in the ensuing weeks. These subsequent articles appeared on the front page six times, often written with somewhat more sensationalistic prose than the typically sober *Free Press*, whose offices were next door on McDermot Avenue, then known as "Newspaper Row."

I held out little hope of ever finding articles from the city's third daily. The *Winnipeg Telegram* was founded in 1898, although it had originated four years earlier with a different name: *The Daily Nor'Wester*. Closely aligned with Canada's Conservative Party, the *Telegram* published daily editions every morning until 1920, when it was purchased by the *Tribune*. Its iconic Newspaper Row building, designed by William Hodgson and built in 1882, still stands at the corner of McDermot Avenue and Albert Street in the downtown Exchange District, and has been designated by the city as a historic site. The paper's archives are not available online, nor included in the *Tribune* archives, but are held on microfilm at the Legislative Library of Manitoba—as I belatedly discovered. With reporting that relied more than its competitors' on direct quotes from interviews with primary sources, the *Telegram* ran five stories about the murder, two of which appeared on the photo-free front page, starting on August 2, 1913.

Of course, most of Winnipeg's recent Jewish immigrants at the time weren't reading the English-language dailies. They were getting their news from the newly founded Yiddish press.

I don't speak or read Yiddish. My story is typical of a lot of North American Jews: My immigrant great-grandparents spoke Yiddish as their first language, my English-speaking grandparents spoke it as a second language, my parents picked some up from their parents but never became fluent, and my generation knows the occasional word or expression but not much more. Still, I'd spent years as an editor at the *Forward*, the English edition of the century-old Yiddish newspaper the *Forverts*; I knew where to turn for help to locate and translate Yiddish articles.

Der Keneder Yid/*The Canadian Jew* was founded in Winnipeg in 1910 as a weekly Yiddish journal; it would later change its name to *Dos Yidishe Vort*/*The Israelite Press*, and begin publishing daily. At the time of Sarah's murder, *Der Keneder Yid* was the city's main source of Jewish news, with offices at 216 Dufferin Avenue in the

North End. The murder appeared on page two in the first issue of the paper to be published after it happened, on August 7, 1913, under the headline "The Horrific Tragedy at 520 Magnus Ave."

I knew from the sheer number of stories I'd found that my great-grandmother's murder was big news in Winnipeg, but I hadn't anticipated that it had made headlines far beyond the city. In their Saturday editions on August 2, 1913, two Toronto dailies ran similar brief items, albeit riddled with errors. "Woman Murdered" read the page twenty-eight headline in *The Globe*—the precursor to today's *Globe and Mail*; "Girl is Arrested, Mistress Murdered" read *The Toronto Daily Star*'s headline, on page five. Both reports begin identically, with identical typos, indicating to me that this was a story that went out on the wire: "The murdered body of Mrs. David Finestein was found in her home at 520 Magnus Avenue at 11 o'clock this morning. Neighbors were attracted by the cries of her little girl who had been beside the body from the time she had awakened from her night's sleep and found her mother missing. A bullet wound was found in her head." Beyond misstating the time her body was found and incorrectly noting that it was neighbors rather than young Harry who'd heard the baby crying, this short story's most implausible claim is that the murdered woman's body somehow went "missing" after being shot in the head. The *Globe* story wraps up quickly, stating that no arrests had been made, and that David was in Canora, Saskatchewan, at the time of the murder. *The Daily Star*, on the other hand, notes that a servant girl had made threats and had been arrested with "a male friend": "Their names are Carrie Duggan and Tony Egan," the story reports, giving the suspects unlikely Irish surnames that appear in no other accounts of the murder, before concluding with one final error by noting that David was in Kenora, Ontario—a town of roughly five thousand people at the time, near the provincial border with Manitoba—rather than Canora, Saskatchewan.

In Montreal's daily Yiddish newspaper *Der Keneder Adler/The Canadian Eagle*—founded in 1907—the story made the front page on August 3, 1913. "Jewish Woman Killed in Winnipeg" read the headline, atop a story that noted that "the horrific, mysterious death of a young Jewish woman…devastated the entire Jewish population of Winnipeg."

The Brandon Daily Sun—the newspaper of the second-largest

city in Manitoba, one hundred thirty miles west of Winnipeg—put the story on its front page on the afternoon of August 1, 1913, referring to my great-grandmother as a "Russian Jewess," and again four days later. In Portage la Prairie, a town of a few thousand between Brandon and Winnipeg, *The Weekly Review* covered the murder by printing re-edited versions of stories from the *Winnipeg Tribune*. Fifteen hundred miles farther west, *The New Westminster Times*, a daily paper outside Vancouver, also followed the case on multiple occasions, printing slightly revised versions of *Manitoba Free Press* articles.

My great-grandmother's murder wasn't just a legend in my own family; it was truly a national story. Sarah Feinstein's name was known all across Canada.

But what was her name, exactly? Feinstein, which probably had a stable pronunciation and consistent spelling in Yiddish (using the Hebrew alphabet), saw its spelling change many times on English-language documents. What was usually Feinstein at the time of my great-grandmother's murder would become Fainstein several years later, with a number of variations along the way. And when it came to newspaper stories about the murder, the spelling changed even more.

This wasn't unique to my family. Foreign-sounding names were particularly inconsistent in English-language newspaper reports: The Feinsteins' neighbor Lucy Kesler was originally referred to in press reports as Lena Castle, and the *Telegram* consistently called her Lucy Kochin; the man the *Free Press* called Stefan Kushowsky was known in the *Tribune* as Stefan Osadchuk, while the *Telegram* couldn't decide, calling him "Kushkowski or Osatche."

When it came to these names, I tended to favor the spellings that came up most often, or in the most direct and detailed ways: For instance, the man who claimed to have seen the shooter was identified as C.D. Polson in the *Telegram*, and as James Fulson in the *Free Press*. But while the latter mentions him briefly in passing, the former offers many more details—his address and his occupation as an auctioneer, as well as long direct quotes—that indicate a more careful attention to accuracy. Other times, I searched Manitoba's Vital Statistics or Canadian census reports to see which spelling was the most plausible. For example, the Feinsteins' next-door neighbor is sometimes called Kastner and other times Kasner in newspaper stories; I couldn't find any records at all for a Robert Kastner in Winnipeg at the time, but there was a record for a Robert Kasner—a Jewish immigrant from Russia—around the time of the murder, so I deduced that this was the correct name.

I could make this kind of educated guess with names. But when it came to other information around the murder—witness testimony, police reports, newspaper stories presenting purported "facts" only to contradict them almost immediately—it was harder to know exactly what was true. Beyond problems of inconsistent spelling, poor translation, uninformed sources, rumors taken as truth, and melodramatic prose, there were conflicting reports about basic facts. Details were omitted, or reported arbitrarily. One newspaper's record conflicted with another's.

I could use the multiple newspaper reports to weave together a relatively complete account of the murder and its aftermath, with one article filling in the blanks left by another. But I still needed more sources, if not to give me definitive answers, then to help me use my best judgment to come up with likely ones, to suggest which threads of the narrative to believe and which ones—after decades as a journalist—I should view with skepticism.

To mitigate the imprecision of the newspaper reports, I relied on official documents—birth certificates and death certificates from Vital Statistics, census reports cataloged online—whenever possible. I assumed these would be more consistent and reliable, with information verified at the time by government officials, rather than being open to interpretation, and misinterpretation, by reporters who often didn't speak the same language as their sources. Even so, these papers were themselves riddled with mistakes, rife with spelling errors—perhaps resulting from poor translation from Yiddish to English. Some of these documents were filed days or even years after events took place, so the dates recorded on them with apparent certainty were subject to the vagaries of memory, and themselves unverifiable. The more errors I found in these documents, the less I trusted the rest of the information they contained.

Still, these were particularly useful for gleaning small bits of information, from dates and addresses to people's exact ages—and names, including my great-grandmother.

A complicated last name in Yiddish or Russian could get changed by—or for—a clerk taking notes for a census or immigration form or birth certificate. So it was possible that a name like Auerbrook or Awerbruch might become something simpler for an Anglo-Canadian clerk to understand.

Her maiden name, however, is inconsistent in official Canadian records—both in its original, longer form, and its possibly Anglicized, shortened form: On her own death certificate from 1913, it is listed as Averboock. But most of the time, Sarah's maiden name appears in a shortened version. Her marriage certificate from 1906 lists it as Book. On her children's birth certificates, Sarah's maiden name was sometimes listed as Brook, and other times (including my grandmother Ethel's birth certificate) as Brooks. Any of these may have been the anglicized version she adopted for herself in North America, or they may have been the closest things the Canadian clerks who filled out the forms understood when she said Auerbrook or Awerbruch. Or perhaps it was both—a name that an English-speaking clerk originally wrote down incorrectly that my great-grandmother then adopted for its simplicity when it came to making herself understood on the rare occasions that other such documents needed to be filled out.

These changes weren't consistent; not everyone in Sarah's family adopted a more Anglo-friendly name. Her youngest sister Gertrude immigrated to Canada in April 1908 when she was seventeen, accompanied by her twelve-year-old brother Ben and seventeen-year-old cousin Rachel Ditlowitcz on board the *Dominion*, servicing the same shipping line from Liverpool to Quebec City that Sarah had traveled two years earlier on the *Southwark*; the passes issued in Kiev allowing them passage abroad listed their last name as Averbuh, and the ship manifest spells it Averbuch. At the time of Sarah's death, Gertrude was living with her husband Louis Gelmon, a grocer, in Sturgis, Saskatchewan; from this point on, she took her husband's last name, but when their only child Sydney was born in 1916, his birth certificate listed Gertrude's maiden name as Averboock. Sarah's other sister, Ida, who'd immigrated in 1910, was also living in Sturgis, where her husband Harry Chodorcoff ran a general store; her maiden name was never shortened, although the spelling on official documents varied from Averbuch to Auerbuch to (on her children's birth certificates) Overboch.

Sarah's male relatives, for whom the family name was used more frequently and prominently, were more consistent: Ben went by Ben Brooks once he arrived in Canada. And although Sarah had left Russia before they were born, she had four half-siblings, after her widowed father married his second wife, Rachel; two of them eventually came to Canada as well, arriving a decade after Sarah's death. These two half-brothers, Max and Al, also went by Brooks. The idea of adopting this anglicized name most probably came from Sarah, who was the oldest in the family and the first to immigrate to North America—although this doesn't necessarily mean that she used Brooks as her maiden name consistently, or from the very beginning of her time in Canada, years before her siblings arrived.

While I couldn't be certain of Sarah's maiden name—in its original form or a shortened version—I ultimately concluded that my mother's notion that my Jewish immigrant great-grandmother from Russia went by the improbably English name of Sarah Brooks was entirely plausible, and even likely to be true.

"That's what my mother said," my mother told me when I shared what I'd surmised—as if the bulk of her mother's story about Sarah Brooks hadn't been fictitious.

Official documents and newspaper reports both had their shortcomings; they were inconsistent, sometimes contradictory, and unreliable. Even a simple question could yield inconclusive answers; Sarah's exact age and year of birth, for instance, vary from source to source, with some suggesting she may have been born as early as 1885 rather than 1887. But the more information I gathered, the more I felt I could extrapolate the facts about Sarah's murder with a reasonable degree of certainty.

To flesh out the story beyond those simple facts, I started researching the history of Jewish Winnipeg, to get a sense of context for my great-grandmother's life.

The Jews in Manitoba, published in 1961 by Rabbi Arthur A. Chiel, traces the rise of the community in Winnipeg, and explores the internecine battles between rabbis, newspaper editors, and community leaders over the years. Reading it punctured any rose-tinted notions I might have had about the early years of the North End's "New Jerusalem" being a simple idyll for poor Jewish immigrants. "A much more correct designation was that applied to it by the Jewish residents themselves—*Mitzrayim*, the Hebrew name for Egypt, a name it well deserved," he writes. "The struggling human beings with which *Mitzrayim* teemed drudged like serfs in the service of a harsh master—physical survival."

The Jews of Winnipeg, a short 1973 documentary directed by Bill Davies and produced by the National Film Board of Canada, includes a few black-and-white still images from the North End that gave me a sense of what the area looked like around the time of my great-grandparents' arrival—wooden houses lining dirt roads, peddlers' carts, garment factories. The movie also discusses the city's longstanding Yiddish culture; when the film was made, more than one-third of the Jews in Winnipeg were thought to speak Yiddish as their home tongue, and the local community television station broadcast a program called *The Jewish Hour* in Yiddish. Comedian David Steinberg, a Winnipeg native, appears in the documentary talking about growing up in a Yiddish-speaking household.

But while *The Jews of Winnipeg* paints a picture of enduring Yiddish continuity in Winnipeg, the language was already on the decline in 1973.

In 1914, just one year after Sarah Feinstein's murder, Yiddish instruction for children began in Winnipeg. The city quickly became home to a wide network of Yiddish-speaking Jewish day schools—including the secular Peretz Schule, which was the largest Yiddish school in North America in the thirties, by which time Yiddish was taught to Jewish children to a larger extent than was true in any other city on the continent. The Jewish community could support a daily Yiddish newspaper—*Dos Yidishe Vort/The Israelite Press* was the first daily Yiddish newspaper in Canada when it converted from a weekly in 1914. But even though the Jewish community stayed strong, Yiddish eventually started to decline, which the paper's fortunes illustrated. *Dos Yidishe Vort* eventually went from a daily back to a weekly, and from all-Yiddish to half-English, before closing entirely in 1981.

I got the best sense of the old North End, and Jewish Winnipeg as a whole, by reading *Coming of Age: A History of the Jewish People of Manitoba*, a 2009 book by Winnipeg-based historian Allan Levine, who grew up in the North End. At a time when the city as a whole was "teeming with enthusiasm" and "alive with excitement" after the turn of the century, he writes, the noisy North End had become "a full-fledged ghetto" rife with disease, crime, and "grinding poverty." When the Chicago-based magazine *The Reform Advocate* published a special issue about the neighborhood in 1914, Levine notes, the reporter deemed it repulsive: "We find a row of dwarfy cottages—neglected; unsanitary with unclean yards and junk and crippled disjointed riggs, express wagons and push-carts—and almost every yard enriched with what was dignified with the appellation 'stable.'"

In *Coming of Age*, Levine offers rich detail about the working lives of the immigrants, and the many internal battles, both religious and cultural, in the community. And he charts the progress of the old North End, from the opening of Oretzki's Department Store on Selkirk Avenue in 1910 to the paving of Magnus Avenue and other nearby streets in the twenties.

Levine also wrote a 1997 novel called *The Blood Libel*, a fictional account of a murder in the Jewish North End in 1911; being a historian, he filled even his made-up story about "the wickedest city in the Dominion" with facts about important real-life Winnipeggers of the period, from Police Chief John MacRae to *Free Press* editor John W. Dafoe. I contacted Levine by email to see if he'd ever heard about my great-grandmother, whose case was contemporaneous with the one he'd created in his novel. He told me he'd never come across the Feinstein murder in his research; "otherwise I certainly would have included it" in *Coming of Age*, he wrote. But more broadly speaking, Levine was well acquainted with crime and policing in the area at the time, and he knew crimes against Jewish immigrants didn't get much attention from police. "Given the times and attitudes towards immigrants (and Jews, in particular) the police would not have expended huge resources" on my great-grandmother's murder, he told me.

The books and the documentary gave me a good sense of what the North End was like when my great-grandmother lived—and died—there. But, I knew, the best way for me to get a feel for the area would be to go there myself.

In all my years of traveling, I'd been to Canada probably twenty times: Toronto, Montreal, Quebec City, Ottawa, Vancouver, and Campobello Island in New Brunswick. But I'd never been to Winnipeg, the city that held my family's history.

Perhaps, I thought, the time has come.

די שרעקליכע טראגעדיע אין 520 מעגנוס עוו.

תאפארת ישראל שהל וואו הרב ה.ו.
נאראפסקי האט נעמאכסם דעם הספד,
פון דער תאפארת ישראל שהל האט אים
נרויסע סהרה מים קענקרעסעסאן לעבען צום
בית עלמן. אוא גרויסע לויה האט
די פאמיליע פון דער עדמא־
דעמא

די ערמארדעטע מים איהר מאן, מים דעם איהר יאהר צוריג.

Above: *Keneder Yid*, August 7, 1913

Right: *Weekly Review*,
from Portage la Prairie, August 6, 1913

Below: *Brandon Daily Sun*,
August 1, 1913

Winnipeg Woman Believed Have To Been Murdered While She Slept

Winnipeg, Aug. 1—Lying peacefully on her left side as if in prayer, Mrs. David Fienstein, a Russian Jewess, aged 28, 520 Magnus avenue, was found at three o'clock this morning by Victoria Komanowska, her hired girl, with a bullet hole through her right temple and blood and brains spattered over her two year old baby, Fanny, who was sleeping beside her.

At three o'clock the maid was awakened by the six year old son, who told her that the baby aged seven months was crying. She went into the room and tried to awaken the mother but without success. Being frightened she went to the next door neighbor who rushed in and discovered the murder. No trace has as yet been found of the revolver. The maid, Victoria Komanowska and a girl who was dismissed a week ago, Mary Manastaka, are being held by the police awaiting investigation.

Woman Murdered While She Slept

A Baby Was Sleeping Beside Her

Brutal Crime Perpetrated in Winnipeg Home Near Midnight

Winnipeg, Aug. 1—Mrs. David Feinstein, a prominent member of the Winnipeg Hebrew colony, was found in her home early this morning, lying in bed, murdered, with a bullet hole in her temple, while her life blood gushed forth in streams upon the seven months old babe lying beside her. The woman's expression was peaceful. There was no sign of a struggle having taken place and not an article in the room was disturbed. In a cot at the foot of the woman's bed lay three young children who wept bitterly for the mother who, having passed the great "divide" could not hear them.

No Trace of Perpetrator

No trace of the perpetrator of the deed has as yet been discovered. There were no signs of a struggle in the room, and practically nothing which would lead to the identity of the miscreant could be found. What might be considered in the nature of a clue was found in the shape of a "box of Russian fuses. These matches are not sold in Winnipeg, but are often seen in the possession of immigrants from South Russia and Austria. The finding of these seems to give color to the rumor that the deed was committed by the lover of a girl named Mary Komanowsky, who is a servant and who quarrelled with Mrs. Feinstein on Friday last.

Victoria, the servant girl, was not awakened by the sound of the shot being fired. Questioned later, she stated that one of the children, Harry, aged 7 years, came to her and told her he could not awaken his mother and that she was bleeding.

She had hurriedly gone into the woman's room and also tried to waken her mistress. She was told by Harry that he had awakened by sounds of the other two children crying. On her attempt ing to awaken her mistress, she had noticed the blood, but did not know what it meant. She had never seen anything like that before.

Husband a Cattle Dealer

The murdered woman was the wife of Dave Feinstein, a cattle dealer, who has resided in Winnipeg for the past ten years. Seven years ago he was married to Miss Sarah Auerbach, who just recently came from Russia. By this union they had four children, all of whom survive. They are Harold, aged 7 years, Ethel, aged 4, Fanny, aged 2, and seven-months-old Annie, who slept beside her mother at the time of the tragedy. Up to the present time Feinstein was paying a battle in the Canora district, he having left the city on his business trip on Sunday last. After many efforts, the news was telephoned him this morning and he is returning on the first train.

Servant Girl's Alarm

The first news of anything extraordinary having occurred came to Abraham Shourman, a young Hebrew residing nearby, who was called by Mrs. Feinstein's servant. The Mrs. sleeps and I won't wake, she said fearfully.

On going straight through to the woman's bedroom, at the end of the hall, leading from the front door, and on opening the door a terrible sight met his eyes. There on the bed lay Mrs. Feinstein in a posture which gave one the impression of peaceful sleep. In her right temple, however, was a terrible bullet hole, the bedroom sign of which seemed to indicate that the shot was fired at close quarters. The woman's hands were on the pillow and under her head, and the bed clothes were not

disarranged to any great extent. By her side lay the seven months old baby girl. She was crying loudly, for the hot life-blood flowing from the mother's brain, was pouring in a torrent upon her little face and body, while the bed beneath the two was steeped in the crimson fluid.

BIG WOOD BUFFALO

Many Bands Still Range North of Alberta Wilds

There are yet vast areas in Northern Canada consisting of stunted forests and open grasslands and muskeg, of which practically nothing is known, save what can be gathered from the stories of trappers and explorers who have penetrated this northern wilderness. Such a country exists on the extreme north boundary of Alberta, to the west of the Slave River, and from this country have come remnants of large bands of wild buffalo, the only remnants, not in captivity, of the great herds which once roamed the Western plains.

To verify these rumors and to take steps to prevent the extinction of these herds, the Forestry Branch of the Dominion Government sent out an investigation party, working under the direction of Mr. A. J. Bell, the Government agent at Fort Smith in the North West Territories. The report sent in reads like a book of adventure and will be contained in the Annual Report of the Director of Forestry, which will shortly be printed.

The existence of at least three herds of buffalo, was proved, one herd consisting of bulls, cows and yearlings, to the number of about forty-five. In appearance they closely resemble the plains buffalo, of which they are the remnant, but, being forced by necessity to live in the hilly woody regions remote from settlement, they have changed their habits somewhat and are fleeter of foot and more agile than their ancestors of the plains.

In summer, they may be found in twos and threes, roaming through the birch woodlands, but in winter they travel in large bands for greater security against wolves. In winter, when passing from one feeding ground to another, they travel in single file through the snow, making a narrow trail on which the snow is packed as hard as a rock. When they come to a grass grown slough or marsh, they stay there until all the feed is exhausted and then, while the cows and yearling make good their escape.

Several pictures of the wild buffalo were obtained. The Indian Chief, Pierce Squirrel, who accompanied the party and who is most familiar with that region, estimated the number of the buffalo there to be at least two hundred. Their worst enemy, at present, is the timber wolf, and attempts will be made to exterminate this destroyer, by raising the bounty in this region.

Following the curtailment of expenditure issued by city commissioners, of Edmonton, some ten days ago, close to 300 men have been laid off in 2 departments and streets.

WOMAN MURDERED.

Winnipeg, Aug. 1. The murdered body of Mrs. David Finestein was found in her home at 520 Magnus Avenue at 11 o'clock this morning. Neighbors were attracted by the cries of her little girl, who had been beside the body from the time she had awakened from her night's sleep and found her mother missing. A bullet wound was found in her head.

No arrests have been made. D. Finestein, husband of the murdered woman, was in Canora, Sask., at the time of the murder, and has been wired for. He is a cattle dealer.

GIRL IS ARRESTED, MISTRESS MURDERED

Winnipeg Woman's Body Found With Bullet Wound in Head.

CHILD BY HER SIDE

Special to The Star.

Winnipeg, Aug. 1.—The murdered body of Mrs. David Finestein was found in her home at 520 Magnus avenue at eleven o'clock this morning. Neighbors were attracted by the cries of her little girl who had been beside the body from the time she had awakened from her night's sleep and found her mother missing. A bullet wound was found in her head. A servant girl who was dismissed last Friday and made threats as she left the house has been arrested with a male friend. Their names are Carrie Duggan and Tony Egan. The husband of the woman, who is a cattle dealer, was in Kenora, Ont., at the time.

Above: *Toronto Globe,*
August 2, 1913

Left: *Toronto Daily Star,*
August 2, 1913

Opposite page:

New Westminster Times,
August 9, 1913

Keneder Adler, August 3, 1913

WINNIPEG MURDER STILL A MYSTERY

Police Search for Galician Whose Moves Puzzled Them—He Disappears.

Winnipeg, Man., Aug. 8.—The city police department is now making desperate efforts to aprehend a Galician whose name is believed to be Stefan Kalowcha, the lover of the girl Mary Manastaka, who is held as a material witness in the mysterious murder on August 1 of Mrs. David Geinstein, at her home at Magnus avenue, since learning that Stefan was in the store of Mrs. Feinman, at 192 Andrews street, a little over a block away from the scene of the tragedy on the evening of the murder.

Questioned as to what transpired in her little general store, Mrs. Feinman stated that Stefan, whom she knew well on sight—he having been at her place more than once in company with the girl Mary—came into the place at about 8:45 o'clock. He ordered a bottle of aerated water and sat on a box and drank it.

"What has happened on Magnus avenue?" he asked casually.

"Why, don't you read the paper?" asked Mrs. Feinman. "Did you not know that Mrs. Feinstein was shot at 3 o'clock this morning?"

"I didn't know. I don't read English." Then he asked: "Is anyone arrested?"

"Oh, yes," replied the storekeeper, "Mrs. Feinstein's girl, the one that used to come here with you."

Was Much Affected.

At the words Stefan started visibly. "Who?" he asked, speaking rapidly. "You mean Mary." As the woman acquiesced a pallid tinge crept slowly across the Galician's swarthy face. His lips quivered, and suddenly the bottle from which he had been drinking fell with a crash to the floor. He stared stupidly at the wreck for a moment and then without a word turned and fled through the doorway, and soon was out of sight in the fading twilight.

This information was given to the police department by Mrs. Feinman, who advanced the additional information that Stefan until the day before the crime had worked in the C. P. R. yards as a laborer. Enquiries in this district elicited the information that since quitting on Thursday night at six o'clock he had not been seen by any of his workmates.

Every means of exit from the city is being watched and the police have practically encordoned the city, making it impossible for this man to escape before he has given an account of himself and his movements on the night of the tragedy.

Some remarkable stories are being circulated by the friends of the murdered woman, who stand around, a morbidly curious throng in the vicinity of the little cottage, telling and retelling the gruesome details of the tragedy. Incidents in the dead woman's life are freely forthcoming. Few of these, however, have any bearing or tend to throw any light on the case.

אידישע פרוי געמוירדעט אין וויניפעג

געשינען לינענדיג מיט א רעוואָל־
ווער קול אין קאָפף, צוויי יאָה־
רונג בײבי בײ איהר זײט אַבענע
שפריצט מיט בלום, קרוסעליכע
דיענסטמיידעל אַרעסטירט.

וויניפעג שבת, — א שרעקליכע
מארד געהיימעניס פון א יונגע אידישע
פרוי, וועלכע איז היינט פריה דא געשו־
נען געוואָרען טויט אין איהר צימער,
האָט אויפגעשטערטם די נאַצע אידי־
שע בעפעלקערונג פון וויניפעג. די אונ־
גליקליכע איז מרם. פיינשטיין, 28 יאָהר
אַלט, פון 520 מאַגנעס אווע. זיא הײ נע־
פונען געוואָרען לינענדיג מיט א רעוואָל־
ווער קויל אין איהר רעכטען שלײף, אין
בײ איהר זײט אין נעלעגען איהר צוויי
יאָהרינע קיירעלע סעניט, אין באַשעען
בעשפריצט מיט רוא געהירען און בלוט
פון דער מומער.

אַרום דריי אוהר מאָרמאַ האָט מרם.
פיינשטיינ'ס קלאסמער דעקם יאָהרינער
אנגעל אָנגעטויעקם ווערע קריסטליכע
דיענסטם וויקטאָריא קאַמאַנאָוואַסקא, און
ער האָט איהר געזאָנט דאָס די בייבי'
אין ארײנגעקומען אין צימער פון מרם.
פיינשטיין אין דאָם, געוואַלט אויסזאָל־
קען זיא יונגע אידישע מומער, וועהענדינ
אַז זיא מעגהט ניט אויף האָט זך די
קריסטליכע דיענסם דערשראָקען און איז
ארײנ אין דער צוויימער היי צו א שכן
און דערצעהלם. דער שכן אין אריינגע־
קריכען האָם ער געפונען דיא פרוי טויט.
פון רעוואלווער האָט מען קיין שפור
ניט געפונען. דיא פאָליציי האָט ארעס־
טירם דיא דיענסט קאַמאַנאָוואַסקא אין א
צוויימע דיענסט מיידעל, מער באַנאָס־
מאַ, וועלכע אין צעלאָסען געוואָרען
מיט א ווארך צורים.

9: PASSOVER TO PASSOVER

Passover has long been my mother's favorite holiday. She was born on the night of the first Seder in 1940. "My father used to make a fuss and celebrate my birthday every year at the Seder, regardless of where it fell on the English calendar," she said. "The fondest memories of my childhood were from Passover."

Hosting the Seder always made her happy—even the parts that seemed like drudgery: switching out the pots and pans for the Passover sets she kept in the basement, getting rid of any food that wasn't kosher for Passover and stocking the cabinets with special salad dressing and mayonnaise and breakfast cereal, washing dozens of dishes when the Seder was over. It took weeks to prepare for the holiday every year, but she loved creating a Seder filled with tradition and good food.

Passover became my favorite holiday, too, and remained so even after I grew up and gave up on most other holidays, Jewish and secular alike. It is one holiday I have never missed, even as our family Seder changed over the years.

When I was little, my grandpa Henry—my mother's father—used to lead the Passover Seder at our house in suburban Maryland. Soft-spoken and even-tempered, he presided over a thorough reading of the Haggadah in English and Hebrew, skipping nothing. It took hours, and was a very earnest affair.

My grandma Ethel, who was neither soft-spoken nor even-tempered, would needle him as things started to drag: "Henry, get on with it!" He never picked up his pace, though. Periodically, at the risk of slowing things down even further, he would stop and ask us, his young grandchildren seated around the dining room table, "Do you have any questions?" At this point my grandmother would retire to the gold velvet sofa in the next room, where she would lie down and bellow in a not-so-subtle rebuke: "Don't ask him anything! We'll be here all night!" He'd ignore her, something he often had reason to do as a way to endure an unhappy marriage. My mother stayed mum—part of her own strategy for dealing with her parents; she had her own hands full during the Seder, ladling out soup, setting out bowls of stuffing and sweet potatoes and trays of brisket and turkey.

Henry died when I was six. My father took over the Seder for a few years. Then my brother, a rabbinical student at the time, ran it for a few more years, until his rabbinical duties—and later, a family of his own—meant that he couldn't come home for the holiday anymore.

Leading the Seder fell to me, when I was halfway through college in the late eighties. I wasn't worried; I knew all the songs and prayers, and I could read Hebrew well enough to get through the Haggadah on my own. But I wanted to make it a very different evening from the one Grandpa Henry had once led—I didn't want a long, dull evening where I'd drone on while Mark heckled me from the velvet sofa.

I created a new Hoffman Seder, with more jokes, more songs, more politics, and less rabbinic commentary in Aramaic. But even if I dispensed with some traditions, it still included the same extended family and my mother's food.

Our Seder, which had already included Doris and Don Herman and their children, expanded further: My aunt Marilyn started flying in from Houston every year, and her son Jason joined as well. As the members of my generation got older and started having families of their own, our numbers swelled, and the folding tables now stretched from the dining room into the living room. I'd run the service from one end, while my parents sat at the other end, my mother in the seat closest to the kitchen so she could keep an eye on the stove as dinner heated up.

When Passover came around in 1990, I'd been dating Mark for nearly a year. My parents knew him—he'd spent many weekends at their house. But there was still a level of discomfort, partly because he was a man dating their son, but partly because he wasn't Jewish.

"Most people would look at Mark and say he's drop-dead gorgeous," my mother told me several years later, when we wrote a story together for an anthology about gay men and their mothers. "It's horrible to say, but my first reaction was that he looked like a *shaygitz*," a non-Jew; Mark is blond, blue-eyed, and fair-skinned. "If you were going to be with a guy, I had at least hoped he'd be Jewish."

Mark knew how much I loved the Seder, and he wanted to be invited. I told him that only spouses got invited, that there wasn't enough room at the table for another guest, that he'd be bored. He didn't believe me. I told him that I didn't want to cause a fuss, or make my mother uncomfortable at the Seder, since it was so important to her. That was true, but it was also a cover, an excuse I made. I was the one who was afraid to have him there, to risk being judged, to change the definition of family so cavalierly on such an important day.

"I didn't want him there," my mother told me later, "because everybody else at the table was having a 'regular' planned life, and you would be different. I didn't know if I was ready. But I didn't *not* invite him. If you had pushed for Mark to come—if you had even just asked me—he would have been there. Yes, I would have been uncomfortable, but he would have been there if you had asked."

The next year, I did invite Mark, and he came. By 1991, my parents had grown comfortable with him, and with us as a couple. "I don't remember it being a big deal that Mark was there," my mother said later. "I don't think we ever discussed whether or not he'd come and I don't think I worried about what anybody would think. I guess enough time had passed that it didn't matter anymore. It was no longer important."

Over the next decade, our extended family around the Seder table—some two-dozen strong—grew more and more nontraditional. Interfaith couples came to outnumber the Jewish couples—and in my generation, every couple had one Jewish and one non-Jewish partner. My mother had grown up in an Orthodox family, and had raised us in a traditional Conservative home, in a time when Judaism's Conservative movement was still fairly rigid and judgmental about everything from feminism to gay rights to intermarriage. But this eclectic array of people around her Seder table only motivated her to be more open, more welcoming, more flexible. The diversity at our table became a point of pride for her, especially as those couples started having children: "Our Seder is an important part of their Jewish education," she'd say. Welcoming people from different backgrounds became the norm.

The families around the table weren't the only nontraditional part of our Seder. We also took liberties with the service itself, sometimes straying far from the Haggadah. One year, in honor of my mother's birthday—which often fell during Passover—I wrote limericks for everyone to read after the Four Questions, because my mother enjoyed a bit of wordplay:

To these questions I must add one more
"Whom are we gathered here for?"
For Elijah, that's true
But more truly, for Sue
She's the birthday girl we all adore

She has taught us what Passover meant
A time to feel joy, not lament
In the game after dinner
Everybody's a winner
In our famed Afikoman event

After all of this food Susan makes
She's always got more, for Pete's sakes.
She'll say, "What could it hurt?
Have a little dessert.
After all, I've got seventeen cakes!"

For her birthday, I'll make three small wishes
Before eating her dinner delicious
One, for Susan's good health
Two, for increasing wealth
Three, for somebody else to do dishes

That's enough of this huffing and puffing
Let's get back to the Seder, no bluffing
We'll sit round this table
As long as we're able
Or till somebody eats all the stuffing

My parents always made room for the occasional extra guest—
someone from their synagogue who had nowhere else to go, or an
out-of-town business associate's child who was studying nearby at
the University of Maryland. Those guests often added something
delightful to the evening. There was the professor from Israel who
explained the deeper meaning of a Hebrew song we always sang,
or the woman from my parents' congregation who read a poem her
grandson had written, or the elderly neighbor who gave us all a
little scare and a big laugh when she came inside and announced
that she couldn't find her keys: Mark went outside to look for them
on the lawn, only to find that she'd left them in her car—in the
ignition, with the engine running and the door open.

But my favorite surprise guest was Mark's mother, Clarissa.
She came up from Florida in 2011; it was only the second time
she'd met my parents. The night before the Seder, she told stories
over dinner about growing up poor in Schenectady, challenging my
mother and my aunt to see whose childhood had been the most
tragic, deprived, and therefore hilarious in retrospect. ("The only
toy we had was a piece of used chalk that we used to draw hopscotch on the sidewalk," Clarissa would say. "You had chalk? You
were rich!" my mother would reply. "We had to use coal that fell off
the coal truck," my aunt would add.)

Mark and I decided to do something during that Passover that
we'd discussed for years: get married. He had proposed—and I had
accepted—some eight years earlier while we were on vacation over
Thanksgiving in Slovenia; that was before same-sex marriage was
legal anywhere in the United States. We weren't in a hurry, so
we'd watched patiently over the next few years as marriage equali-
ty became the law in one state after another. When a marriage bill
died in the New York State Senate in 2009, we figured we could
wait a bit longer; when Republicans took control of the State Senate in 2010, we figured we'd have to wait much, much longer. And

watching my mother's memory lapses get larger and more alarming, we realized we might not have as much time as we thought, if we wanted her to know what was happening. So we decided to elope over Passover in 2011.

A few hours before the Seder, we drove into Washington, D.C.—the city where we met back in 1989, where we had both lived in the nineties, and where same-sex marriage was already legal. With my sister Stacey and Victor as witnesses, we held a very quick and informal ceremony by the fountain on Dupont Circle: We were in jeans and button-down shirts, and our officiant was dressed just as inconspicuously. (Mark had found him online, and I had laid out a few requirements for our bare-bones nuptials: "No vows, no God, and if you show up wearing any kind of collar or robe, I'm leaving.") The ceremony itself lasted about five minutes. I read a poem by Cummings, Mark read a poem by Whitman, and we exchanged rings—one he'd had made for me in Oaxaca, one I'd bought for him in Jerusalem. There was so little pomp and circumstance, it was hard for passersby to realize what was happening. In fact, a group of tourists behind us by the fountain interrupted me in the middle of my poem. "I'm sorry," said one teenage girl, holding out a disposable camera, "would you take our picture?"

I held up one finger in the air. "Can you give me one minute?" I asked. "I'm in the middle of my wedding."

She looked confused, unsure if this was some sort of joke. Victor assured her it was not. Then he offered to take their picture.

I filed this away as a story we could tell later at the Seder.

That night, surrounded by the usual Passover crowd—plus Mark's mother, Clarissa—I started the Seder normally. But when we got to the Four Questions, I added a fifth. "Why is this night different from all other nights?" I asked. "Because tonight, we are married," Mark and I said, holding up our hands, adorned with silver rings.

Clarissa, for whom this was her very first Seder, asked Mark, "Is this a regular part of the Seder?"

"Yes, Mom," he said with characteristic sarcasm. (His sense of humor—"so dry it could blow away"—is what had attracted me to his personal ad all those years before.) "Every year, a different couple has to get married."

My mother was caught off guard, but she understood what was

happening—which was one of the main reasons we hadn't wanted to wait any longer. She wasn't thrilled that we'd eloped; she'd missed the wedding, such as it was, and couldn't share the moment with her friends and family. The woman who'd cautioned me years earlier not to "tell everyone" now wanted to spread the news. So I told her we'd plan a brunch a few weeks later, where she could invite people to the house and have a proper wedding celebration.

"Only *simchas*," she told guests who came to the wedding party in May—meaning we should always have happy occasions to celebrate.

As my mother's memory started to fail, we made minor adjustments to the Seder, particularly in the planning. I took over some of the logistics, ordering tables and chairs to be delivered, making sure we had enough plates and glasses, coordinating travel schedules and making sure everyone had a place to stay.

Cooking soon became an issue. It's not that she forgot how to cook completely. But as is common for people with Alzheimer's, the planning involved in this kind of complex task—when to order the brisket from the butcher, when to thaw the turkey in the fridge, how exactly to make the stuffing she'd been making for decades— became trickier, and the realization that her faculties were slipping caused her tremendous anxiety. We turned Seder preparation into a family affair; my mother was still in charge, but she wouldn't have to do it all alone. I'd come down from New York a few weeks before the holiday to help with the shopping and the scheduling; my aunt Marilyn would fly in from Houston a few days early to help her with the actual cooking.

But even this quickly became too much to handle, and she had to start giving up tasks she had done for decades. One year, I ordered side dishes from the kosher supermarket, and bought cakes online to be shipped to the house, so she could focus on the main dishes. She still had to make the brisket and the turkey and the matzo ball soup—with help from Marilyn—so it still felt like Passover to her. By the next year, I ordered the turkey and the soup from the kosher supermarket, so all she had to do was make a brisket; a year after that, I ordered the brisket as well.

My mother had little to do to prepare for the holiday by this point, but she still knew what was coming, and her stress level would rise as the holiday grew closer and even though I'd reassure her that I'd ordered everything and had it all under control, she'd worry that everything wouldn't get done on time.

In 2013, she had her first truly disastrous Seder, and we all knew that a line had been crossed.

It started off well enough, pretty much the way it did every year. Our usual crew gathered in my parents' living room, sitting on rented plastic chairs squeezed around an irregular horseshoe of folding tables. This year, our unexpected guest was a woman my father had gone to high school with. She had recently relocated to the area, so he had invited her to come, with her sister, for the evening. They seemed to like our admittedly nontraditional Seder. That night after everyone left, my mother was in a good mood.

The next afternoon, my father's high school friend called to thank my mother for such a lovely evening. And that's where something short-circuited.

Perhaps it was her tone. Or maybe it was just the long-simmering adolescent resentment my mother had always felt toward people who had gone to my father's high school—middle-class Jews from Newark who looked down (or so she thought) on her, a working-class girl from an immigrant family living on the wrong side of Jersey City. Whatever it was, my mother's mood quickly soured.

By the following day, the Seder guest's phone call had been transformed in my mother's retelling from an apparently gracious thank-you that may (or may not) have included a condescending tone ("It's not what she said; it's the way she said it!") into a nasty call where the woman said horrible things about how rotten the Seder had been, and how much she had disliked the irreverent way I'd led the evening. The day after that, my mother erroneously recalled the woman actually standing during the Seder and telling me to shut up. By the next day, her memory included me bursting into tears at the table; at this point, my mother was angry more about how I'd been treated than how she'd been slighted, and she was calling my sister to check up on me because I had allegedly been devastated by what had happened. "If I had a gun when they were here," my mother told my sister, "I would have shot them."

That was the last time we had unexpected guests for Passover.

From then on, my sister and father and I decided, we wouldn't invite new people for the holiday. Seders would be family affairs, just as they had been when Grandpa Henry used to lead them.

But for my mother—and, as a result, for all of us—the definition of family had evolved into a broader, more accepting group. We were no longer brought together strictly by tradition, or even by my mother's brisket. Passover was now, first and foremost, about relationships.

10: TO WINNIPEG

The day after Passover ended in 2013, I bought a ticket to Winnipeg. I wanted to fill in more blanks in the story I'd been researching, so that I could share everything with my mother before it was too late for her to comprehend what I was telling her. After her distressing Passover, I knew I shouldn't wait much longer.

Before I went to Winnipeg to explore my mother's maternal family history, however, I went on a sort of dress rehearsal, to look into my mother's paternal family history.

It started as a business trip to Poland; the editorial staff of my magazine spent a week in Warsaw, reporting on Jewish life in the capital. But Mark joined me and the two of us took a side trip to Plock, the Polish town where my mother's father Henry grew up, before immigrating to the States as a teenager shortly after World War I. Poland was not a place my grandfather ever recalled fondly—"It was awful; that's why we left" was pretty much the only thing Grandpa Henry ever said about it.

The exact address of my grandfather's house had been lost, and in any event, the building was likely destroyed long ago as wars decimated much of Plock. But even without finding his specific house, I got a sense of the neighborhood where he lived, and the once large Jewish community there, now vanished. I went inside the one small synagogue still standing, a place my grandfather surely visited as a child; today it is a museum explaining the town's

Jewish history—run by non-Jews, since there are no Jews left. A Jewish population that stood at 12,000 in the early twentieth century fell by a quarter before World War II, when Jews, including Grandpa Henry's family, emigrated; almost all who remained were shot in the forest outside town as soon as the Nazis arrived. After the war, the city's Jews numbered in the single digits, and every last one of those has since left or died.

Even if I couldn't trace the exact details of my family's history, because parts (like their exact address) had been forgotten and other parts—the much grander Great Synagogue, the ritual bath, the Jewish cemetery—had been obliterated by the Nazis and then the communists, I realized, I still learned a great deal about the city where my grandfather had once lived and what his life there might have been like.

I hoped going to Winnipeg would give me a similar sense of place, so I could better understand our family's history there, too. And I hoped I'd be able to dig up a bit more family history in Winnipeg for my mother's sake, to ask the questions she never asked and get the answers she never knew.

Before I left for my trip, I wanted to see if any relatives might give me leads to follow up when I was in Winnipeg. There was one person in particular I wanted to track down: my mother's cousin Judy.

When my great-grandmother Sarah was murdered in 1913, my grandmother Ethel was just three-and-a-half years old, and her sisters Fanny and Anne were still babies. Ethel was probably too young to remember the murder itself, and might not ever have known the real story. Instead, she heard, or concocted, a tale about a drive-by sniper—a story I never really believed, and that I now knew was not true.

Ethel's older brother Harry had been nearly six when their mother Sarah was killed, and he was the one who found her body. If any of the children had known first-hand what had actually happened to their mother, and what had ultimately come of the investigation, it would have been him. And maybe, I thought, if Harry did know what happened, he passed the story down to his only child, his daughter Judy—my mother's cousin.

I set out to find Judy, to see what her father had told her, and what she remembered hearing about the murder. The problem was that I didn't know how to find her, and at this point neither did my mother, who hadn't seen Judy since they were children. I wasn't even sure what Judy's last name was, what country she was living in, or whether she was still alive.

I tried Google, but without any solid details, my search went nowhere. I tried online directories, but those weren't useful without more specific parameters. So I turned to Facebook. And after trying several possible names and locations, I came up with one likely candidate and sent her an email.

It was not the right Judy. But it wasn't just a random person: This other Judy was related to the family by marriage—and she said she had contact information for the right Judy. She forwarded my note to her, and I waited for a response.

It never came.

I nudged the other Judy again as my trip got closer.

"Judy may not be interested/willing to dredge up old family stuff," the other Judy wrote.

I had come close. But for whatever reason, this long-lost cousin—who may have already known the answers I was hoping to find—apparently wanted to remain unfound.

The first thing I did when I arrived in Winnipeg at the beginning of May 2013 was walk to The Forks, the area where the Red River—which flows north through the city—meets the Assiniboine River, which cuts eastward across town. This was the neighborhood where Jewish immigrants from Russia once lived in temporary barracks before finding more permanent homes in the North End; I could only assume that for my great-grandfather David and some of his siblings, this was their first home in North America.

A century later, however, The Forks is a tourist attraction: There's an outdoor amphitheater, a children's museum, a tony inn, a skateboard park, and an indoor retail market housed in converted horse stables once owned by the railway companies. I bought a Winnipeg T-shirt with a moose on it, and ordered the most Canadian Jewish thing I could possibly find in the food court: pierogi poutine.

Like my ancestors, I didn't say long in The Forks.

I met Allan Levine, the historian I'd emailed about my great-grandmother's murder, for coffee in the city's South End, which is where most of the city's fifteen-thousand Jews live today in neighborhoods like River Heights and Tuxedo, areas that once excluded Jews altogether. The Asper Jewish Community Campus—a two-hundred-fifty thousand square foot complex named for Izzy Asper, a Jewish media magnate and former head of Manitoba's Liberal Party who died in 2003—opened in 1997 close to those two neighborhoods, just south of the Assiniboine River. It includes a Jewish day school with more than six hundred students, a massive Jewish community center with extensive recreational facilities, a library, a museum, a restaurant, offices for community organizations and social service agencies, and the Jewish Heritage Centre of Western Canada.

A retired teacher now devoting his time to writing, Levine was knowledgeable about his city's Jewish history and happy to share what he knew—both traits I'd find echoed in everyone I dealt with in Winnipeg.

Long home to the third-largest Jewish community in the country—after Toronto and Montreal—Winnipeg has now slipped behind Vancouver and is roughly tied for fourth with Ottawa. But new immigrants from Argentina, as well as Russian Jews moving from Israel, have bolstered the community's numbers in recent years, he told me. And Winnipeg's Jews maintain a prominent profile in the city of three-quarters of a million. As Levine pointed out, Sam Katz, a son of Holocaust survivors who was born in Israel but grew up in the North End after his family immigrated when he was an infant, became Winnipeg's first Jewish mayor in 2004; he was still in office when I visited in 2013. And the late Izzy Asper, the man whose name graced the Jewish Community Campus, had also been the force behind the city's Museum of Human Rights, Canada's first national museum outside Ottawa, which was due to open the next year. "Jews are as vibrant as ever in Manitoba," Levine wrote in *Coming of Age*, noting the pressures on the community but keeping an optimistic outlook.

But the purpose of my trip wasn't to explore the city's current Jewish community. I had come to Winnipeg to walk in the footsteps of my great-grandparents, to see where Sarah had lived, and died. For that, I'd need to head to the North End.

I drove up Main Street through downtown to the North End. While the downtown business district had wide streets and sidewalks lined with tall blocky business towers of brick and glass, the North End was mainly a residential area of quiet side-streets and single-family houses. Selkirk Avenue, the main commercial strip a hundred years ago, remains so today, with its churches, butchers, and pawnshops; there are still signs in Ukrainian, Polish, and Hungarian, if not Yiddish. Magnus Avenue, however, is entirely residential: Small houses covered in siding or stucco, with chain-link fences enclosing modest yards, line each block, with cars parked along the curbs. I slowed down, hoping to spot the house where my great-grandmother once lived—and died.

But there is no house at 520 Magnus Avenue today.

In 1914, the William Whyte School opened around the block from David and Sarah's house. It faced Manitoba Street, one block south of Magnus, with the rear of the school facing the backs of the houses along the south side of Magnus Avenue across the alley. The ornate, four-story brick building was named for a railway executive who had died that year. Under the leadership of English-born principal Lizzie Redman in the 1910s and '20s, the school would serve the children of the North End's immigrants, most of them Jewish. In 1976, the original building was torn down and replaced by the boxy, nearly windowless school that exists today, facing Powers Street; the rest of the entire block from Manitoba to Magnus, Powers to Andrews—including the spot where David and Sarah's house once stood at 520 Magnus, as well as the house at 502 Magnus that David's brother Harry once shared with his wife Pauline, and the alley that ran behind both of them—was torn down to make way for playing fields for the school.

Tens of thousands of residents call the North End home today, including large numbers of indigenous Canadians (First Nations, Metis) and Southeast Asian immigrants. Remnants of older and now smaller Eastern European communities are evident on Selkirk Avenue. But there aren't as many obvious remnants of the old Jewish community. The area's last kosher butcher—Omnitsky's, at the corner of Main Street and Poulson Avenue—closed in 2008.

The few Jews who still live in the North End have moved much farther north than Magnus Avenue. In 2002, three historic North End synagogues—Beth Israel, Bnay Abraham, and Rosh Pina, which my great-grandfather David's brother Harry had helped to found nearly a century earlier—consolidated to serve these remaining residents in a new Conservative congregation called Etz Chaim, a mile and a half north of the old Jewish area. The only synagogue to remain from the Jewish North End of my great-grandfather's day is the Ashkenazi synagogue, opened by Lithuanian immigrants in 1922 at Burrows Avenue and Charles Street; it's the city's oldest existing synagogue, holding an Orthodox minyan every weekday morning.

"It's not the place, so much as a way of life that's disappearing," the narrator announces at the end of the documentary *The Jews of Winnipeg*, noting how the neighborhood had already become a shadow of its former self when the film was made in 1973. "It was the people who made the North End what it was, and perhaps the memory of the old North End will just fade away, like those old Jews from another century."

Driving through the North End, it was possible for me to get a sense of geography, of the closeness of the houses and the scale of the streets. I could imagine what my great-grandmother's Winnipeg looked like, just as I had done when I'd visited my grandfather's hometown in Poland or my mother's childhood home on York Street in Jersey City. But while some of the North End's buildings, and a handful of businesses have survived for a century, the neighborhood is clearly not what it once was. "New Jerusalem," I discovered, is long gone.

11: THE FUNERAL

Three thousand people gathered to pay respects to Sarah Feinstein early in the morning on Sunday, August 3, 1913, in front of the family's home at 520 Magnus Avenue. The house, which had been cordoned off by police since Friday's murder, was opened to visitors for the day.

The crowd was extraordinary for Winnipeg, which had roughly one-hundred-fifty thousand residents at the time. "Winnipeg had never seen such a big funeral," Der Keneder Yid/The Canadian Jew, the Yiddish newspaper, reported. The Tribune noted that it was "attended by practically the entire Hebrew colony of this city."

"The street in front of the house was thronged with a morbid crowd who scrambled and fought for an opportunity to gaze in at the windows of the innocent-looking little cottage which was the scene of the crime," the Telegram reported. When the crowd grew too large and unruly, police had to call in an extra squad to control it.

A brief service was held in the house, after which the casket was brought outside to a waiting carriage. Seeing his children sobbing, the newly widowed David—who had returned to Winnipeg from a business trip in Canora, Saskatchewan, the previous morning— was overcome by emotion and fainted. A sympathetic neighbor kept him from falling to the ground and Dr. Abram Bercovitch, who had been called to the house on the night of Sarah's murder, took him outside for some fresh air until he could stand on his own again.

*Police strained to hold back the crowds so that the mourners'
carriages could pass. The coffin was brought to Tiferes Israel, a
synagogue that had opened that year just around the block from
the Feinsteins' home, at Manitoba Avenue and Powers Street—the
same street corner where David and Sarah had been married sev-
en years before. The service began at eleven in the morning, conducted by Rabbi Israel Isaac Kahanovitch, leader of the Beth Jacob
Synagogue on Schultz Street, the largest synagogue in the North
End, seating some seven hundred worshippers. A short man with a
long beard, Kahanovitch was born near Grodno—then part of the
Russian empire—and studied in a yeshiva in Slobodka, Lithua-
nia, before coming to North America in the wake of the pogroms of
1905, ultimately arriving in Winnipeg in 1907 after a short stint
in Scranton, Pennsylvania. He became the city's chief rabbi. Despite his prominent position, he was not paid a full-time salary in
Winnipeg and lived on Flora Avenue—the street David and Sarah had lived on a few years before—in a modest home where his
wife Rachel kept a vegetable garden, a chicken coop, and several
goats. Barely forty years old at the time of Sarah Feinstein's funeral, Kahanovitch was already one of the leading Jewish authorities
in Western Canada, revered by both secular and religious Jews in
Winnipeg and beyond as he built Hebrew schools, orphanages, and
old-age homes. His followers were so devoted that in Manitoba's
1911 census, many Russian immigrants reported their religion as
"Beth Jacob" rather than "Hebrew," as most Jews did at the time.*

*But Beth Jacob, which had opened in 1907, was not the only syn-
agogue in town—some Romanian Jewish immigrants, for instance,
reported their religion on the same 1911 census as "Beth Abraham,"
naming a different congregation—and Kahanovitch was not the
only rabbi. One younger rival, Rabbi Jacob Gorodsky, arrived in
Winnipeg in late 1912 and became a community rabbi for several
new synagogues in the North End in the 1910s. Dubbed the "second chief rabbi" in the Yiddish newspaper, Gorodsky sometimes
challenged Kahanovitch's authority on subjects such as his super-
vision of kosher slaughter, and his support for Zionism. Gorodsky,
too, spoke at Sarah Feinstein's funeral—a sign of unity in the city's*

sometimes-divided Jewish community.

Gorodsky eulogized about Sarah's tragic end, and consoled the grieving crowd by assuring them that even if the identity of the murderer was not yet known for certain, God saw the truth and would eventually punish the culprit. Police had not yet apprehended Stefan Kushowsky, who was still the prime suspect.

It was seventy-six degrees and fair, a beautiful summer day, as the funeral procession began. The route spanned more than five miles to the Children of Israel cemetery on Almey Avenue, across the Red River in Transcona—a town that had been incorporated only two years earlier and didn't even have a proper sewer system yet, serving mainly as home to repair yards for the railroads. Several hundred people made the full journey to the gravesite, on foot or in horse-drawn carriages. By the time they arrived, it was mid-afternoon.

Winnipeg's first Jewish graveyard, Children of Israel had opened thirty years before, in March 1883, the land purchased for eight hundred dollars. The first people buried there were five infants who had died the previous winter. They had originally been buried temporarily in a flood-prone cemetery on Thomas Street, in what was then the city's red-light district, before being moved to the new site. By the time of Sarah's funeral, there were just a few dozen graves at Children of Israel. A plot cost about five dollars.

David had gotten through much of the day without breaking down, as the Telegram *wrote: "For the most part he stood staring straight before him, as if unable to realize the depth of meaning in the scenes which were taking place before him." But when his wife's body was taken out of the hearse, David threw himself on her casket. "It is impossible to describe the harrowing effect this tragedy has had on him,"* Der Keneder Yid *reported. As the casket was interred, David lost all control, throwing himself on the ground and screaming in anguish until the rabbis calmed him down and escorted him home—or, rather, since his house at 520 Magnus Avenue was again behind a police cordon, back to his brother Harry's house down the block, where his children had been staying with their aunt Pauline since the murder. They would all remain there for the next week, sitting* shiva *in observance of Jewish mourning rituals.*

12: FINDING SARAH

One hundred years after Sarah Feinstein's funeral, on my trip to Winnipeg in May 2013, I visited her grave.

The Children of Israel cemetery has been out of use since 1935. Today it is overseen by the Conservative synagogue Shaarey Zedek, the city's oldest congregation, which moved from its original location in the North End in 1950 to a massive new building south of downtown that can hold up to fifteen-hundred people—more than twice the entire Jewish population of Winnipeg when its original building opened in 1890.

Shaarey Zedek's maintenance supervisor Bill Croydon picked me up outside my downtown hotel in his four-wheel-drive truck; there was no way for me to find the cemetery on my own, he told me. We drove across the Red River into Transcona, which is hardly the remote outpost it was a century ago. Absorbed by the city of Winnipeg during the 1972 amalgamation with surrounding towns and cities, Transcona is now a working-class suburban area that is home to more than thirty-thousand people. Driving down Reenders Drive, past fast-food restaurants, we stopped just after we passed the parking lot for Kildonan Place mall. Croydon signaled a left turn, which surprised me, because we weren't at an intersection; he crossed the lane coming the opposite direction, jumped the curb, and drove across the grass, disturbing a family of geese before finally coming to a stop alongside a field of knee-high thistle that spread out along the edge of a wooded area. There, backed up against the trees, was a twelve-foot-high chain link fence surrounding the cemetery. It was almost invisible from the road. Even standing a few feet away, it was hard to appreciate what it was. The only sign was barely larger than a sheet of paper, hung next to the locked gate. And the gravestones inside were flush to the ground, so even standing a few feet away, it wasn't obvious that this was a graveyard.

The stones had been lain flat and set in cement a few years early, Croydon explained, to protect them from decay or possible vandalism. Already many of the markers had been damaged.

The headstones there once illustrated the great range of wealth in the Jewish community at the time: Some were wooden—although only one wooden one survives today—while others were marble. Some were in Yiddish or Hebrew, while others were in English. Some had neat lead lettering, while others were hand-carved and sloppier, their letters crushed against one another.

There are only several dozen gravestones in the cemetery. It didn't take long to find my great-grandmother. Appropriate for someone who lived in the middle of the North End—not right next to the rail yards with the poorer residents, but not as far away as the wealthier families—her tombstone was somewhere in the middle of the lot in terms of its appearance. It was made of marble, with cement roughly patching a few large cracks, although it was impossible to know if they'd been caused by vandals or time and weather. At the top were three simply carved doves. At the bottom, in neatly carved English, it gave her name (although it was spelled Fainstein—which was more familiar to me, since that's how the family spelled it by the time I was born—rather than Feinstein, which is how it had appeared in most official documents, newspaper reports, and census forms before Sarah's death), her age (twenty-eight, although this also did not match most official documents or reports), and her date of death: Aug. 1, 1913. Above that, in three arcs of legible but tightly squeezed, hand-carved Hebrew letters, it listed her date of death on the Hebrew calendar (27 Tammuz 5673), her Hebrew name (Shifra), and her father's Hebrew name (Aharon Michael), and noted that she was "a righteous woman."

The Hebrew text concluded with an acronym meaning "May her soul be bundled in the bundle of the living."

I took pictures of the gravestone with my phone, and as Croydon drove me back to my hotel, I emailed them to my father, so he could show them to my mother. I called her that night and told her, "I finally found Sarah."

Sarah's gravestone in the Children of Israel cemetery

13: THE MYSTERY OF FANNY

My great-grandmother's murder wasn't the only mystery I was hoping to solve in Winnipeg.

The story my mother heard when she was a young girl about the drive-by sniper included a brief coda about what happened to the family after the murder.

"After my mother was killed, my father remarried," my grandmother Ethel told my mother. David's second wife was Bella, whom my mother had already met on her trip to Winnipeg in the early forties, and knew as Bubbe Bayla, Yiddish for Grandma Bella. "My father already had four kids, and Bella already had one from her first husband, who'd died, and together they had three more."

Even as a child who wasn't particularly good at math, my mother knew those numbers didn't add up: Four plus one plus three is eight, but her mother was one of just seven siblings.

"Who's missing?" she asked.

"Fanny," said her mother.

"What happened to her?"

Ethel said plainly: "They gave her away."

No further explanation was given, and my mother never demanded more detail.

I'd heard the same bit about Fanny when I was growing up and my mother would tell me the sniper story. While the part about the drive-by killer struck me as a *bubbemeiseh*—a ridiculous legend—I hadn't spent much time thinking about whether the specific bit about Fanny might be true.

Once I called bullshit on the whole story, though, I also told my mother how unlikely the part about Fanny sounded. "They gave away one of their children?" I teased. "How did they decide which one? Did they draw straws? And where did they leave her? On the sidewalk?"

Now that I'd spent time digging into family history, Fanny had become a serious source of intrigue for me, a second mystery wrapped up in the larger mystery about my great-grandmother's fate. And after my research, I knew one horrible detail about Fanny's childhood: She was the closest to her mother when she was killed. It was Fanny who lay in bed with her mother when the gunman entered the bedroom and shot Sarah. When the newspapers reported the gruesome details of the scene, they all described the blood soaking Fanny's nightgown as she continued to sleep next to her mother's body.

I had learned the truth about Sarah. I thought finding out what happened to Fanny would be easier, and I could answer even more questions that had hung over the family for a century.

On the last day of my 2013 trip to Winnipeg, I stopped by the Asper Jewish Community Campus in the South End, to do research about Fanny at the Jewish Heritage Centre of Western Canada. The Centre's Genealogical Institute has photographed nearly sixteen-thousand gravestones across Manitoba, and entered information about the deceased into a database—a project that required some twelve-hundred hours and thirty-five volunteers to complete. In those files, the Centre's archivist Ava Block-Super found records for someone named Fannie Fainstein, who was buried in the Hebrew Sick Benefit Cemetery, four miles north of Magnus Avenue in the city's North End.

"That's got to be her," I said. There was nobody else with a remotely similar name in the computer.

Using the information from the database, Block-Super found a snapshot of the grave in one of the meticulously labeled boxes on a shelf. She handed it to me, and I held it by the edges, careful not to smudge the glossy print with my fingers.

Unfortunately, the photograph wasn't very clear; the all-English lettering on the black headstone was difficult to make out. We could both see the name, but the date was in shadow. Block-Super pulled a magnifying glass from her desk, but even huddled together over the photo and squinting through the glass, we couldn't be certain. Our best guess was 1919.

I wanted to take a ride back to the North End, to see her grave in person, but I was leaving Winnipeg later that day and didn't have time.

It seemed I had finally found my grandmother's missing sister, the little girl her father allegedly "gave away." But I wished I could be certain.

The photo of Fanny's grave was all I had, but it was still a big deal to me—it was the first picture I'd ever seen that had anything to do with her. In the jumble of photos my grandmother Ethel stuffed into the plastic bag that eventually ended up in my parents' closet, she had shots of her other siblings, but none of Fanny. They were only two years apart, and I imagined they must have been close as children. Ethel was the oldest girl; Fanny would have been next in line to wear her hand-me-downs as both girls got older. Somewhere, I imagined, there must have been a photo of the children when they were young, Fanny standing by Ethel's side, wearing the dress that had belonged to her big sister a year or two before. But I had never seen such a picture.

Fanny wasn't only missing from family photo albums; she was nearly impossible to trace in official records.

Fanny's older siblings Harry and Ethel have official birth certificates on file with the province of Manitoba, papers that attest to their parents' names and addresses, their dates of birth, and the doctors who delivered them. But Fanny has something different: a brief one-page document titled "Form 9" issued by Vital Statistics, Manitoba. It includes far less information: Her parents' names and addresses are there, and correct. But the date, written out multiple times, is wrong: It says she was born on November 15, 1909. Most other official documents, and newspaper reports, suggest she was born in 1911—and this particular date in 1909 seemed impossible, coming just two weeks before her sister Ethel, my grandmother, was born.

Fanny didn't appear in the 1911 census because, I believed, she hadn't been born yet. But in the 1916 census, she is listed as being seven years old, slightly older than my grandmother Ethel, who was six at the time. So when exactly was she born: 1909, or 1911? And if she was born in 1909, how would that have been possible?

I called Vital Statistics to ask about the inconsistent dates. Almost anything might have gone wrong, a helpful clerk named Andrea explained. Often, she said, these forms were filled out years—even decades—after the fact, and the information on them was frequently incorrect; this was, in fact, the case with some minor details on the birth certificates: For instance, Harry's birth certificate was filled out a full twenty years after he was born; it was filed by his father David in 1927, and listed the number of children born to his mother Sarah as four—a number that was correct when he filled out the form, but not at the time when Harry, the oldest, was born in 1907.

It was even possible, Andrea suggested, that Fanny's certificate had the right date, and it was Harry and Ethel who had the wrong birth years on theirs. But Harry and Ethel's birth years are consistent across a slew of official documents and newspaper reports—and I believed my Grandma Ethel was born in 1909 because she told me so herself when I was a child. So I chalked up Fanny's mysterious birth year to human error.

The 1916 census was the last official government record I could find that mentioned Fanny. The only thing my mother had ever heard was that Ethel's sister Fanny had been "given away" after their mother was killed—but in 1916, three years after the murder, Fanny was still there. And since the rest of the story my mother had learned about Sarah's demise contained so many inaccuracies—the drive-by sniper, the porch-side breastfeeding in winter—it was hard to lend her story about Fanny much credence.

There was one thing about Fanny I was fairly certain about: My aunt Marilyn's middle name is Fay, and the day that I called bullshit on the drive-by sniper story, she told me that she was named Fay after Fanny. "Ethel must have had some kind of close relationship with Fanny that she wanted one of her children to be named after her," Marilyn later told me. But beyond that, it also indicated another thing: My Grandma Ethel, who had a deep well of superstitious beliefs about tempting the evil eye, must have been absolutely certain that her sister Fanny had died before Marilyn was born in 1943, or she wouldn't have named a child after her—

naming a child after a living relative would have been taboo in an Ashkenazi Jewish family with Eastern European roots. (Sephardic and Mizrahi Jews, who trace their lineage to Spain, North Africa, and the Mediterranean, have entirely different traditions and taboos around names.)

If Fanny died in 1919, that lined up with everything else I knew. It explained why she vanished from records after 1916, and how my grandmother could be certain her sister was dead by 1943. But how exactly did she die?

The year on the tombstone—1919—remains significant in Winnipeg's collective memory. A massive General Strike lasted some six weeks that spring, pitting local politicians, businessmen, and newspaper publishers against thirty-thousand workers, including many Jews, who walked off their jobs demanding collective bargaining rights and higher wages.

In addition to the strike, 1919 stands out in Winnipeg's history for another reason. Canada, which had enlisted hundreds of thousands of volunteers since war was declared against Germany in 1914, only instituted a military draft in 1917. My great-grandfather David's brother Isidor—twenty-seven years old and still unmarried at the time—was the only one in the family to be drafted; he was discharged in April 1918 so he could join the Jewish Legion, as part of a battalion of Jewish Americans and Canadians fighting with British forces against the Ottoman Empire in Palestine, most notably in the decisive Battle of Megiddo that September.

As American and Canadian soldiers returned home in late 1918, they brought influenza with them; by the end of 1919, half a million Americans and sixty-thousand Canadians had died of the disease. The first deaths in Manitoba hit in October 1918. Schools were closed, and public gatherings of more than six people were banned. By January 1919, nearly thirteen-thousand people in Winnipeg had fallen ill, and more than eight hundred had already died. Young people were particularly susceptible to the virus, and once infected, more likely to die.

Perhaps, I thought, Fanny had been one of the victims. I could imagine the panic in Bella's mind, trying to care for one sick child while being terrified that Fanny might infect the rest of the kids in the house—and the horror of losing a little girl to the disease.

Winnipeg's Jewish community had been hit hard by the epidemic. On November 10, 1918, the day before Germany signed an armistice with the Allies that effectively ended the war, Rabbi Israel Isaac Kahanovitch and Rabbi Jacob Gorodsky—the same two rival rabbis who had come together to perform Sarah Feinstein's funeral in 1913—came together again to hold an unusual "wedding of death" to ward off the disease. The first event of its kind in Canada, the ceremony combined the wedding of Harry Fleckman and Dora Wiseman at one end of the Shaarey Zedek cemetery in the city's North End, a ceremony that drew more than a thousand Jewish and gentile guests, with a minyan of ten Jewish men conducting a funeral for an influenza victim at the other end of the graveyard.

The *Tribune* reported: "The ancient Jewish 'Song of Life' was played. On the west side of the cemetery, at the same time, Jews were chanting the wail of death, as a body was committed to the grave. Ancient Jewish chapters reserved for these ceremonies were chanted by the rabbis, and so repeated by all Jews present as the wedding procession marched out of the cemetery."

I'd never heard of a ceremony like this; apparently, it wasn't common back then, either. (Rokhl Kafrissen wrote in Tablet, the magazine I edit, about a similar ritual called the *mageyfe khasese*, or plague wedding, which was performed among Russian Jews to fight cholera epidemics in the late 1800s, and later at least once during the flu epidemic in New York.) As Esyllt Wynne Jones recounts in the book *Influenza 1918*, although the event in Winnipeg raised four-hundred fifty dollars for charity, the city's Yiddish daily newspaper *Dos Yidishe Vort/The Israelite Press*—formerly the weekly *Der Keneder Yid/The Canadian Jew*—criticized the rabbis for violating both Jewish tradition and official health recommendations around burials: "It is a misdeed of our religious leaders to undertake performing a wedding at a cemetery and bring together such a large crowd. If the sick will use medicine and doctors and not wait for miracles and wonders to cure them, that is all right. But if they rely on such miracles, many of them will surely die."

This story, I thought, made much more sense than the one my mother had been told. I was pretty proud of myself—I had solved another mystery—so I called my mother to tell her what I'd learned: Fanny hadn't been "given away" by her father after her mother's death. She died of influenza in 1919, when she was just eight years old.

That explained why she died and disappeared from family stories. But it didn't explain what my grandma Ethel meant when she said her sister had been "given away." I had solved part of the mystery, but more remained unknown.

14: A FREE MAN

At seven o'clock on Sunday evening, August 3, 1913, just hours after Sarah Feinstein's funeral, Stefan Kushowsky walked into Winnipeg's central police station and asked to see Mary Manastaka, who was being held as a material witness in Sarah's murder. He was sent upstairs to see one of the Polish-speaking detectives, but when he announced his identity, he was immediately placed under arrest.

A few hours later, Stefan walked out of the station a free man.

He had been the prime suspect in the investigation since Friday, August 1, the day the crime was committed. Most residents of the North End had placed the blame on him, as had most of the journalists covering the story, relying on a widely repeated story about Mary Manastaka, his alleged girlfriend, being fired by Sarah and vowing revenge. Further details had bolstered the case against him, from the neighbor who claimed to have heard someone shout "Stefan!" at the time of the murder, to the owner of the confectionery shop around the corner who told reporters that Stefan dropped his bottle of aerated water on the floor and ran out the door when she informed him about the police investigation later that evening.

But when the police questioned Stefan, they discovered he had a solid alibi—and that much of the information they had heard about him was untrue. Their initial reports, for instance, told of Stefan being seen on Magnus Avenue near the Feinsteins' house late at night on Thursday, just a few hours before the crime was committed, and they assumed he'd still been on the scene hours later; now police confirmed that he had been home asleep at the time of the murder. Police originally were informed that he had skipped work on Friday, the day of the murder, but now confirmed that he had, in fact, been at work at the Canadian Pacific Railway on both Friday and Saturday, as usual. In addition, said Stefan, Mary Manastaka wasn't even truly his girlfriend; they had only gone out walking, or to Feinman's confectionery shop, a few times. Detective Sergeant George Smith made inquiries around the North End about Stefan's claims, and found him to be telling the truth.

"Miracles occur," reported the Yiddish newspaper Der Keneder Yid. "However outlandish it might be, the fact is that after the Ukrainian detective questioned him, he was released."

Alone among the city's newspapers, the Telegram had always been dubious that Stefan was the killer: After all, the paper reported, he didn't match the description offered by C.D. Polson, the man who said he'd seen the shooter. The night of the murder, Polson had told Telegram reporters that he'd been coming home with his wife at one in the morning, returning to his house on Andrews Street, when he saw a man heading toward the Feinsteins' house, which was three doors east of Andrews on Magnus Avenue, "running across lots and between the houses." He estimated that the runner was fifteen feet from him, and noted that "although it was rather dark at the time I had a fair look at him and think I could identify him." He said the man in question was "short and of heavy build, with a dark suit of clothes." Stefan was short but slight, and wore a light suit on the night in question. The Telegram also noted that Stefan had a "rather pleasant face" (in contrast to the Free Press, which wrote about the "pallid tinge" that spread across "the Galician's swarthy face") and that during questioning by police, he maintained "the appearance of an innocent man."

The motive—getting back at his girlfriend's employer for firing her—also didn't satisfy the reporters at the Telegram: "It is difficult to believe that so brutal a murder arose from so trivial a cause."

And yet, even as the Telegram *defended Stefan, it painted an ugly picture of him because of his background. But ironically, in this instance, a sort of casual racism led journalists to believe he was innocent.*

Stefan couldn't possibly have planned this kind of crime, the Telegram *asserted on August 4, the day after his release: "It is felt that the murder was too carefully committed to bear the stamp of the work of a Galician. These latter people, in their vendettas, usually leave a broad and well marked trail, while in this murder there is nothing in the way of direct evidence to point to any individual," the paper reported, noting that the "investigation is being carried on along the line that the man who committed the deed was one of more than usual cunning."*

With Stefan's official exoneration, what had just one day earlier seemed to everyone else like a fairly simple case, with a plausible motive and a likely culprit, was suddenly a muddle. The Telegram *impugned the immigrant residents of the North End as a group for telling stories that are often at odds with one another: "Out of the mass of contradictory evidence gathered among the foreign residents of the vicinity of the crime, the police hope to be able to sift something that will be of service. These people are naturally very excitable and prone to give credence to any rumor, however wild and improbable. So long as it grips the imagination it is sufficient. And with alert imaginations to feed upon the stories have attained weird proportions."*

The Telegram, *again the exception among local newspapers, had been wary of North End gossip from the outset—although broad ethnic stereotypes were again a key part of its reporters' reasoning: "The difficulty of getting anything like a connected story from any of the highly excitable residents of the district is almost insurmountable, until they have had an opportunity of calming down," the paper had reported the morning after the murder, before Stefan had even been arrested. "There are rumors of every description afloat... but few of them have any evidence of authenticity."*

Now that the case against Stefan had collapsed, police and other reporters were belatedly beginning to realize how much of the information they had gleaned from witnesses and neighbors was faulty, or based on gossip. On top of that, multiple language barriers—within the North End's jumble of immigrant tongues, and between those residents and the local authorities—would lead to a frustrating array of false leads, miscommunications, and outright fabrications. "Very few clues of any importance were found by the police and they are working at a disadvantage, as they have to work with the Jews and Galicians, whose language they are unable to speak," reported the Free Press, *whose front-page headline on Monday morning, August 4, declared: "Murder Mystery No Nearer Solution."*

"The more it is investigated the deeper the mystery seemingly becomes," read the Telegram's *story the same day. Police, who called the crime "one of the most brutal in the annals of the force," announced that they were now searching for another man, described as "five feet nine and a half inches in height, dark complexion. He wears a moustache, and is generally smiling, showing a strong set of strong white teeth." This suspect's identity was either unknown or "being withheld for good reason," the paper wrote. But his profile didn't seem to match the one offered by C.D. Polson immediately after the murder—five feet nine and a half was hardly "short," especially at the time—so this description must have come from someone else.*

New theories and mysterious suspects came almost immediately from residents of the North End. The Telegram *mentioned a story about a man who was "persecuting" Sarah in the days before the murder, who had "tried to force himself into the house, but was repulsed." There was no discussion in the paper, however, about whether this might be the unnamed, mustached man with the strong white teeth.*

While police made lists of new male suspects, the only two people they kept in jail were women. Rumors of international intrigue soon surfaced, explaining why this was the case. "At the funeral yesterday, there were many groups talking over their version of the affair and in three different groups it was heard that Mary Manastaka and Victoria Komanowska…were members of a secret society in

Russia," the Free Press reported. "The day previous it was rumored that Mrs. Feinstein had been a member of a secret society in that country before coming to Canada and had left the fatherland without the consent and against the wishes of other members. These two rumors put together might lead to something definite. Did the girls belong to the same society as Mrs. Feinstein? Were they here to look her up and possibly do the very deed which has been committed?"

Soon after Stefan's release, the Tribune ran an entire story about Russia's "secret societies," in light of "the recent tragedy on Magnus Avenue." Its reporters interviewed "a well-known Russian professional man in Winnipeg with a view to gaining some information about the work of the secret societies in Russia, and more especially the feature of modern sensational romance, Nihilism." But the unnamed source, identified as a Nihilist himself, was dubious. "Can you tell me something of this great secret society?" the reporter asked. The man replied: "No, I cannot, because there is no Nihilist society in Russia and one never existed outside the pages of a novel....I will tell you what I can, but I am afraid that if you print it, it will spoil the thrill of many who now enjoy an hour gloating over the terrors of the initiation into the non-existent society."

Police didn't seem to put much stock in secret societies, even if such speculation did sell newspapers.

"The greatest difficulty we have to contend with," Chief of Detectives Eli Stodgill told the Tribune, "is the many garbled stories which are told us by people who either knew, or think they knew the story of the woman's life."

The day after Stefan's release, Mary Manastaka was also released. Once again, language barriers and gossip from people who knew far less than they claimed seem to have muddied the facts: Mary, it turned out, never worked for Sarah Feinstein at all.

She worked, instead, for Joseph and Esther Hershfield at 526 Magnus Avenue, three doors down from the Feinsteins. And while she had indeed once quarreled with Sarah, they had reportedly remained friendly afterward, and she had even helped care for the Feinstein children on occasion. She told police she'd been at home *the night of the murder, and after police corroborated her story, she was sent home at five in the afternoon on August 4. The* Free Press *announced the news the next day: "Girl Suspect in Feinstein Murder Case Released."*

15: THE KEY

While he called the murder of Sarah Feinstein "the work of a most steady hand and a heart of stone," Chief Constable Donald MacPherson said that "not a really tangible clue was left" at the scene—except for one puzzling piece of evidence.

There were three keys to the Feinsteins' house, one of which Sarah typically carried, while the other two hung on a ledge in the house. David Feinstein never carried a key to his own house, since his wife was always home to let him in, and the hired girl Victoria Komanowska didn't need one either since, as the Free Press reported, "she never had a night off, as she was not permitted to go out, and did not want to." Coming in through the one window that had been left open a few inches would have made too much noise, police said. So it seemed likely that the perpetrator had used a key to enter the house, probably through the front door that had been mysteriously unlocked when Victoria ran to alert the neighbors after the shooting. When David returned to Winnipeg from his business trip to Canora on Saturday, the day after his wife's murder, neither he nor the police could locate the keys that normally hung on the ledge. Where was the key that the murderer probably used to open the front door? "It may be at the bottom of the Red River for all anyone knows of it at present," the Free Press offered.

Perhaps the murderer was already in the house when Sarah went *to sleep. That person might have come in without a key by climbing through the coal chute and hiding in the cellar until the middle of the night before coming into the house via the basement stairs. This was a remote possibility, although nobody noticed coal dust tracked through the house. More likely, the murderer had taken the key before the killing, or had the key passed along by someone inside the house—a hired girl, for instance. Or maybe a key had been taken or passed along some days before the murder and simply duplicated; the door had a standard Yale lock, whose key could easily be copied by a locksmith.*

Whatever the exact story, police believed that the key to solving the crime was, literally, the key. "There is little question but that the perpetrator of the crime had a key to the place," wrote the Free Press, *"and it would be strong circumstantial evidence to be able to find it on anyone."*

Investigators had little other physical evidence to consider. While they could deduce from the flattened bullet removed from Sarah's skull during the autopsy that the weapon that killed her was a .32 caliber revolver, no gun was recovered. A box of "Russian fusees" were found, and as the Tribune *noted, "these matches are not sold in Winnipeg, but are often seen in the possession of immigrants from South Russia and Austria"—although that didn't do much to narrow the list of suspects in a neighborhood filled with immigrants, with more arriving from Russian and Austrian lands every month.*

This lack of evidence didn't stop Winnipeg's journalists from publishing story after story speculating about the case. The murder stayed on the front page of the city's newspapers for days in early August 1913, alongside reports of train wrecks, grain production, revolution in Venezuela, and provincial cricket tournaments, as well as other less sensational headlines, such as "Drowning Man Saved by Moose" or "Chicken Shooting Begins Tomorrow All Over Manitoba."

After the release of Stefan Kushowsky and Mary Manastaka, the Free Press *reported that investigators had already explored "a dozen different plausible theories that looked strong for the time being."*

Dr. William Rogers, the coroner overseeing the inquest into Sarah's death, had ruled out suicide early; if Sarah had killed herself, the gun would have been found in her bed. A domestic dispute— the cause of several other much-publicized murders in Winnipeg in 1913—was taken out of consideration after neighbors were unanimous in their observation that Sarah and her husband had rarely quarreled, and that "David Feinstein always treated his wife with consideration, gratifying her every whim whenever possible," according to the Free Press. *("The only trouble the couple ever had was shortly after their marriage and was about relatives coming to see them," the paper noted, adding that "for the past several years they have lived happily.") The possibility of an extramarital affair was also dismissed: "Jealousy, the most common motive for murders in all police records, is hardly worthy of consideration in this case," the* Free Press *wrote. "Although questions along this line were put to hundreds of people since the murder, not a word has been heard against the woman's faithfulness or character." Sarah, the newspaper concluded, lived "a particularly clean and wholesome life, and no dark spot can be located since she has been in Canada." Despite the fact that the Feinsteins were relatively well-off by this point, with a reported net worth of twenty-thousand dollars, robbery also did not appear to be the motive, since expensive fur coats that were stored in the attic remained untouched—and even in the bedroom where the murder occurred, a fancy watch and valuable jewelry were lying right out on the bureau, but were not taken. Nor was the attack sexual in nature: "The woman was not assaulted," the* Free Press *discreetly reported, "as the bed clothes lay unruffled over the lifeless form."*

Anti-Semitism was widely assumed—by police, journalists, and the Jews of the North End—to be part of the motive for murder. But that didn't help to significantly narrow the list of possible suspects since, as the Tribune *noted, such feelings were "more or less rampant amongst certain of the foreign element in this district."*

While police were investigating and journalists were reporting on the Feinstein murder case, local politicians also got involved. Altar

Skaletar, the newly elected alderman for Ward Five representing the North End on the City Council—the district's second Jewish alderman, a member of the Conservative Party, and a onetime Canadian correspondent for the Yidishes Tageblatt Jewish newspaper in New York—asked the city's Board of Control on August 4 to provide reward money for information leading to the murderer's capture. "There is a prevalent opinion among the foreigners of the city that they are not given the proper protection because they are foreigners," Skaletar said. "I have often tried to correct this opinion but it seems hard to combat."

"That is one of the reasons why I would like to see the capture of the murderer in this case," Skaletar told the Board of Control. "I think it would have a good effect in showing the foreigners that they are dealt with justly by the authorities."

Controller William Grigg Douglas agreed that more protection was warranted in the North End, but said there wasn't enough money for more police; besides, he argued, even "one hundred extra policemen" wouldn't have prevented the Feinstein murder, which he called "one of the worst crimes in the history of the city." The Board of Control further insisted that providing a reward was a provincial, not a municipal, matter, but agreed to comply if the police commissioner recommended it. The commissioner did, and Douglas kept his word, offering a motion to the board, which carried it unanimously. The following day, on August 5, the provincial government and Board of Control each put up half of a five-hundred-dollar reward. Mayor Thomas Russ Deacon said, "We are trying to assist justice in this matter, and we hope that the murderer will soon be in the toils," but he maintained that in the future such things really should be up to the provincial government, and said he wanted to make sure this wasn't seen as a precedent.

The Free Press reported that the reward might soon grow: "Individuals among the Hebrew population of Winnipeg have expressed themselves as ready to contribute if they decide that the offering is not enough to prove significant inducement to the greatest effort to bring about the arrest of the criminal."

Overcome with grief in the days following his wife's funeral, and still sitting shiva *to mourn her, David couldn't bring himself to file Sarah's Official Notice of Death for the Province of Manitoba. So on Tuesday, August 5, 1913, he sent his brother Morris to handle the paperwork. He didn't remember his sister-in-law's birthday, and incorrectly listed her parents' names as Morris and Annie.*

Sarah's maiden name was written as Auerbrook, although that may not be exactly right: The information was being spoken aloud by Morris, a non-native English speaker who may not have known the precise facts about his sister-in-law, and written down by a clerk based on what he thought he heard. Morris didn't fill out the form in English himself; he couldn't even sign his name in English, so he made an "x," which the registrar identified as "his mark."

In the evening on August 5, just hours after the death notice was filed, the coroner's juried inquest into the case was set to convene. Many witnesses had been subpoenaed, and the Tribune *reported that "it is expected that startling developments will take place during the hearing of evidence." The* Free Press *ratcheted up the anticipation, claiming "the police may have some other witnesses that they will spring at the right moment."*

But the most startling development that day came before the inquest even began. In the afternoon, the missing keys were found: They were sitting out in the open atop a jewelry box on a bureau in the rear bedroom—the room where Sarah had been murdered, which detectives had thoroughly searched a few days before. Police surmised that someone had sneaked the keys back into the house on Sunday, when the cordon around the house had been lifted for the day of the funeral, and hundreds of friends, relatives, neighbors, and even strangers had come to pay their respects. The detectives were flummoxed.

"What were at first thought to be good clues have developed into blind leads, so that the officers are working practically in the dark," the Telegram *reported.*

In the final moments before the inquest was supposed to open— the jury had been seated and curious spectators had already arrived—coroner Rogers called for a week's postponement. The inquest, which only two days earlier had seemed like a simple matter where the jury would declare Stefan Kushowsky the murderer and Mary Manastaka his accomplice, was rescheduled for the following Tuesday.

"This is a hard case," Stodgill told the Tribune. "It is one of the most brutal murders in the history of Winnipeg and the proposition of unraveling the tangled skein of mystery which apparently surrounds the whole tragedy is an extremely difficult one." He claimed that new information had been recently found, and said that "things look much clearer than they did," but cautioned that no further arrests were imminent after Stefan's release.

After they found out that the inquest slated for that evening had been canceled, residents of the North End continued to speculate about who might have committed the heinous crime. "Some remarkable stories are being circulated by the friends of the murdered woman, who stand around, a morbidly curious throng in the vicinity of the little cottage, telling and retelling the gruesome details of the tragedy," the Tribune reported. The Free Press also commented on the rumors, noting that "little weight can be attached to any of them as they are told by excited people whose imagination has run riot and every little thing that has ever happened is stretched until it assumes the proportion of a plausible theory."

Realizing that the Feinstein murder would not be resolved as quickly as he had hoped, Chief Constable Donald MacPherson told the Free Press: "It is one of the most difficult murders we have ever had in the history of Winnipeg, and it will have to be sifted out by a slow, steady process which will likely take a long time."

Sarah Feinstein's death certificate,
filed by her brother-in-law Morris,
pages 1 and 2

PART 3

CHAPTER 16: WHODUNIT?

After I returned from Winnipeg in May 2013, I started to plan my parents' annual summer visit to the Catskills. This time, I invited four of their oldest friends to join us. Distant memories were still fairly sharp in my mother's mind, and I thought having people around who could reminisce about things that happened decades earlier would allow her to participate in conversations with less anxiety.

These friends lived in New Jersey. For many years, they had typically met my parents for a weekend now and then in Philadelphia, roughly halfway between them, but now even a short overnight trip made my mother anxious: unfamiliar hotel beds, noisy restaurants, confusing museum exhibits. I thought that if I played host, I could take care of the cooking and cleaning and transportation, leaving them free to tell stories and talk about old times.

Phil Feintuch was my mother's oldest friend. They grew up ("poor, but not destitute," he explained) across the street from each other in Jersey City in the forties, and their mothers—Ethel and Ida—had been lifelong confidantes. Phil and his wife Bibi were best friends with another couple my parents had known for more than fifty years: Carole and Arnie Felberbaum. Carole had gone to college with my mother at Jersey City State in the late fifties.

When I was growing up, my brother and sister and I often heard about the Felberbaums and the Feintuchs, but since we only met them in person a handful of times—at bar mitzvahs or major family events—and they were always together, we didn't remember who was who. We couldn't tell Carole from Bibi, even though one was blond and the other brunette; we knew their husbands' names, but couldn't recall which husband went with which wife. We referred to them as a collective foursome, who we dubbed "the F's." It was only when I became an adult, when Mark and I got to know Carole and Arnie better—we shared passions for theater and travel—and met them a few times for dinner in New York City, that "the F's" had become four individuals in my mind.

Over Fourth of July weekend, we had long, animated meals around the dining room table, where the peals of laughter filtered through the open bay windows; this was not a quiet group, nor one where each person waited to speak in turn. My mother laughed when she remembered how Phil's younger brother used to stop by her house on York Street to use the bathroom if he was outside playing.

"Why didn't he just come home?" Phil asked. "We lived across the street."

"Because your apartment was up too many flights of steps," my mother said, "and he really had to go!"

Phil, in turn, told my mother about her mother Ethel's visits to his house, where she'd sit at the kitchen table and talk with his mother Ida. In addition to complaining about their unsatisfying marriages (my aunt Marilyn once described them as "two lonesome women leading very empty lives") or just kibbitzing, the women would talk about their kids.

"She'd always praise you," Phil told my mother. "'You won't believe what Susan did! And how smart she is!'"

"I never heard her say any of those things," my mother replied.

"A hundred eighty degrees different from what she told you to your face," Phil said. "She was probably worried about tempting the evil eye."

"Would it have killed her to tempt it a little?" my mother asked.

We sat in rocking chairs on the porch over evening cocktails and they told more stories—about Jersey City, and their parents, and their lives before they all had children. My mother could still follow a conversation, but she rarely added anything. She still understood when something was funny, but she often wasn't fast enough to join in with her own stories, or even to interject a comment here and there. "We couldn't wait to see her, usually. She was the entertainment," Phil told me later, after the visit was over. But this time, he observed, "She didn't have that *joie de vivre*, she wasn't bubbly. She was more retired, more reserved."

After meals, as I cleared the table and listened from the kitchen, I noticed that I rarely heard my mother's voice.

"We used to say she could have done stand-up," Carole told me. "Her timing was great." But in the Catskills, it was different. "She remembered some stories, but she wasn't the storyteller anymore. It was sad. We saw her begin to fade."

I had my own story to tell on the porch that weekend, about the research I'd done about my great-grandmother. The F's had all known my grandma Ethel, and they were intrigued by the story of Sarah's murder. "So who did it?" they all wanted to know.

Mark chimed in: "David."

"Why do you think it was David?" the F's asked.

"It's always the husband," he explained.

Heads shook all around the table. "He wasn't even there," I said.

Mark was insistent: "So he ordered the hit."

A skeptical chorus of "why?" followed. Mark had his theories about money, an affair, the Russian mafia. Nobody else at the table was convinced.

"Who do *you* think did it?" he asked me.

Even after all my research, and my trip to Winnipeg, I still didn't have an answer.

As a journalist, I'm always looking for a peg, a reason why a story is important right now. There's a reason we publish stories about summer camp in June rather than December, and essays about holiday recipes in the days leading up to those holidays rather than in the weeks afterward. Anniversaries, particularly anniversaries with nice round numbers, are always an appealing peg. And the summer of 2013 would mark one hundred years since my great-grandmother's murder.

It seemed like the perfect time for me to solve the mystery. After all, 2013 was shaping up to be a year of disorientation in my own family, as my mother's condition changed everything about her, and everyone around her at the same time. It seemed an appropriate mirror for 1913, a pivotal *annus horribilis* for my ancestors, the year when the family was shattered by loss, thrown off course, broken in a way that could never be fully repaired.

I wanted to answer the question that left me stymied over the Fourth of July: "So who did it?" But if I wanted to fully understand what happened on August 1, 1913, by the time August 1, 2013, came around, I only had a few weeks left to figure out who'd killed my great-grandmother.

17: THE INQUEST

"Who walked into the house with no other intention than to shoot to death an inoffensive mother?" the Free Press *asked, in typically purple prose, after police released railway worker Stefan Kushowsky, their main suspect in the murder of Sarah Feinstein. "Who contemplated the placid features of the sleeping woman as she lay with her hands beside her face as though in prayer? Who was cold-hearted enough to send a bullet crashing into the beautiful forehead to abruptly end a young and happy life, to leave motherless four tiny children, one of whom had its curly head pillowed on the mother's breast when the assassin's bullet ended her life? What could have been their motive? The prospects of ever having these questions answered look very slim at present."*

Speculation ran wild in the North End of Winnipeg, and in the city's newspapers, after the inquest was postponed on August 5, 1913.

David Feinstein was never considered a serious suspect in his wife's murder, because he was hundreds of miles away in Saskatchewan at the time of the incident—nor did any newspaper reports imply his indirect involvement. David's siblings and their spouses, most of whom also lived on Magnus Avenue, were similarly free of suspicion; this was not, the police believed, a family affair.

The Feinsteins' servant Victoria Komanowska was held in jail as a material witness for several days, even as rumors of a Russian secret society circulated in the press. She was eventually called before Winnipeg's Police Magistrate Hugh John Macdonald—son of Canada's former Prime Minister John A. Macdonald, who'd first welcomed immigrants from Russia to establish a "Jew colony" three decades earlier. But detectives believed Victoria was telling the truth about the events of August 1: Not only had her story been consistent throughout several police interviews, but her description of how she locked the doors—thus placing herself as the only adult other than Sarah definitively in the house at the time of the murder—could have potentially implicated her in the crime. A simple lie might have gotten her off the hook, if she had instead claimed not to have locked the front door before going to sleep that night; the fact that she continued to tell a story that might incriminate her inclined police to accept her story as truth.

There was a new suspect: Mary Manastaka had been incorrectly identified by police as Sarah's former employee who had sworn revenge after being dismissed, or "given her conge," in the lingo of the day's journalists. While this turned out to be false—she actually worked for another family down the block—the rest of the original story surrounding her still held some water: There was, in fact, a different servant named Mary whom Sarah Feinstein had fired some months earlier. All the suspicion that had once surrounded the now-exonerated Mary Manastaka fell to this other woman. "Two months ago, a girl who is known to the neighbors in the vicinity of 520 Magnus Avenue as 'Mary' was given her conge by Mrs. Feinstein because of her promiscuous love affairs with young men whose reputation was in doubt," the Free Press *wrote. "It was this girl who vowed vengeance on the victim of the murder. It was she instead of the Manastaka girl who really worked for the family and who became mixed with the latter in the first accounts of possible clues published." Residents of the North End couldn't recall her last name or much else about her, but they claimed to have seen this other Mary after the murder; they said she ran off, frightened, when they started asking questions, which only bolstered their suspicions about her. She was alleged to be working in a nearby restaurant.*

When police found this other Mary—Platak was her last name—
she acknowledged that she had left her job at the Feinsteins' house,
but she said the reason was not anti-Semitism, nor her "promiscuous love affairs," as the Free Press had charged. She had left,
she said, simply because the wages were too low. She did recall a
time when a boy she didn't know stopped to talk with her outside
the house, and Sarah overheard and told him to leave, at which
point the boy used a filthy expression. But Mary Platak said she
had never threatened Sarah, who had always been good to her. Police, satisfied with her explanation, erased another likely suspect
from their list.

With the obvious suspects cleared, suspicions returned to the de-
mon in Sarah Feinstein's distant past—not a mysterious "secret society," but a more specific individual. An unnamed woman claiming to be one of her relatives told the Tribune about "an unfortunate
love affair" Sarah had back in Russia before she immigrated to
Canada: "A young man of position and wealth in their native town
had become infatuated with her and had for a considerable time
been enforcing his attentions on her," the Tribune reported. "She
was said to have rebuffed the ardent lover's advances and he, on
receiving his final conge, had gone away vowing vengeance 'if it
took him a lifetime.'" The story was dismissed as "an idle tale" when
Sarah married David, but in the wake of the murder, the newspaper reported, "this rumor has again been brought into the limelight,
and quite a number of people in the vicinity are inclined to believe
that in the following up of all this phase of the matter in all probability would be found the solution of the matter."

When Chief of Detectives Eli Stodgill questioned Sarah's uncle—
the one she'd initially stayed with upon arriving in Winnipeg, for
the few months before she married David—he did not reject outright the notion that this earlier affair might have some connection
to her murder. But he told police he hadn't inquired about it further
among relatives still living in Sarah's native town in Russia. Chief
Constable Donald MacPherson told the Free Press that the police
"may have to have an investigation of Mrs. Feinstein's life in Russia
before we can make much headway" regarding that angle. But in a

police department already strapped for resources and short on language skills, such an investigation would never occur.

The Yiddish newspaper Der Keneder Yid *slammed the city's English-language newspapers for publishing "sensationalistic" stories about the murder—and about Sarah Feinstein's past: "The* Free Press, *for example, hooked on to the information that there is an underground group in Russia that believes whoever commits a crime against them must pay for it with their life. And because Mrs. Feinstein crossed that secret organization, they sent a hit man from Russia to kill her. The* Tribune *reported that a lover of Mrs. Feinstein took revenge on her. The truth is that both contentions are false and unfounded."*

But such rumors were all the newspapers had to report, in the absence of any solid leads.

Neighbors also told reporters about a man who had been "persecuting" Sarah, trying to gain entrance to her house in the days and weeks leading up to the murder. "It is said that on different occasions, he tried to force himself into the house, but was repulsed," the Telegram *reported. But no details were ever forthcoming in the press about who the man might have been, what he looked like, or what he could have wanted in the house.*

Dr. William Rogers, the coroner overseeing the inquest into the murder, swore in the jury on August 12, one week after it had initially been scheduled. But rather than beginning to hear testimony, he announced: "We find that we are in the same position as a week ago. The police are unable to proceed just at present." He adjourned the inquest without any hearing.

The jurors were "decidedly dissatisfied," as the Tribune *put it. This was the second time they'd assembled for a hearing that was postponed at the last minute. Rogers assured the jury that the following week the police would finally be ready to present their case. The jurors were nervous that the process would drag out even longer. One asked if they might hear preliminary evidence that night, and the rest of the evidence the following week, to speed things along; Rogers told him, "No, we shall be through in one night." Another juror said he had already postponed an eye operation so he could be present on August 12, and didn't want to put it off any longer; Rogers excused him from the next week's meeting. "I should like to get through with this as quickly as possible," one juror told Rogers, "and I know there are some others who would like to get away soon."*

The afternoon after the inquest's second postponement, the Tribune reported on August 13 that police had "nothing of value to add" since the previous week: "Practically all their efforts to locate even a motive for the murder have been fruitless, and they are as far from a solution of the mystery today as they were on the day of its happening."

Since the murder on August 1, the dailies had covered the story almost every day. But the August 13 Tribune item noting the delay—just three sentences long—marked an end to that. The newspapers fell suddenly silent, publishing nothing about the case in the ensuing week, leading up to the inquest's newly rescheduled date.

A throng of reporters and other observers was on hand when Rogers seated the jurors a third time, swearing them in at eight in the evening on Tuesday, August 19. This time, after two weeks of delays, the police were finally ready to proceed, with Rogers and Charles A. Ritchie, the acting coroner who had examined Sarah's body on the night of the murder, sharing the bench during the proceedings.

The inquest took nearly four hours, as the jurors questioned each witness. "Some of the members seemed particularly anxious to dwell strongly upon certain points," the Free Press reported—in particular the missing key, which had already earned a great deal of attention in the newspapers, as well as a story about a possible new suspect who had never been brought up in press reports. Because of the language barriers in the room, such questioning took a long time. "Nearly all the witnesses were unable to speak English," the Telegram reported, "and procedure through an interpreter was slow."

At one point, a disagreement over English translation brought the proceedings to a complete stop. David's sister Fina Dorfman recounted the details of Sarah's last evening at home, dictating letters in "ordinary family style." At one point during her testimony, one member of the jury—presumably one of the Jewish members, such as Moses Finkelstein or Max Goldstein, who probably understood Yiddish—objected to the English translation being offered by the interpreter. "He subsided, however, when the witness reaffirmed her statement as it had been given to the court," the Telegram wrote.

Lucy Kesler, the neighbor who had seen Sarah on her front porch around eleven o'clock on the night of the murder, testified about their last conversation, which she claimed lasted just five minutes—during which time, the hired girl Victoria Komanowska had also been on the porch, praying. David and Sarah's other neighbor Robert Kasner, who built the Feinsteins' house, testified about the kind of locks he'd put on the doors, as well as the scene he found when he was called to the house the night of the murder.

Abram Schurman also spoke, noting that he had been at the railway depot—on Higgins Avenue near Main Street—until after midnight, waiting for an uncle who was due to arrive from Russia; his uncle never arrived, and rather than go to his parents' home at 373 Athole Avenue, he walked to the Kasners' house at 516 Magnus Avenue and went to sleep around one in the morning, only to be awakened by Victoria two hours later. Abram was the only witness who was asked directly by the coroner, "Have you any idea who shot Mrs. Feinstein?"

"No," he replied. "I have no idea. I was in bed at the time, and when I got there, other people had arrived before me."

Mary Manastaka and Mary Platak—the two servant girls who had been suspects but were later cleared—both spoke about their relationship with Sarah. Mary Platak, who had worked for the Feinsteins, testified that she had left her job on good terms—and that she had never quarreled with Sarah, or vowed to get even with her, as the newspapers had reported. Mary Manastaka, who actually worked a few doors down but had been confused for the other Mary when the investigation began, said she had indeed had "words" with Sarah the previous Friday; the Tribune said Mary Manastaka "had been hindering Victoria" from working, "and had been sharply ordered about her business" by Sarah. But, Mary testified, she and Sarah had been friendly to one another since that time—she'd even taken the Feinsteins' baby, Anne, out for a walk. Mary had been inside the Feinsteins' house again two days before the murder, she acknowledged in response to questioning, but only to chat with their hired girl, Victoria.

Victoria was herself a "star" witness, according to the Tribune, and the journalists were waiting in anticipation to hear what she had to say. One juror found it suspicious that she'd been praying outside a few hours before the murder, when Lucy Kesler had come to visit.

"Why were you praying outside on the veranda?" he asked.

"It was better for me to pray outside than inside," replied Victoria, a Ukrainian Christian who had immigrated from Austria that spring.

"Is it usual for you to pray outside?"

"I nearly always do," she said.

Victoria told the jury that after saying her prayers, she had gone to bed at midnight and fallen asleep quickly, and had not heard a gunshot. As she recounted the details of that night—entering the rear bedroom to find the body, and then running out the front door—the jurors examined a floor plan of the house so they could follow along.

"How was the front door when you tried to go out?" the coroner asked.

"It was not locked," Victoria said, "but it was shut."

"Could anyone come in from the outside in the condition the lock was?"

"Yes," said Victoria.

More questions about the key followed, but Victoria insisted that she had never used the key herself; she had no need for one because she never had a night off, and she never went out without Sarah.

Then Victoria brought up something that hadn't been mentioned in the numerous newspaper stories published to date: a young man who'd allegedly come calling for her at the Feinsteins' window. That caught everyone's attention. The jurors then asked her several questions about this new and mysterious character.

"Who was the boy who was calling you through the window?"

"He never did anything but make signs for me to come out," said Victoria.

"Did you go out?"

"No, I was afraid," she said.

"Do you know who he was?"

"No, I don't know who he was. I got afraid at his calling and looking through the window."

"What time was it when he did this?"

"It was after ten o'clock at night, but I cannot remember the date."

"Did he call more than once?"

"He knocked a lot at the window that evening, but I did not go out."

Coroner Rogers interrupted to clarify the timeline: "When was this?"

"About three weeks before the tragedy," said Victoria.

The newspapers had a new prime suspect; perhaps this was the same man whom neighbors had claimed had attempted to gain entrance to the Feinsteins' house—or maybe not. Either way, it was fodder for more speculation on the part of reporters and North End residents, even if there weren't enough concrete details to give police any usable leads.

However remarkable Victoria's testimony was, the Free Press asserted, "probably the most important evidence was that of the husband."

David Feinstein "gave his testimony in a low, thick voice, and showed he was still deeply affected," according to the Telegram. The house key was a major subject of discussion. Jurors asked David about the coal cellar, to see if the intruder might have been hiding inside the house rather than using the key to enter the front door. He explained that the cellar was seven feet deep, with a chute leading to it, as well as four windows—three of them closed and one with a screen. David testified that the chute was closed up when he returned home from Canora, the windows were intact, and the screen had not been moved. So it appeared that the intruder had not entered through the cellar.

Winnipeg Crown Prosecutor Elias R. Levinson—a Jewish native of Australia who'd been appointed the previous summer—picked up this line of questioning.

"On Saturday morning, when you came back, did you search for the keys?" he asked.

"Yes, with the police," said David, "and we could not find them."

"Who put the keys in the bureau afterwards?" asked Levinson.

"I don't know," said David.

The Free Press *later reported that David's "testimony in regard to the keys deepened the mystery, if anything. The funeral having been held between the time of the first search for the keys and the time they were found made it possible for the murderer to return them."*

Coroner Rogers asked David what he'd heard from Sarah about a mysterious man who'd been trying to get Victoria's attention by scraping the windows: "Did you ever hear of anybody having a quarrel with your wife?"

"No," David replied. "Once, after I had been out, however, the misses told me that a boy was scraping at the window and disturbing" Victoria, whom he referred to as "the new girl."

"Who was that boy?" the coroner asked.

"My wife did not tell me," said David, "because she did not see him."

"Why was he scraping at the window?"

"To disturb the girl."

"That would not mean that there was a quarrel," said Rogers. "Was it some young fellow who was going with the girl?"

"I don't know," David answered.

Based on the testimony that evening, it seemed clear that the killer most likely used the key—however and whenever it had been obtained—to enter the house. And it also seemed likely that the mysterious boy at the window might somehow be involved. But neither of those theories led the jurors any closer to the killer's actual identity.

The remaining witnesses testified in their professional or official capacities, and were more straightforward and definitive in their statements.

Jurors were shown four photographs of the victim as Dr. George

Hirsh Kalichmann and Dr. Abram Bercovitch, who had arrived first on the scene and pronounced Sarah Feinstein dead, shared their observations about what they found: the body, the bullet wound, the bloody sheets.

The only police officer to testify was Sergeant Rice of the North Winnipeg police station, who told of getting the call and going to the scene at 520 Magnus Avenue with Patrol Sergeant Livingston and taking charge of the scene until detectives arrived. No detectives spoke at the inquest.

Coroner Frederick Todd Cadman, who had assisted Dr. Gordon Bell in the autopsy, testified that the course of the bullet was nearly straight across the brain on a level with the eyes, slightly upward and backward. Death, he said, was sudden. As he testified, the jurors examined the flattened bullet, identified as coming from a .32 caliber revolver, that had been taken from Sarah's brain.

Gun expert Alfred Paterson, who worked in the sporting goods department of Ashdown's hardware store, testified that a silencer was probably not used on the gun that killed Sarah. Detectives initially thought such a device might have been used, since nobody in the house claimed to have heard the shot, but Paterson explained that silencers could not be used on revolvers, since the sound would escape from the cartridge chamber. He said that few silencers were sold, and the sale of one for a gun larger than .22 caliber was extremely rare.

In all, eighteen witnesses were called. But as the Free Press *reported the next day, "none of them threw any light on the mystery." The testimony lasted until just before midnight, but deliberation took a mere ten minutes. The jury—"all of whom are well-known citizens," the* Telegram *assured readers—returned an open verdict, signed by foreman H. E. Isaacs, indicating that they had been unable to come to a definitive conclusion about who committed the murder: "We, the jury empanelled for the purpose of inquiring into the death of Sarah Feinstein, find that she died on August 1, 1913, about three o'clock in the morning, at 520 Magnus Avenue, of a bullet fired into her right temple." The culprit, they concluded, was "some person or persons unknown."*

18: A RICH REWARD

The morning after the official investigation into Sarah Feinstein's murder reached its inconclusive conclusion at the coroner's inquest, the Free Press *reported on the findings in an August 20 story headlined "Jury Baffled by Feinstein Murder." The* Telegram *echoed the sentiment, proclaiming: "Little Progress Made Towards Solving Murder."*

After a weeklong lull in coverage, the city's daily newspapers were back on the case. Reporters wrote a flurry of new stories about the murder after the jury returned its "open verdict," refusing to drop the subject. Investigators didn't let it drop, either. Nor did the victim's family—specifically, David Feinstein and his brothers and sisters.

The Feinsteins' hired girl, Victoria Kamanowska, was kept in police custody for two more weeks while detectives searched for more suspects. Police didn't believe that she had committed the murder, but surmised that she might know more than she had admitted to the jury—in particular, about the mysterious man at the window she'd testified about at the inquest. She claimed she hadn't seen his face, and hadn't talked to him, but the fact that a young man had been lurking outside the Feinsteins' house, scraping the window to get her attention, meant that the killer might have been someone she knew.

Police also kept a close eye on Abram Schurman after he testified at the inquest. On August 27, Abram—who had come to Victoria's aid on the night of the murder, calling for a doctor and the police—was taken into custody on "an ordinary charge of vagrancy, in which he is accused of having no visible means of support," the Free Press *reported the next day. The* Telegram *noted that he had no trade, no steady work, no regular abode; he had come from Russia with his family the previous year, but his father Eli had since banished him from their house on Athole Avenue. In fact, it was Eli, the* Telegram *reported, who had called the police about Abram's vagrancy.*

Schurman was held for a week, during which time suspicion about him began to build. The Free Press *accused police of "keeping back information" about the reasons behind the arrest: "Although [Schurman] is being held on a charge of common vagrancy, it is understood that he is really held in connection with the murder," the paper reported on September 1.*

A full month after the murder, and more than a week after the inquest, the case had fallen off the front page. But Schurman's arrest put it right back. "Big developments are momentarily expected in the case," the Free Press *reported. "It is not supposed that [Schurman] had anything whatsoever to do with the case himself, but the belief of those who have been following the case closely is that he knows something about it that will assist in bringing justice to the assassin."*

Big developments never came. Schurman was released, Victoria was released, and reporters found fewer and fewer pegs for new stories.

What seemed like a new break came on September 2, when the Tribune *reported that an unnamed boy already being held in the boys' ward of the local jail was believed to have inside information about the case. "Police Believe Youth Knows About Feinstein Murder," read the front-page headline. Was this the infamous young man at the window? Further information from the boy known simply as "the youth" never materialized.*

Frustrated by the lack of leads, David deposited with police a check for an additional five hundred dollars to help find the killer, as the Tribune *reported on its front page on September 8: "Mr. Feinstein would not state whether or not he believed that this additional reward would stimulate the police to further efforts, but he is under the impression that the large sum may succeed in tempting someone in possession of valuable information to turn the same over to the police." At the end of September, the police took out an ad in the* Tribune *and the* Free Press *advertising the reward, now totaling one thousand dollars—the original five hundred from the city and the province combined, plus another five hundred from David. Reporting on the impressive sum in its final front-page story about the case, headlined "Police Making Further Efforts to Find Slayer," the* Tribune *noted on September 30, "The advertisement of the large reward has been made in the hope that someone, an accomplice, perhaps, may be led to turn king's informer and so deliver the slayer to justice." Detectives, the paper implied, were out of ideas: "The police authorities are absolutely in the dark. Every clue they have been able to obtain so far has led into the ground, and not the slightest evidence as to the discovery of the murderer has been discovered."*

For three months, there was no newspaper coverage of the murder.

Then, on New Year's Day 1914, the Free Press *reflected on the previous year in crime. Winnipeg had witnessed 178 violent deaths in 1913. People were killed by sunstroke, elevator accidents, and electrocution. Workmen fell from buildings they were erecting. Two men froze to death. Three babies were smothered while sleeping with their parents. Twenty-one people were killed in railway accidents, while twenty-eight drowned—including twenty-two accidental deaths, three suicides, and three cases of children who drowned in rain barrels. A man died after being punched in the jaw in a streetcar fight. One man committed suicide after a lover's quarrel, while another killed his new bride by setting her on fire. One week after one man was killed in a car crash, his young daughter died by accidentally drinking a saucer of fly poison.*

There were also six murders that the newspaper singled out be-

cause they "held the public interest to the greatest degree." One man shot his married paramour and then himself, and another did the same with his wife. One man killed his own baby, while a domestic worker cut the throat of her employer's baby. One man shot his sister-in-law and was sentenced to be hanged. And then there was the Feinstein murder—the only one on the list that remained unsolved.

The Tribune published a story in February 1914 about the case, noting that the attorney general had raised the reward to the unprecedented sum of three thousand, five hundred dollars. Even though Winnipeg had the country's highest average wages at the time, this was still nearly four times the average annual wage for the city's working men. "For weeks, the entire detective force made an endeavor to bring to justice the perpetrator of the foul crime; but without avail," the Tribune reported. But even with such a rich reward, the newspaper noted that police were "as far from a solution as they were in August."

"The murder of Mrs. Feinstein," the Tribune wrote, in the last article any newspaper would publish about the case, "was without doubt one of the most mysterious occurrences ever recorded in the annals of this city."

19: UNLIKELY SUSPECTS

The official investigation into Sarah Feinstein's murder had ended inconclusively. Even Winnipeg's dogged journalists had ultimately given up. But as the hundredth anniversary of my great-grand-mother's death approached in the summer of 2013, I wasn't ready to concede defeat quite yet. I started to look beyond the newspaper reports and official documents I'd accumulated.

Maybe, I thought, the culprit had eventually been caught, and there had been a second trial—one that the newspapers chose not to cover. I called the Clerk of the Courts for Manitoba to see if there had been a trial beyond the initial inquest, but their records only date back to 1984, and everything before that had been destroyed.

I called the Winnipeg police to see if I could get any more infor-mation on the case. Ross Read in criminal investigations told me the city's police department records only went back to 1914, and there was no mention in them of the Feinstein murder. But I still wasn't convinced: Perhaps a trial had taken place, but it had been considered a 1913 case since that's when the crime took place. Per-sistent, I sent an email asking for more help.

James Ham, the web services coordinator for the Winnipeg Po-lice Department, forwarded my inquiry to the Police Museum, where curator/historian Jack Templeman—who'd advised local historian Allan Levine about *The Blood Libel*, his fictional murder mystery set in the North End that bore a slight resemblance to my great-grandmother's case—wrote back that this appeared to be an unsolved murder. He said he found the newspaper reports curious, thought it strange, as I had, that no detectives appeared at the inquest, and wondered why they let the case drop in an age with so few murders—unless they were at a complete dead end. He also wondered about the "convenience of the husband being away" and the possible involvement of the hired help. "I guess," he wrote in an email, "someone got away with murder."

Whenever I'd bring up the murder to my mother that summer, I'd go back over the story about the newspaper reports, the phone calls, the emails, my trip to Winnipeg. I'd tell her everything I'd learned about what happened to Sarah: Someone came into the house in the middle of the night, when her husband was out of town, and shot her while she slept—with one child next to her in bed, and another nearby in the crib. Police initially suspected the boyfriend of Sarah's disgruntled former servant, but that theory had soon been discarded.

My mother would circle back to the same question: "So who killed her?"

I'd have to respond, "I don't know."

The next day on the phone, the cycle would begin again.

I began to feel discouraged. I'd been researching the case for months, and I still didn't have an answer. If detectives and journalists were unable to solve the crime at the time, there was no reason to think I could solve it a century later and a thousand miles away. There was no new evidence to uncover, no new suspect to interrogate. All I had was what I'd already gleaned from my research—and that had led to a dead end.

But even though there hadn't been a definitive resolution of the case, I had come across details that seemed suspicious to me, clues that might have pointed to the killer, even if they hadn't been conclusive enough to secure a conviction. I went back through all the newspaper reports, with all their inconsistencies, to try to build a logical case of my own based on what I'd learned.

I tended to believe at this point that the initial suspect, Stefan Kushowsky, was innocent. Not because his alibi seemed airtight; it would probably have been simple enough for him to slip away from his job at the nearby rail yards after two in the morning without being missed. But his connection to the victim was almost non-existent. He wasn't, it turned out, the boyfriend of the Feinsteins' servant; he was a man who'd been to the soda shop with a different servant named Mary Manastaka, who worked somewhere else. And without any connection to Sarah, he had no motive to kill her. The theory the police outlined on the day of the murder had sounded compelling in the newspapers, but it fell apart almost immediately.

In falling apart, the case against Stefan also showed how unreliable the neighbors were as witnesses. What of the neighbor who claimed to have heard someone shout "Stefan!" at three o'clock in the morning? Was this a detail that the neighbor "remembered" after investigators had already named Stefan as the main suspect? What about the other neighbors who recalled Mary Manastaka's threats against Sarah? Were these memories, too, offered up after police named Mary as an accessory—in error? Neighbors were quite free sharing unsubstantiated rumors and gossip, much of which turned out to be false—for instance, pointing the finger at the wrong Mary in the first place.

That didn't mean the Feinsteins' hired girl Victoria Komanowska—or her real predecessor, Mary Platak—played no role in their employer's death. One of them may have passed a spare key to someone else to be copied, and may have provided the killer information about when Sarah's husband would be out of town, essentially abetting and facilitating the murder. But who could have enlisted them in the plot—they were rarely out of Sarah's sight, and didn't even have house keys of their own—and why would either of the women have consented?

The most likely suspect in my mind was someone whose story didn't add up: Abram Schurman—the neighbor who wasn't really a neighbor at all, the young man who gave up waiting for an uncle who never arrived and decided, for no apparent reason, to show up on a friend's doorstep in the middle of the night, just feet away from the murder that would soon take place. Unlike the other suspects, he lied to the police (and reporters) in the beginning, initially telling them that he lived in the house next door to the Feinsteins, and when he was later arrested, his alibi (the uncle allegedly coming from Russia) never checked out.

Maybe, I hypothesized, Abram was "the man at the window,"

whose identity was never certain; if he was friends with the Kasners, who lived next door to the Feinsteins on Magnus Avenue, he would have had ample opportunity to stand outside their window without arousing much suspicion on previous occasions when he came to visit his friends.

I couldn't figure a solid motive for Abram in particular, meaning he didn't seem to have a direct connection to the Feinsteins, or any apparent reason to kill Sarah. But perhaps he was a hired hitman, paid to commit the crime; after all, he was—unlike Victoria, Stefan, and both Marys—a vagrant with no other visible means of support. Even his own father had cut him off. He needed money. Maybe that was motive enough for him.

But even if Abram was paid to pull the trigger, or if the killer was any random hired hit-man for that matter, that wouldn't explain who was actually behind the murder.

My husband Mark remained certain that my great-grandfather had been behind the shooting. In fact, virtually everybody I told about the case—everybody, that is, except relatives or friends of the family—came to the same conclusion quite quickly: David had his wife killed.

The theory is a staple of *Law and Order* and every other crime drama on television: The husband did it. That's not without reason. In reality, intimate partners—spouses, boyfriends and girlfriends, and ex-partners—are quite often the perpetrators in murder cases. According to Statistics Canada, in 2014 more than one in five homicides were committed by an intimate partner, and in those cases, women were four times more likely than men to be the victim. (Even so, while it's true that complete strangers commit murder relatively rarely, partners and spouses aren't the most frequent assailants—unrelated acquaintances are. In other words, someone who knows the victim well enough to hate her, but not well enough to love her.)

While it would certainly make for a tidy story, I didn't believe that my great-grandfather murdered my great-grandmother.

True, on a personal level, it would be difficult to think about what that would mean, to have my great-grandfather commit such a hideous crime and then spend the rest of his life lying about it to the very children whose mother he had killed. What kind of a sociopath could do such a thing?

But beyond my subjective sense of familial discomfort with that idea, the crime simply didn't fit the most common patterns of spousal homicide.

This wasn't a crime of passion, committed during a heated argument or physical altercation. David was hundreds of miles away in Canora, and had been gone for more than a week, when Sarah was killed in Winnipeg.

There was no evidence of marital discord. Sarah spent her final evening dictating a letter to David, for his sister Fina to write; these letters came up at the inquest, and there's nothing in the record of Fina's testimony to suggest that they indicated any marital problems or disputes. Nor did Lucy, the neighbor who was the last to speak with Sarah just hours before the crime, reveal in her testimony that Sarah had mentioned such strife. While it's reasonable to believe that Fina could have remained quiet to protect her own brother from accusations of wrongdoing, it doesn't make sense that Lucy would have hidden such information—covering up the truth about her friend's death so she could continue to live next-door to the man who plotted her murder.

Police and journalists asked neighbors, friends, relatives, and the hired help about the couple's domestic life, and everybody reported that the Feinsteins' marriage was a good one. These neighbors and friends weren't shy to gossip or spread negative rumors: In addition to impugning the servants and Stefan, they shared tales about Sarah's spurned boyfriend in Russia, and suggested without any substantiation that she might have been part of a secret society before she immigrated to Canada. Even when asked directly, they never said anything about David and Sarah having a bad marriage—and to me, they sounded like the kind of witnesses who would happily have shared this information if they'd had it.

It seemed impossible that Sarah was having an extramarital affair. A mother with four children under six years old, one of whom she was still breastfeeding, with a live-in servant who never left the house, in a close-knit neighborhood where everybody knew everyone else's business? Where exactly could Sarah have met someone else and carried on an affair?

As for David, he did have ample opportunity to have an affair. It seemed unlikely to me that he could have a mistress in Winnipeg without one of his gossipy neighbors finding out about it. But he was often on the road for business—even if Canora, a tiny prairie town where he stayed with his brother, seemed an improbable place to find a new girlfriend. However, if he indeed had a mistress in Canora, and a brother willing to cover for him, why would he have wanted to disturb this easily maintained double life: a wife and children in Winnipeg, and a girlfriend and a perfect alibi hundreds of miles away?

Perhaps he had a mistress who wanted to become his wife. But David would remain a single father of four young children for two years after Sarah's death. He could easily have gained more freedom by placing his kids in the local Jewish orphanage: As Bernie Bellan, editor of *The Jewish Post & News*—Winnipeg's English-language bi-weekly community newspaper, whose roots go back to a weekly called *The Jewish Post* that was founded in 1925—told me, widowed parents or even married couples who'd fallen on hard times financially often placed their children in the orphanage at that time; sometimes this was temporary, other times it was permanent. The city's Jewish orphanage—which David's brother Harry would later run, becoming president of the Jewish Children's Home in 1946—wasn't a sort of Dickensian workhouse strictly for children who had lost both parents. It was a residence for children who weren't necessarily orphans but whose parents had trouble supporting them. Kids there had access to school, a place to sleep, and three meals a day. And it didn't carry the kind of stigma that taints such places in popular memory today.

So: If David had a mistress who wanted to remain his mistress, he had no need to get rid of his wife. If he had a mistress who wanted to start a new family with him, without taking on the burden of raising another woman's young children, he had the chance to send his kids to the orphanage without raising any eyebrows in the community—but he never did. If he had a mistress who wanted to become his wife and was willing to raise another woman's young children, he didn't do anything of the sort for two years, quite a long time for a man to be a single parent a century ago.

It's true that it's not unusual for a husband to kill his wife. But in this case, I couldn't see a motive. Nor did David's actions after the murder seem to indicate anything nefarious.

This was no ordinary crime. It was planned out; the killer presumably made sure David wasn't home and Sarah was asleep, and had a way to get into the house without making much noise—whether he used the spare key, or a copy of the key, or simply picked what was surely a very simple lock to pick. The assassin could have taken any of the valuables that lay in plain sight, because he either wanted the money or wanted to throw the motive into question, but he didn't. This was personal and specific, a premeditated and targeted murder, essentially an execution at point-blank range, and nobody made any effort to make it appear otherwise. It seemed like it was meant to send a message.

But to whom?

To my mind, someone trying to send a message to Sarah—a mysterious secret society, a crime syndicate, or a spurned lover in Russia who inexplicably waited at least seven years after being jilted before sending an emissary across the globe to get revenge—would have actually sent the message to Sarah directly before killing her: He could have broken into her bedroom, woken her up, told her what was about to happen, and then pulled the trigger. He could have threatened her or her children, or her husband, or robbed her, or beaten her, or blackmailed her. But instead, he put the gun to her temple and killed her while she slept, without delivering any message.

Killing Sarah in such a fashion sounded to me more like it was meant to send a message to her husband. A warning of some sort, or revenge? It was plausible that someone else had intended Sarah's murder to send a message to David. But David wouldn't order a hit to send a message to himself.

As the *Telegram* suggested just one day after the murder, at a time when speculation was rampant: "Beyond a possibility that it was for revenge, there seems to have been no motive for the crime." If revenge wasn't the motive, and neither was financial gain, or romantic entanglement, then what was?

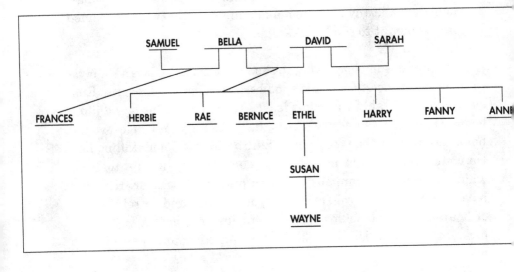

20: DAVID AND BELLA

David Feinstein married his second wife Bella Freedman on May 9, 1915. They were wed by Rabbi Jacob Gorodsky, who had eulogized David's first wife Sarah at her funeral two years earlier. Their wedding was held at Tiferes Israel, the synagogue that had held Sarah's funeral service—on the same corner, Manitoba and Powers, where David and Sarah had been married in 1906.

David already knew Bella, a dressmaker four years his junior. Since the murder at 520 Magnus Avenue, David had moved with his children one block north to 506 Burrows Avenue; Bella lived just a few blocks away on Pritchard Avenue, and the two had several things in common: They were both Russian immigrants who'd become Canadian citizens—she was born in Kishinev or Odessa and sailed into Halifax in 1905 or 1906 (records vary about her hometown and date of arrival) aboard the Montezuma. They were both widowed, single parents. David had four young children—Harry, Ethel, Fanny, and Anne—and Bella had one, a five-year-old girl named Frances, who'd kept the last name of her father Samuel Turbovsky, who had died of pneumonia when she was four. Together David and Bella, who were thirty-three and twenty-nine when they were married, would eventually have three more children.

The family name, which had officially been Fainstein for a few years on the children's birth certificates before turning into Fein-

...ın in census reports and most newspaper stories, ultimately settled again, with some consistency, on Fainstein.

Nine months after David and Bella were married, their daughter Bernice was born in Winnipeg in February 1916. But by the time the census of the prairie provinces of Manitoba, Saskatchewan, and Alberta was taken that June, David and Bella and the children— their exact ages and names were muddled by the census taker; Ethel became Hattie, Bernice became Bertha, Fanny became Flora—were living in Canora, the small town in Saskatchewan where David had been working when Sarah was murdered in 1913. Also living with the family was yet another Mary: Mary Garachuk, a thirty-two-year-old Galician domestic. Their house in Canora, on Third Street, was spartan. There was no indoor plumbing; when it was the children's bath time, they'd boil water and pour it into a basin in the kitchen. But they were not entirely without luxuries: They had a player piano.

David and the other Fainstein brothers were taking turns living in Saskatchewan full-time. Harry, who had been living in Canora at the time of Sarah's murder, left Saskatchewan at the end of 1915 and was now living in Winnipeg's North End with his wife, Pauline—who'd taken in David and Sarah's kids after Sarah's murder—and their two young sons Max and Stanley, at 541 Mountain Avenue. But David's youngest brother Louis, who had lived with David and Sarah when he first arrived in Winnipeg as a teenager in 1907, was now living just down the street from David in Canora, with his new wife, Bessie. David's sister Clara was nearby, too, with her husband Joe Gelmon, who sold dry goods, and their children William and Pearl.

The first Jews had arrived in Canora in 1905, shortly after the Canadian Northern Railway tracks were laid in 1904 and the hamlet was founded. During the same period, Jewish settlers also arrived at other nearby small towns, where they most often ran general stores; Joe Gelmon's brother Louis, who'd married Sarah's sister Gertrude, was one example, running a small grocery store in Sturgis, Saskatchewan, twenty-five miles from Canora. Meanwhile, Jewish agricultural colonies, which had sprung up in

the region in the late 1800s, began to grow and multiply as the Jew-
ish Colonization Association purchased thousands of acres of land
in the early 1900s—giving birth to larger colonies in Saskatchewan
like Sonnenfeld and Edenbridge (known as Yidn Bridge) in 1906.

Jews quickly became a prominent part of Canora. Samuel Korbin
arrived in 1905 with his wife and children, and opened a general
store; within a few years he was a town councilor and in 1912 he be-
came mayor. Sam Cohen, whose family had been among the found-
ers of Winnipeg's Shaarey Zedek congregation in 1880, opened Can-
ora's first hotel, the Canora Hotel, a three-story structure across the
street from the new railway station. Other Jewish newcomers were
butchers and shopkeepers.

The Fainstein brothers were part of this westward migration, ar-
riving in 1908. They farmed three-and-a-half miles northwest of
Canora, and Harry bought a house in town, where the other broth-
ers would stay when they came on business.

Residential lots in Canora sold for as little as one-hundred-fifty
dollars—with discounts of 6 percent for purchases made in full,
rather than relying on monthly or quarterly payments. Sales were
handled through the Canora Townsite Company, located in Winni-
peg; its ads touted the town as "the future railroad and agricultural
center of eastern Saskatchewan."

A History of Canora and District *was published in 1960 to mark*
the golden jubilee, or fiftieth anniversary, of Canora's official in-
corporation as a town. The oversized commemorative paperback,
emblazoned with the town seal and filled with hundreds of brief
articles illustrated with black-and-white photographs and vari-
ous charts and lists, chronicles local progress: Wooden sidewalks
were built and later replaced by cement; a post office opened, and a
school, and a hospital; a local newspaper was founded—originally
called the Advertiser, *but now known as the* Canora Courier, *which*
is still publishing. The book also lists the disasters that struck Can-
ora: Epidemics of scarlet fever, typhoid, and influenza battered the
town; in a 1909 smallpox outbreak, infected guests at the Canora
Hotel were quarantined. Fires razed new wooden buildings. Harsh
winters and summer flooding destroyed crops and livestock.

But Jews continued to come. By 1911, the town of several hundred was more than 9 percent Jewish.

For a tiny town that still had fewer than a thousand people when David and Bella moved in 1916, Canora was surprisingly diverse. David and Bella's neighbors included Chinese waiters and laundrymen, Irish dressmakers and postal workers, German stenographers and carpenters, and Scottish veterinarians and police officers. Alongside the Jews lived Methodists, Catholics, Anglicans, and a large number of Doukhobors—radical Christian pacifists from Russia, several thousand of whom had settled on communes in western Canada after 1900.

The Jews of Canora were a tight-knit group, and became known for their generosity. As Winnipeg's Yiddish newspaper Dos Yidishe Vort/The Israelite Press *reported on October 5, 1916, all twenty-five Jewish families in town—presumably including David and Bella's family—gathered in one resident's home to raise money for Jewish war victims. "The results of the meeting were spectacularly surprising in the full sense of the word," the story said. "From a handful of Jews they managed to raise five-hundred fifty dollars in cash. We are reminded that a mass meeting of thousands here in Winnipeg raises the same amount. We in Winnipeg, then, must be ashamed in the face of Canora Jews who must be upheld as paragons of generosity and compassion."*

It was no surprise, then, when Winnipeg's Jewish orphanage—the same one where David's brother Harry would eventually become president—was soliciting funds a few years later, they sent their representatives to Canora, where the same newspaper reported that the locals "are being asked to fulfill their duty."

By 1921, more than 13 percent of Canora's twelve-hundred residents were Jewish. The community of nearly two hundred—now representing some thirty families—started a synagogue, hired a Jewish teacher, and opened a kosher food store. David and Bella stayed in Canora for several years, long enough to witness the growth of the Jewish community; their daughter Rae was born there, and so was the baby of the family, Herbie, who arrived in 1923.

As the Jewish population of Canora started a dramatic decline in the twenties, leading up to the Great Depression—foreshadowing a trend for Saskatchewan's Jewish community as a whole, which saw its numbers peak at five thousand in 1931 and eventually decline by half—David's family returned to Winnipeg. He bought a house near his brother Harry and Pauline on Mountain Avenue, a major thoroughfare seven blocks north of Magnus Avenue, a significant jump up the North End's socioeconomic ladder. It was a relatively large house, although the children still had to share rooms: Ethel, Anne, and Frances—the three older girls—tripled up in one bedroom. Little Herbie used to sleep on the balcony.

Even though Ethel was a teenager by the time the family moved in, and she only lived there for a few years, this house at 452 Mountain Avenue is the place she would later describe as her "childhood home," the place where she grew up. Everything that came before it vanished in retrospect, including the fact that she spent half her childhood, more than seven years, in Saskatchewan—a detail she never mentioned to her children or grandchildren. In the few stories she passed down, Mountain Avenue in Winnipeg is where her life truly began, with Bella—who'd raised her since she was five years old—as her mother.

21: LETTING THE PAST REST

Every time I discovered a new bit of family history—about my grandma Ethel's childhood in Canora, or what happened to Ethel's sister Fanny—I'd call my mother. Whether she was following every sentence or knew every person's name I mentioned didn't seem to matter. She'd listen, occasionally interject with a laugh, and prod me along.

Sometimes she'd jump in with a detail or two that she remembered, and other times the whole story seemed like something she was hearing for the first time. But she recognized some of the names—her mother, her aunts and uncles, her grandparents—and understood that it was somehow connected to her.

I looked forward to telling her about what I'd found, because focusing on the past gave us something to talk about. The present had become much trickier.

I was still calling my mother every day in 2013. Mornings weren't good anymore, because she'd be anxiously waiting for the driver to take her to Kensington Club and was afraid that taking a phone call would make her miss the doorbell. So I'd call her in the afternoon instead, after she got home.

When I'd visit her in person, she could still carry on a fairly normal conversation: There was context and a common setting, and we could move around and see other people and things that might spark conversation. She would make facial expressions and hand gestures when words failed. And silent gaps didn't seem awkward when we were occupying the same space. But on the phone, things were getting more difficult.

She'd recognize my voice most days, but her questions were rote. She'd repeat a few questions in a rapid cycle several times: Where are you? Is it raining there? When are you coming? Where are you? Is it raining there? When are you coming? Even answering these simple questions would confuse her.

"Where are you?" she'd ask.

"New York."

"Why are you in New York?"

"Because I live here," I'd say.

"Since when?"

"More than twenty years ago."

I knew better than to say I was "home." She thought that meant her house, which would confuse her more.

If she asked, "When are you coming?" sometimes she meant "When are you coming to visit?"—recognizing that I was in a different city, and might come to visit in the coming weeks. But other times she meant "When will you get here?"—as if I were on my way to her house at that moment from somewhere nearby, and she wanted to know if she should hold dinner for me.

I'd try to steer us into a different path, to get out of the endless loop. But if I talked about work, she'd get confused because she didn't remember what I did or where I worked or for how long. If I talked about the news, or a television show, she didn't know what I was talking about. If I asked her about her day at Kensington Club, she couldn't remember what had happened.

I ended up telling her stories, many of them the same ones she used to tell. Of course, I also talked about my great-grandmother Sarah and her murder. My mother listened eagerly, excited to hear both about what happened a hundred years ago, and my own sleuthing to get to the truth.

Then, almost immediately, she'd forget everything I told her—not just specific new details, which she'd had difficulty remembering for a while now, but the fact that I had just visited Winnipeg, or had been doing research into family history at all.

So she would repeat the sniper story she'd learned as a child. I'd explain that now I knew the real story, and she would listen, surprised, and seem to take in the information—a shot through the head while Sarah slept in her bed, not a sniper driving by while she breastfed on the porch. Then, a few minutes later, I'd mention something else about Winnipeg, and she'd chime in with the old story about the sniper again.

"But that's not what happened, Mom," I'd say, trying to be patient, trying not to get frustrated. "Remember? We were just talking about the real story."

"And what was that?" she'd ask. And I'll tell her again. And again, she'd be surprised, and intrigued, and seem to understand.

The next day, searching for something to talk to her about again, I'd mention something else about my trip to Winnipeg, and she'd start all over, *Groundhog Day*–style: "My grandmother Sarah Brooks lived in Winnipeg," she'd say, as if telling the story for the very first time. "And one day she was out on the front porch, breastfeeding..."

When I'd started looking into my great-grandmother's death, I thought I could set the record straight quickly, and share this with my mother. I had since come to realize, in the summer of 2013, that even if I could correct much of the story about Sarah, I couldn't actually come to a place where all my questions would be answered.

I had failed my mother, and myself. I'd started this whole investigation into the past with a snarky comment, calling "bullshit" on my mother's well-worn anecdote, and a large dose of journalistic cockiness, figuring I could find the truth with just a little bit of research, and correct the record in my mother's mind.

Now, I realized, the whole issue was moot anyway. No matter what answers I uncovered or what myths I could dispel, whatever individual pieces of the truth I could reveal, my mother wouldn't be able to join me in this journey of discovery. She could still understand some of what I'd found, but she couldn't retain it. Not only were my mother's memories of the past getting blurrier, her ability to form any new memories or hold onto any new thoughts at all was vanishing.

I could no longer pretend to be digging into this family history just for my mother's sake. At first, I thought I was going to help her remember, to fill in the blank spots in her memory. But now, the job of remembering had fallen entirely to me. This project was now entirely my own. And I wasn't sure it was worth continuing.

Did my mother really need what I'd been offering her—a self-congratulatory editor's note correcting a story she'd enjoyed telling for decades? As the months went on, it became apparent that she needed a great deal of help in the here and now. As the hundredth anniversary of Sarah's murder came in August 2013, I conceded that maybe it was time to let the past rest, and focus on my mother in the present.

PART 4

22: ETHEL

In 1929, sixteen years after her mother Sarah had been murdered, my grandmother Ethel Fainstein—the English spelling of the family name had finally been standardized and adopted by all the relatives in Canada—left Winnipeg.

Ethel had come into her own as a young woman in the community, occasionally appearing in the social column in *The Jewish Post*. An item I found from 1928 describes her attending a bridal "linen shower" where "the rooms were decorated with white bells and streamers" and "the table was centered with gladioli and a miniature bride." Another blurb tells of Ethel working the "novelty and handkerchief booth" for the Do More Girls' Club, raising money for a bazaar to benefit the Talmud Torah school.

She could have stayed in Winnipeg, and continued getting mentioned in the paper, as her sisters did: Frances had tea with family friends, Rae attended a sweet sixteen party, Bernice performed at a piano recital—that's how the girls made news in the twenties. But Ethel had her sights on bigger things, further from home. She was nineteen when she moved out of the house on Mountain Avenue.

Her older brother Harry was attending the University of Chicago, and Ethel lived with him briefly in Hyde Park. But she soon went farther from home: to New York City, where she rented a room in a women's residence on West 88th Street in Manhattan.

Moving more than a thousand miles away to a new country was a bold move for a single woman, without a place to live or any family support system. At nineteen, Ethel was still young—but no younger than her own mother Sarah had been when she left Russia and traveled across the world alone to start a new life in Canada.

Ethel didn't have a job lined up in New York, and there were serious barriers she had to consider. "At that time, there was a tad of anti-Semitism," my mother said, recounting her mother's early life on the video I took of her in 2010. "If you had a Jewish name, you couldn't get a job." So my grandmother adopted a pseudonym, Ethel Ben-Aaron, which she somehow believed sounded less identifiably Jewish than Fainstein. (At this point in the video, I can be heard laughing from behind the camera, asking my mother in disbelief: "Couldn't she pick Smith? Jackson?") She found a job working for R.R. Donnelley and Sons, a company that published a telephone directory of businesses known as Donnelley's Red Book—a precursor to the Yellow Pages. "When it was a Jewish holiday, she would call in sick," my mother told me, so Ethel could observe without giving away her religious background.

One winter, she went skating at Rockefeller Center and fell on the ice. A man a few years her senior—five-foot-six, with red hair and blue eyes—stopped to help her up. Although Ethel was seeing someone else at the time—a scientist known for his punctuality, something she valued tremendously—she agreed to a date with this new man, named Henry. "The man had no sense of time," my mother remembered Ethel telling her, "he was never on time for a date." Nonetheless, after living in New York for seven years as an independent single woman, Ethel married Henry in 1936.

"Why marry someone who makes your life easy?" she would later tell my mother.

Henry was an immigrant from Poland, specifically the town of Plock, where Mark and I would visit almost a century after he left as a teenager once World War I ended; he became a naturalized American citizen in 1930, when he was twenty-four. He never finished high school, but he was skilled at drawing—"that's why he drew my pictures of bugs for biology," my mother told me—and found work as a draftsman. Later, he sold Hoover vacuums door-to-door before taking a job running an army surplus store in Newark owned by his cousins; in his spare time, he made Baby Susan

Snuggies, the underwear named after my mother that he sewed in the back room of their brownstone on York Street. Ethel also worked—sometimes in Newark at her husband's store, sometimes elsewhere—while my mother and my aunt Marilyn went to high school and college.

Even with two incomes, money was tight, and travel was expensive, so Ethel only visited her family a handful of times. In the mid-forties, when my mother was in grade school and Marilyn was still a baby, she took them to Winnipeg. According to the city's 1945 voter registration rolls, David and Bella—who'd belatedly become naturalized Canadian citizens in 1941, many years after David's brothers had done the same—were living at 328 St. Johns Avenue, one block north of Mountain Avenue in the North End, with Ethel's two youngest siblings: Rae, who was working as a saleswoman, and Herbie, who was in the Royal Canadian Air Force. This was the trip where my mother met David and Bella—her grandparents, whom she called Zayde Dovid and Bubbe Bayla—for the first time.

A few years later, in the late forties, Ethel took the girls on a train to Detroit to visit her brother Harry and her sister (technically, her stepsister) Frances and their new daughter Judy—the same Judy I had tried unsuccessfully to find during my research. They stayed for the summer. Harry and Frances' house, with a backyard and a swing, seemed fancy to my mother and her sister, compared to their small apartment on York Street in Jersey City. "We didn't get to go on vacation a lot," my aunt Marilyn told me. "That was one of my highlights."

In 1954, Ethel and the girls took their biggest trip together: to Vancouver, where David and Bella had moved in 1947. Herbie had been stationed with the Air Force on Vancouver Island during World War II, and soon after the war ended, he persuaded the family to give up Winnipeg's harsh winters (and biting black flies in the sweltering summers) and relocate to the West Coast. David had bought first-class tickets for Ethel and his granddaughters to come to Vancouver, where they'd stay with Ethel's sister Bernice and her family. It was not only my mother's first time flying first class, it was her first time flying, period. "We got on the plane, United Airlines, we took our seats in first class," my aunt Marilyn told me, "and the first thing my mother did was pull the shades down. And she told us, 'Don't accept any food, even if it's offered.'"

So while passengers all around them were enjoying in-flight meals, my mother and my aunt ate nothing. "We were only allowed to take chewing gum," Marilyn remembered. "The stewardesses would come and ask if we wanted anything, and we would look at my mother and she didn't have to say anything, she'd give us 'the look.' And that look was enough." The girls certainly weren't permitted to use the restrooms, where untold diseases surely awaited them, just as they did at the movie theaters back home.

The family in Vancouver was noticeably wealthier than Ethel and Henry in Jersey City. Their relatives had large houses, modern furniture, and pets. The girls made friends with their cousins over their summer stay. "If my mother had said to me at that point, 'I'm going to stay here; I can't leave Canada,'" Marilyn told me, "my sister and I would have been fine with that." But it was the last time they'd visit, and the last time they'd see most of their cousins for many years.

It was also the last time the girls saw Bella, who died of pneumonia two years later after having a stroke and suffering for years with hypertension and chronic myocarditis, or David, who died of a stroke in 1971.

When I visited my grandparents as a child in the mid-seventies, Ethel and Henry were living in a small apartment on Tonnele Avenue in Jersey City. It had a galley kitchen, a gigantic Zenith console television, and the slowest elevator I'd ever seen, the old-fashioned kind where you have to fold up the accordion gate across the doorway manually before pushing open the elevator door.

By this point, my grandmother was working in the Empire State Building for a man named Milton, who was in the apparel business. She was technically his assistant, placing calls and running errands, but in a broader sense she was essentially his office mom, making him tuna sandwiches for lunch (just as she'd done for my mother when she was in grade school). One of the perks she enjoyed was access to Milton's WATS line, a flat-rate long-distance telephone service at a time when daytime long-distance calls, especially international calls, were prohibitively expensive. She used it to talk to my mother nearly every day, and to keep in touch with her siblings in Vancouver and California.

While Ethel's brothers and sisters, and their children, on the

West Coast saw each other with some frequency over the decades, Ethel's connection to her family was mostly reduced to these calls.

The rest of us had even less connection to them. As a child, I barely knew the names of my grandmother's siblings. All four of her sisters traveled to Maryland for my brother's bar mitzvah in April 1977—there's a picture in his photo album of the five women posing together outside the synagogue in ankle-length, patterned dresses and open-toe spring shoes—but that's the only time I met Anne, Frances, and Bernice. I met Herbie (and his wife, Ruth) at the bar mitzvah for my cousin Jason, Marilyn's son, in Houston in 1981. And Rae came to visit us in Maryland two years after that; what I remember most from that visit were her menthol cigarettes. I never met Harry, who died of a heart attack before I was born.

I remember visiting Grandma Ethel in Jersey City in the late seventies, after Grandpa Henry died; she was still in the apartment on Tonnele Avenue with the slow elevator and the giant Zenith television. She took my brother and sister and me into New York City. We rode "the tubes," as the PATH train from New Jersey was then known, and transferred to the subway, covered in graffiti and grime. I'd never seen anything so filthy, especially compared to Washington's pristine new Metro system, and I couldn't believe my fastidious grandmother rode this train every day. She had given each of us a five-dollar bill before we boarded. ("Put this in your shoe, in case you get lost," she told us. "Or mugged.") We stuck together quite diligently, though, especially walking through Times Square—back when Times Square was Times Square. I recall seeing what appeared to be rubber penises in a shop window. I asked my grandmother what they were. "I don't know," she demurred, either because she didn't think it was appropriate to tell a child of six or seven, or because she didn't actually know what a dildo was.

When my grandmother retired in 1979, her boss Milton bought her a condo in Kings Point, a senior community near Delray Beach, Florida. Her best friend Ida, who had lived across the street on York Street when my mother was growing up, moved to the same complex. ("They knew everything about each other and in an odd way, they were responsible for each other's survival," my aunt Marilyn told me. "Their loyalty was 100 percent.")

We visited her the following summer, when I was nine. I remember the old men working as security guards, riding giant tricycles.

And the swimming pool that was off-limits to anyone under six-teen, which seemed cruel to all the visiting grandchildren who were surely as bored as we were in granny land.

Ethel had long been a master of playing her children off each oth-er. She never praised my mother or Marilyn to their faces, for fear of tempting the evil eye or giving her girls swelled heads. Instead, she criticized them directly and only praised each one to the other. She built a deep-seated sense of inadequacy in my mother that never lifted, insecurities about her abilities and her worthiness, but mostly about her weight. Even when my mother was an adult, Ethel continued to criticize her, often in humiliating ways: On one of my mother's visits to Kings Point, when Ida came over for lunch, my grandmother pulled the bathroom scale into the living room and told my mother to stand on it. "Can you even believe how much she weighs?" Ethel asked Ida, as the two women squinted over their reading glasses at the dial on the scale. "Now, her sister Marilyn—she has a beautiful figure."

Whatever her shortcomings as a mother, Ethel was a loving grandmother to me, the baby of the family. When she was diag-nosed with lung cancer and had to move into our house in Mary-land in the spring of 1983, I became her helper. I'd carry her walk-er up the steps to my brother's old bedroom—the same room that would be converted a few years later into "the office," where my mother would type legal correspondence for my father—or fetch her something to drink so she could take her pills. When she placed special orders for lunch I'd relay the message to my mother, who'd roll her eyes.

If I wasn't around to be her messenger, she'd call my mother di-rectly: The telephone in her bedroom had a different number from the phone downstairs in the kitchen. (At the time, this was "the kids' line," which would later become my father's fax line.) She rarely used the phone, but sometimes her questions were urgent, or seemed that way to her. "What is the meat of the day?" she asked my mother one afternoon after dialing the kitchen line. "The meat of the day is fish," my mother responded. Ethel had always shopped for her own food and cooked for herself; it wasn't easy for her to let my mother run the house.

Ethel spent much of her time in bed, or on the sofa downstairs watching soap operas and game shows. Our dog Killer, an eight-pound Maltese, was often by her side—something my grandmother, who'd never had a dog, professed to hate. But her true feelings soon came out. Once, when Killer had been given a sedative at the vet, we'd dropped him off at home before we ran out to do some shopping; when my grandmother came downstairs while we were at the store, she found our normally attentive dog sprawled on the kitchen floor, unresponsive. We came home to find her crying on the couch: "You left me with a dead dog!" A few weeks later, when we were going away overnight, we planned to put Killer in the kennel so my grandmother wouldn't have to take care of him. "Absolutely not," she said. "He'll stay here with me."

Ethel was quite ill by this point. Mentally, she remained sharp. But radiation had made her hair fall out, and she was thin and weak and often tired. She could be a tough customer on her best day, and these were not her best days.

During the Passover Seder that year, she came downstairs in a housecoat. She'd decided not to wear her wig, but instead pulled a cheap terry cloth turban over her head—until she took that off as well; she was just "her old, bald self," my sister Stacey said.

Stacey was sixteen at the time, and was deeply embarrassed by our grandmother, who had a knack for saying unkind and sometimes racially insensitive remarks to her friends. ("Your friend Mae is tall...for one of them," she said about one of Stacey's Asian-American friends, who, for the record, wasn't tall by any standard.)

"I didn't want to have people over. It wasn't worth it," my sister told me recently, as we reminisced about the time Ethel lived with us. "It was like someone took my house and made it not my house, and for the most part, that person was Grandma. She was a difficult person to please. I remember Mom being stressed all the time, because she was at Grandma's beck and call. Everything in the household was upside down."

After six difficult months, Ethel's health deteriorated and she moved into a nursing home in Bethesda, across the road from my allergist. After my weekly doctor's appointments, I'd stop by with my mother. Ethel was always good with a zinger, knowing exactly how to devastate my mother in the most efficient way.

"I want pictures of Stacey all over my room," she told my mother during one visit.

"Why?" my mother asked.

"So that she'll remember never to do to you what you're doing to me," came the reply. The boys were off the hook, apparently; she only wanted my sister to heed her lesson. This was something about what mothers expect from their daughters.

Sometime in October, about six weeks after she moved into the nursing home, my grandmother had a stroke and nearly died. She survived the physical ordeal, but mentally, the incident marked a turning point. She was no longer entirely lucid, and she'd babble. Once, she made up a song about my brother and our dog; "Scott and Killer," she sang, "Scott and Killer." My sister teased my brother about it: "She thinks you're a dog!" But my brother teased back: "At least I'm in the song."

Grandma Ethel also became delusional and paranoid. It started when one of her nurses started quoting the New Testament and talking to my grandmother about Jesus. Ethel thought she was trying to convert her—which may not have been far from the truth. But then my grandmother told us that the nursing home was forcing her to appear in television commercials about how they treated their Jewish patients well. In her mind this was part of a larger plan to lure Jews in and then convert them. She started speaking to my mother in Yiddish—my mother understood some Yiddish from her childhood but didn't speak it fluently—so the non-Jewish staff couldn't understand what they were saying.

Grandma Ethel had one last day when she was lucid—meaning she spoke in English and made sense, even though she was still confused. In December 1983, two weeks before she died, my bar mitzvah was on a Saturday morning, with my party following that night. While my brother and sister had more lavish celebrations in the synagogue, with professional bands and guests in their fanciest clothes, mine was a very different affair. We knew my grandmother didn't have long to live, and if she had died before my bar mitzvah, Jewish mourning rituals would have dictated that my mother couldn't listen to live music for thirty days—meaning, if I had a band and dancing, my mother wouldn't be able to attend. So instead, we had a smaller, more casual affair at home, just in case my mother would also be in mourning. My friends and I spun LPs on the record player in the basement and played video games in a "video van" parked in our driveway. My mother felt guilty for depriving me of a bigger affair; personally, I was happier wearing corduroy pants and Docksides, listening to Duran Duran, and playing Centipede.

The day after the bar mitzvah, my mother and I went to visit my grandmother in the nursing home, and she remembered my big day. She forgot about the home; she thought she was back in my brother's old bedroom, where she'd lived for six months. She thought my bar mitzvah party was just getting started downstairs.

"Tell everyone I'll be right down," she told me, smoothing her remaining wisps of gray hair with her hand.

23: LOST

Cars lined both sides of our tiny street in the Catskills on a Saturday morning in September 2013. It was Yom Kippur, the one day of the year when the small Reform synagogue across from our house draws a large crowd and its tiny parking lot overflows in every direction.

I don't observe the holiday—no long day in synagogue, no fasting, no prayers of atonement. So even though I could see the cars and the congregants dressed up in their best suits and dresses through the bay window, I was spending the day inside with Mark, watching Netflix and eating popcorn on the couch.

But back in Maryland, I knew, my parents would be spending endless hours at services that day. So I was surprised when my cell phone rang early that afternoon. I assumed it was my father, since my mother had never called my cell phone before. This time, for the first time, it was my mother, with a seemingly simple but devastating question.

"Where's Mom?" she asked, without a hello.

I paused, trying to figure out what she meant.

"Whose mom?" I replied. "You're my mom."

"My mom," she said.

"Your mother died in 1983," I told her, as calmly and clearly as I could manage.

"What about Dad?"

"He died in 1977," I said.

"Ah," she said. No discernible emotion, just registering what I'd told her; she was confused but not panicked.

"Why are you asking?"

"Because we're at their house, and your father is taking a nap, and I want to make sure he's up before they get back."

My father probably was taking a nap between services; this was common enough for a Yom Kippur afternoon when he'd gone all day without food and coffee. But the rest of what my mother said didn't compute. I didn't want to rattle her, so I tried to be logical and concise.

"Are you in a house right now?" I asked.

She was.

"Your parents never had a house," I said. "They always lived in apartments. Remember?"

"Right," she said. She was quiet for a few seconds. "Then whose house is this?"

"It's your house," I said.

"Since when?"

"For the past forty-two years," I said. "Since I was a baby."

She asked where she'd lived before that house, and I told her. She asked about the place before that, and the one before that, until I finally got to Chicago. My parents lived there for a year when my brother was a baby, and it was a painful time. They had trouble making new friends. (My mother's hopes had been raised one time when another young mother found out that my parents had a new chip-and-dip bowl, and asked if she could use it for a New Year's Eve party—but didn't ask my parents if they'd like to come, too. "Our chip-and-dip bowl got more invitations than we did!" my mother would say.) Between the social isolation, the frigid weather, and my father's job, they were miserable. ("I've only seen your father cry two times," my mother would later tell me. "When Kennedy was shot, and when we lived in Chicago.")

"I remember Chicago," my mother replied in a tone that made it clear she had no nostalgia for the city.

"That was in 1964," I told her. Six years before I was born.

Whether she fully grasped what I'd told her or not, about the house and about her parents, she sounded relieved. "I knew you'd have the answers," she said. "That's why I called you."

After she hung up, I could drop the pretense of taking this surreal phone call in stride. I stood in the doorway of our living room and, for the first time since she was diagnosed, I cried for my mother.

Up to this point, my mother's memory loss had been many things to me. Most often it was simply tedious, as I'd have to repeat things over and over. Sometimes it was frustrating, if there was something I wanted her to understand and there was no way to penetrate the fog. Occasionally it was even amusing—for both of us—when she forgot something; she could still laugh about her lapses when she knew they were happening. But now, with this phone call, things had reached a new level. This wasn't something trivial: someone's name, what day it was, an article in the newspaper. It wasn't even like her grandmother Sarah's murder—new details of which I'd tried to share with her that she couldn't retain. This was an important part of her own personal history that she was losing.

How could someone forget that her own mother was dead?

But I was also shaken for a more personal reason: If she was losing her memory of everything that had happened in the last fifty years, I worried, as a forty-two-year-old, that meant she might soon forget about me entirely. Would my entire life vanish from her mind? If she could forget that her mother died, couldn't she just as easily forget that her son had been born? Ever since she'd been diagnosed, I'd dreaded the day I'd lose my mother. But on that Yom Kippur, I started to worry about a much more awful possibility: that my mother might lose me first.

It didn't take long for this fear to become more concrete. A couple of months later, my mother forgot my birthday for the first time. Every year, she'd not only send a card, but she'd also call just before six in the evening and tell me: "Just about this time, back in 1970, a beautiful baby boy was born—just in time for dinner." I was a very large baby: ten pounds, eight ounces, the kind of baby who looked like he never missed a meal. Every year, she'd tell me the same stories about my birth. How my father had tried to bargain with the obstetrician before I was born: "Your father said, 'I'd rather have one baby at fifteen pounds than two at seven-and-a-half,' and I told him, 'You try to push a fifteen-pound baby out of your body. That's like giving birth to a Thanksgiving turkey!'" Or how my father went to look at me in the incubator after I was born; very large babies lose body heat quickly. But that meant I was in a room with lots of tiny preemies, and looked like a giant next to them, with a full head of brown hair. "Everyone was looking at you, and saying, 'Somebody forgot to take their baby home,'" my mother would recall.

For the previous few years, I'd called my mother to remind her of my brother and sister's birthdays; I assumed they'd done the same about mine. But this time, even calls and reminders weren't enough. I waited for my annual call but it never came. When I called her the following day, I mentioned that my birthday had been the previous day. "Happy birthday," she said, almost reflexively, but this realization didn't trigger the rest of her annual routine. The first story my mother—or anyone—ever told about me had been forgotten.

Despite the often testy relationship my mother had with her mother—my grandma Ethel—she became increasingly obsessed with her as the Alzheimer's progressed.

It would usually start with the simplest question: Where's Mom?

At first, reminding my mother that her mother was dead was a straightforward affair, just as it had been with that Yom Kippur phone call. She was looking for information, and once she had it, she seemed satisfied.

Then she began to include follow-up questions. I answered as best I could: In 1983. Lung cancer. King David Memorial Gardens in Virginia.

I had to recount the history of her mother's final years frequently—sometimes once a week, but later multiple times in a single conversation. But for the time being, she seemed temporarily satisfied with the answers, even if she couldn't retain what she'd been told.

In the spring of 2014, my mother had a minor operation: inserting a mesh to relieve bladder complications she'd had since her hysterectomy a decade earlier. She didn't entirely comprehend the details of the surgery—"They're going to shove everything back up there," she told me, which was probably as specific as she ever would have been regarding such things. She came home from the hospital with a urinary catheter, held in place with a small balloon, which she'd need to keep in for two days.

The following day, my father found her pants covered in blood in the bathroom. She had pulled the catheter out, balloon and all.

Physically, she hadn't done any serious damage. But when I asked her on the phone what had happened with the catheter, she told me: "My mother helped me take it out."

She had been asking about her mother for months, but this was the first time she seemed to believe she had actually seen her.

"First of all, your mother died thirty years ago," I told her. "And second of all, even when she was alive, she never helped you do shit."

The first part of what I'd said didn't register, but the second part elicited a knowing chuckle.

Asking for her mother became a daily affair. (She asked for her father, too, but only occasionally, which was a shame because she had warmer and less complicated feelings about him.) And after the surgery her questions became attached to a specific action: She began packing to "go home."

"Home," at this point, meant York Street in Jersey City, where she hadn't lived since high school, and where nobody in her family had lived since the fifties.

Every morning, she'd take a suitcase out of the closet in my old bedroom, and pack for her trip to see her mother, whom she insisted was coming to pick her up. By this point she couldn't pack with any rhyme or reason, so she simply stuffed the bags until they were nearly impossible to close or lift, filled with a random assortment of objects: her necklaces, a cordless phone, my father's sweaters, a cutting board, a tape dispenser, a salt shaker, my father's car keys, one shoe, fitted sheets, panty shields, a box of rotini. She'd ask about her mother each day, sitting with her packed bags by the front window, and my father would tell her that she wasn't coming, going over the story about Ethel's death in 1983. Then he would unpack the items and put the bags away, and she'd forget about going home until the next morning, when she would begin anew.

"Again with the fucking bags," my father told me on the phone, as his frustration started to mount.

Eventually he got an idea: He started leaving the bags packed, hoping to at least cut out one step in this routine, but each day she would pack more bags anew, filled with a different assortment of random objects from around the house, regardless of what had already been packed previous days. Small things started to "disappear": her engagement ring, my father's driver's license, her glasses, credit cards. My father would dig through the suitcases until he found most of the items tucked inside. Some, like her ring, he never found.

Fed up with this routine, he started hiding the suitcases so she'd have nothing to pack. My mother filled garbage bags instead. One day, he told me, she spent twelve hours straight packing bags and waiting by the door.

Her emotions finally started to infuse this routine; her mother's death was no longer a simple fact to be remembered or forgotten. Suddenly, hearing that her mother was dead—long dead—caused her terrible distress: "She's been dead all these years and we never buried her?" I'd assure her that we had, and I'd tell her where the cemetery was. "Why didn't anyone tell me about the funeral?" she'd ask, in a panic. I tried to calm her down—"Don't worry, you were there," I'd tell her, "we were all there"—as she worked first through her anxieties about being a less-than-dutiful daughter.

Grief came next, the entirely understandable grief of finding out that your mother has died: racking sobs, the kind I overheard from the basement when I was thirteen and my mother got the phone call from the nursing home on Christmas, two weeks after my bar mitzvah, telling her that her mother had just died. Only now it was every day, sometimes multiple times a day, that she learned this horrible news. "It's like you're telling her for the first time, every time," my sister, who had the same conversations with our mother, told me.

It's not unusual for people with Alzheimer's to forget about the deaths of loved ones, so there's plenty of advice on the subject online. The conventional wisdom suggests being candid—but also staying mindful of the fact that for the person with Alzheimer's, this information seems new, and their grief may be overwhelming, again and again. We had tried being candid. But after a while, we couldn't keep telling her the truth. It no longer resolved her questions; now it exacerbated her despair. And it was more important to avoid upsetting her, we agreed, than to make sure she knew the details of her mother's death.

But going along with her delusions wasn't productive, either. If we concurred that her mother was on her way, then my mother would sit by the front window, bags packed, coat zipped up, waiting and waiting for her mother to arrive. My father finally figured out a solution: "If your mother shows up, I'll come and find you," he'd say, and that would eventually persuade her to leave her post for a while, until her mind drifted to other things.

My mother's desire to go home wasn't necessarily rooted in any sense of great nostalgia for her family's brownstone in Jersey City. She had some wonderful stories from her childhood, but her early years weren't exactly idyllic.

Part of her desire to go home, we realized, was about where she wanted to get away from, more than where she wanted to go: She no longer recognized her own home, where she had lived for two-thirds of her life—not the kitchen she had renovated, not the tchotchkes that she'd accumulated, not the bedrooms where she'd raised three children. The Yom Kippur phone call had been the first time this was apparent to me, but it was not the last. Her home—which had, for much of my own life, been my home, too—had become simply a house.

I'd talk to her on the phone, and she'd say, "I don't know where I am."

"You're in your house," I'd say.

"This isn't my house," she'd say.

"Turn around," I'd say, knowing she was in the kitchen. "Are there pictures of your family on the refrigerator?"

There were, and she still recognized some of the people in them.

"That's because it's your house."

My parents bought their house when I was an infant; with three kids, the family had outgrown its small apartment. My father has never had any patience for shopping—a trait I inherited from him—so he told my mother they could look at exactly three houses, and if they didn't like any of them, they'd stay in the apartment for another year. They considered a home in Potomac, then a tony suburb of horse farms and hilly lawns west of Washington. "I'm not a country squire," my father protested, so they ended up in Silver Spring, a middle-class area north of the city, where a more racially diverse collection of government employees and other mostly white-collar professionals lived in subdivisions of new cookie-cutter colonials with backyards big enough for swing sets, and Chevys and Ford station wagons parked in the carports.

But this house was now unrecognizable to my mother, and before long, my efforts at explaining this to her stopped working.

She greeted me at the door in tears late one night on a visit to Maryland. "There are strangers in the house," she whispered, pointing upstairs. I knew my aunt Marilyn was visiting. I asked her to take me upstairs and show me the strangers. She led me to the doorway of my sister's old bedroom, where my aunt was already asleep.

"Who's in there?" she asked.

"Your sister, Marilyn."

She took me into her own bedroom. "And whose room is this?"

"This is your room," I said. "Look, here are pictures of you and Dad on the dresser. And here are your clothes in the drawers."

But the world had progressed beyond recognition for her. She didn't see herself in the photos—not the framed black-and-white wedding portrait from 1962, nor the more recent color prints that sat in Lucite frames atop her hutch next to the small wooden box of Killer's ashes with his baby blue dog collar on top. She didn't recognize my father in the photos, either, even though she had just seen him seconds before. The plush carpet she'd chosen years before, the bedclothes she'd color-coordinated with the comforter when she redecorated the bedroom, the leather rocking chair she'd bought on our trip to Costa Rica—nothing registered as her own. Even her clothes were foreign to her, so hearing that the blouses hanging in the walk-in closet and the shoes on the shelves were hers didn't soothe her; it terrified her even more. Nothing made sense, and the more I tried explaining things, the more surreal it became.

She collapsed in my arms—something she had never done—and held on to my shoulders as she heaved in tears.

"But how can it be?" she asked, as I tried to keep her upright. "How can it be?"

24: THE DOWNWARD SPIRAL

My mother ducked into my bathroom before bedtime and came out with three toothbrushes in her hand—two from her toiletry kit and one from the sink. "Which of these is yours?" she asked.

Mark and I live separately in the city, in shoebox studio apartments—we are both writers who need our own space to work—so there's only one toothbrush on my sink: mine. I don't know what color it is; whatever the dentist gives me after my semi-annual appointment, that's what I have. It's never been important to pay attention, since it's normally the only one in the apartment.

"Now that they're all in your hand," I said, "I have no idea."

She understood the quandary, and we all had a laugh. It was nothing to get upset about. We threw out the toothbrushes and bought three new ones at the CVS on the corner.

My parents were spending the night in New York because the next morning Mark and I were taking them on a weekend trip to Montreal, to celebrate their seventy-fifth birthdays—his just past, and hers several months in the future. My father still wanted to travel, and even though it's not far away, Montreal feels like a big trip: passports, currency exchange, a new language. We thought my mother might be able to handle a very quick trip—a one-hour flight, no time change. We planned it to be as leisurely as possible: Over Labor Day weekend in 2014, they'd come to New York for a night and we'd have dinner and see a show. We'd fly to Montreal the next day for two nights, and on the way back, they'd stay one more night in New York before heading back to Maryland. No rushed connections, no day entirely eaten up by traveling.

And Montreal was a place with some meaning for my parents. Before we took our first trip together to Paris in 1999, they'd gone to Montreal on their own in the summer of 1997. That was a trip that my brother, sister, and I got them as a present for their thirty-fifth wedding anniversary. We'd put them up at a hotel downtown, next to the summer's annual outdoor jazz festival. They had enjoyed that trip, but hadn't been back since. In 2014, when I proposed returning—this time, together—they jumped at the idea.

There had been troubling signs at the beginning of the Labor Day trip. My parents arrived at my apartment with four suitcases, which seemed like an awful lot for a weekend. My mother had packed; she had always been the one to pack, and my father didn't want to take away the few things she still considered her own domain. Trouble was, she didn't pack his pajamas, or socks, or undershirts, or bathing suit. These things were easy enough to borrow from me or replace—but what was in those bags? Sweaters, a closet full of them, all my father's, and none necessary for a late summer weekend.

The next morning was more troubling, as she tried to squeeze into a new pair of pants from Chico's that my father had bought for the trip. She was having trouble pulling them up over her hips, and she started to cry. "I'm just a terrible person," she said to herself. "I'm a terrible person." This, I knew was the inner voice that her mother Ethel had cultivated through decades of persistent criticism about her weight—and the deep personal shortcoming that being overweight represented. She couldn't remember if her mother was alive or dead, but she remembered this lesson that she'd learned in Jersey City many years before.

Once we got to Montreal, however, the trip went more smoothly. We took a duck boat tour along the Saint Lawrence River—something I'd never done on a dozen previous trips to Montreal. We strolled around the cobblestone streets of the Old City, stopping in the historic Notre-Dame-de-Bon-Secours Chapel; Mark and I have always loved the views over the port from its tower, the ornamental boats that hang over the pews (the church was a haven for sailors in the nineteenth century), and the kitschy, hologram- and diorama-filled museum in the basement in tribute to the founder of the church, St. Marguerite Bourgeoys. My father bought a new swimsuit so he could enjoy the pool in our hotel; he was an avid swimmer but hadn't been able to go to his local pool for a couple of years, since he'd been taking care of my mother at home.

I showed my parents Square St. Louis, my favorite spot in the city, a small park surrounded by brightly colored Victorian rowhouses, where we sat by the fountain and watched locals walk their dogs. And while we didn't visit any zoos—the dogs were as close as we got to seeing animals in the wild—we did get to the requisite "Jews" part of any trip with my parents. We took a cab up to the Plateau neighborhood, where we bought the city's legendary Fairmount bagels and ate them —still warm from the oven, with a schmear of cream cheese—on a park bench while we discussed the relative merits of Montreal and New York bagels.

We even had dinner with my old friend Laurent—the Montreal native who had helped show my parents around Paris when we celebrated their sixtieth birthdays back in 1999. He had been there on the first big trip I took with my parents, and now he was there for what seemed like it might be the last.

We went to Au Petit Extra, a restaurant that's been my favorite since my first trip to Montreal more than twenty years earlier. For Laurent, a local, the place is a bit of an old chestnut by this point, a traditional French bistro with a chalkboard menu, white paper tablecloths, and waiters wearing white aprons. But for Mark and me, it's a must on any Montreal trip—and for my parents, it was a novel delight, from the crusty baguettes on the table to the crème brulée they shared for dessert.

Laurent had enjoyed meeting my mother in Paris, and I was worried that their second meeting might be less successful—that she wouldn't remember him, or that he'd have trouble following her sometimes confusing sentences. I was relieved that none of that happened: Whether she was having a particularly good night, or was merely faking it well, she was as warm and charming over dinner in Montreal as she had been with him over dinner at the restaurant Aux Trois Petits Cochons in Paris years before, when Laurent had convinced her to try her first kir royale as an aperitif and later, when the drink loosened my mother's tongue, the two of them compared notes on which waiters were the cutest.

I was happy that the trip had been a success, after its rocky start in New York. For a moment, I grew hopeful that we might still have a few trips together: Even if big adventures were off the table, because they were simply too much for my mother to handle, quick weekends away could still be in the cards. I made a list of places that were close enough to do in a long weekend but that could still feel like big trips: Quebec City, Puerto Rico, even a return to Costa Rica to see the animals.

Our trip back to New York was uneventful. A quick meal at a diner in Greenwich Village, and then the bus ride back to Maryland the next morning.

When they got home, my mother called—I assumed—to let me know they'd arrived safely.

"So what did you do this weekend?" she asked.

I wasn't sure how to answer.

"I was with you this weekend," I said, hoping it'd jog her memory.

"You were?"

"We went to Montreal."

"You did?"

"No, we did," I said, now frustrated at her forgetfulness. "You were with me. You just left my apartment a few hours ago."

There was no "of course" moment for her—only one for me: Of course, she didn't remember; people with Alzheimer's forget recent events and holidays and trips, instantly and completely. Nothing came back to her. Not the meals, not the boat tour, not the hotel pool. Not even the bus she had ridden less than an hour earlier. It was as if the entire trip had never happened.

For the first several years of my mother's illness, her decline seemed like a straight line on a graph, her memory steadily but gradually fading, her self-awareness gently ebbing, her abilities eroding perceptibly but rarely in a sudden way. Even the occasional new developments—getting lost in the car, lashing out after Passover—stood out as one-time events, rather than full-fledged trends.

It was easy for my father—and for me—to take much of this in stride. The downward slope was mostly gentle, if persistent. And whenever she had a truly exceptional episode, my father would say, "She had a really bad morning...but by the afternoon, she was back to normal," or "Yesterday was bad, but today she turned the corner." I'm not sure if he believed his own words; I often didn't. But for the first few years after my mother's diagnosis, I'd still found comfort in the notion that her disease would progress in a measured, predictable way.

Over the course of 2014, that situation had started to shift. Once she'd started asking about her mother, she would never stop. Soon after she began packing suitcases, it became a daily occurrence. Then came the imaginary dinner guests, people who had allegedly called or stopped by to say they were coming for dinner. My father would come home from work to find the dining room table set for eight and heaps of extra food on the stove. At first the guests were specific people she claimed to have spoken with that afternoon, and later it became unnamed people whom she couldn't identify. She'd refuse to let my father sit down until the guests arrived—and she often included enough plausible details that my father wasn't certain if she was making things up until after the guests' purported arrival time had passed.

"Things started making no sense at all," my sister later recalled. "There was repeating before, there was forgetting, but there wasn't this very obvious detachment from reality."

Even as her behavior had grown stranger and she'd shifted from forgetting things that actually happened to inventing things that hadn't happened and people who didn't exist—another common development as Alzheimer's progresses—we still had a general sense that my mother was my mother. Her humor, thankfully, remained. She could still have a brief chat on the phone, albeit in a fairly superficial way. She still knew who I was. She couldn't hold on to the past, the present was baffling, and the future was coming unmoored from reality. But she could still have a conversation, enjoy a meal, or appreciate a joke. There was still, at her core, the most basic essence of what made her Susan.

For me, that trip to Montreal—for all of its difficult moments— would prove to be the last time my mother seemed like herself. The next time I saw her, she wasn't the same person at all.

When I went to Maryland on Christmas in 2014, something was definitely wrong with my mother.

The dining room table was set for one of her imaginary dinner parties. But it wasn't just the extra place settings that were off.

Next to each plate was a fork, and also several sugar packets. Instead of a vase, in the middle of the table there was a tiny replica of the Liberty Bell, a souvenir I'd bought as a child—not in Philadelphia, strangely, but on the Freedom Trail in Boston—that had long sat on the desk in my bedroom. When I went to check on the chicken she was planning to serve, I found that she had put a sauce over raw chicken parts, but never bothered to cook them. I opened the refrigerator to see what else might be ready to serve, and I found expired cottage cheese, old cartons of dozens upon dozens of eggs, and rotten meat. My mother, who was always overly cautious about expiration dates—"better not to risk it," she'd say, a mantra I inherited from her—would never have kept such things in her fridge when she was in her right mind.

The next day she asked me all sorts of questions about when I was going to finish high school. I told her I finished high school a long time ago and I was living in New York. She asked when I'd be starting college. I wasn't exactly sure if she recognized me as her son but was flashing back to my own senior year of high school, the last time I lived with her for any length of time, or if she was confusing me with her youngest grandson Ethan—my brother's son—who was indeed in his final year of high school on Long Island.

Then, when it was time to leave for a movie, she asked me, "What are we going to do with the baby?"

"What baby?" I asked.

"Our baby," she clarified. And now I was pretty sure she had realized I wasn't a high school student, but a middle-aged man—but she now thought I was my father.

"I'm your baby," I said, stroking my gray beard, "and I'm driving you to the movies."

She seemed to cycle around for the rest of my visit, sometimes knowing I was her son, other times thinking I was her grandson or her husband—sometimes a teenager, sometimes a man in my forties. There was no fixed answer for her, and she could switch back and forth in the course of a single sentence. I checked Alzheimer's resources online and found, again, that this was a common occurrence in the "moderate" stages of the disease. But it was new to me.

My friend Will—one of my closest friends from Springbrook High School, whose mother still lived near my parents—came over for brunch while he was visiting from Chicago. He said he wanted to thank my parents for being so supportive of him when we were younger; many of my friends had challenging relationships with their parents when we were teenagers, and they were all envious that my parents were less uptight, more encouraging, and generally easier to be around. Will understood the seriousness of my mother's situation and wanted to see her before it was too late. I had talked to my mother about the visit in advance to make sure she understood who he was, and she seemed to recall a few details I mentioned about him from our high school days: the day our dog Killer bit him, or the time his crappy 1972 Pinto broke down and my father had to go pick him up, or how he was such a klutz that our friend Matt's father had put up Lucite "Will protectors" around his expensive stereo equipment.

But once Will arrived, a forty-something bald man with a bushy beard and a big gut, she couldn't connect any dots to the gangly blond teenager he had once been. She was polite to him, but it didn't register consistently that this was the same person we'd been discussing an hour earlier: Will, one of my old friends she'd always adored, who'd spent countless hours in her house. While she acted like she was following the conversation, she was clearly confused.

Will and I were talking about concerts we had seen, and I mentioned seeing Madonna on a recent tour.

My mother chimed in: "Did you see Madonna at Springbrook?"

To Will, it had seemed like my mother understood the conversation up to that point; she was laughing at the right places, making eye contact, smiling, nodding along. But now, Will looked intently at my mother, and then back to me to see how I'd respond to the notion of a pop superstar appearing at our suburban high school.

"No, Mom," I said calmly; I was trying to take her odd question in stride. "It was Madison Square Garden."

Will texted me that evening: "You guys are really rolling with the punches with your mom," he wrote, noting that the bit about Madonna was "an exchange for the ages."

What he didn't appreciate was that I was focusing on her remark in a different way: So what if she had ridiculous ideas about Madonna? The fact that she remembered where I went to high school, and remembered, even for a minute, that Will was one of my high school friends, was the important part to me.

Later, after we went to bed, my mother walked into my bedroom in the middle of the night and stood there in the dark, looking around. Then I heard her go down the hallway and open the doors to my brother and sister's old rooms, now empty.

The suitcases she continued to pack were lined up by the front door. Rather than confronting my mother about them or immediately getting rid of them, my father had resigned himself to this routine by this point, leaving them there for a few days without comment before finally unpacking the bags, and starting the whole process over again. While I was visiting, she took a few things out of my own suitcase and packed them for herself, until her bags were too heavy to lift.

That visit shook me up.

The only fortunate part, so to speak, is that my brother came to visit later that week, and my aunt Marilyn right after that. And we all witnessed the dramatic changes that my father couldn't fully appreciate because he saw her every hour, every day. For my brother, my aunt, and me, the decline over the previous few months was more alarming than anything we'd witnessed in the previous several years. All three of us had talks with my father after that week, and the fact that we'd all observed the same things finally allowed my father to step back from his immediate concern—trying to get through each day—and focus on the bigger picture.

Things were getting dramatically worse, and quickly, we realized. Now that my brother, my aunt, and I had gone home, there was only one person who could be in charge of addressing my mother's downward spiral: my father.

25: 'HI. I'M SUSAN.'

My parents raised a family in a manner that would now be dubbed "traditional." My father had his career. Until my final semester of high school, when she went to work for the county's Division of Elder Affairs, my mother was a homemaker—what was then called a "housewife," in charge of cooking, cleaning, organizing carpools, taking the kids to doctors' appointments and Hebrew school, and generally keeping us out of trouble.

Growing up, I don't recall ever seeing my father wash a dish, do a load of laundry, push a vacuum, or cook anything more complicated than a hot dog or a hard-boiled egg. It's not that he considered those things beneath him. It's simply that the role of homemaker had already been filled. Those things were my mother's job.

Now, unexpectedly, after decades where this division of labor seemed to serve them well, he knew things had changed.

So, in his seventies, when most people think it's too late to change, my father changed. With help from his kids, he learned how to cook a chicken, make a bed, wash clothes, do the dishes, and even host a brunch. He kept track of my mother's doctor's appointments, and checked that she took her pills on schedule. He made sure they saw friends and relatives, setting up dinners and movies and social outings—taking over "the calendar," which had always been my mother's domain.

Logistically, these changes—cooking, cleaning, planning—

weren't a major challenge for him; "I was reasonably confident that I could plug those holes," he told me. Wrangling those chores away from my mother, on the other hand, was sometimes more difficult. "She fought like a steer to maintain her role as sole cook in her kitchen," he said. "She was far more flexible and willing to cooperate in other areas."

Even once he'd persuaded her to let him do more housework, he said, psychologically the shift in duties around the house made him feel "piss poor."

"It's a sign that you've moved on to another phase of your life, and it's not going to be reversed," he told me. "The finality of it is what gets you. The realization that there's no turning back."

The new division of labor in the house was obvious; I'd notice the changes on my visits home. But the more important changes were ones I didn't see—changes that were affecting the very nature of my parents' marriage.

"The major losses were her counsel and support, her sense of humor, the warmth of another body in the bed, and enforced abstinence," my father later wrote to me in an email. "For the tangible losses, I can compensate, or at least try to do so with fair success. As for the intangible losses, there is no way to compensate."

In addition to taking over the household chores, he became her primary caregiver, handling as much as he could, and finding other people to do the things he could not.

My father was still working at the law office downtown, so he couldn't always be around when my mother's driver dropped her off at home in the afternoon after her day group at Kensington Club. But at the beginning of 2015, he realized she couldn't be left alone in the house anymore, waiting a few hours until he got home from the office, so he hired a home health aide.

Genete had worked at Kensington Club and already had a rapport with my mother. An Eritrean immigrant with a soft accent and a long supply of patience, Genete would paint my mother's fingernails, or read to her, or take her for a walk. But her main job was to keep my mother out of the kitchen. Left alone, he now understood, my mother might start a fire in the kitchen, or eat something she wasn't supposed to eat. Her problems with food had grown vastly more problematic, and even dangerous—to herself and my father: She started eating cat food—while putting her own pills in the cat's food dish. She served pods of dish detergent with dinner. She put plastic in the oven, melting it over the metal racks, and tried to cook a steak without any pan at all.

As often happens among people with Alzheimer's as their disease progresses, my mother's speech also took a dramatic turn around this time. She was still communicative, but oftentimes her sentences turned into "word salad," an incomprehensible collection of words arranged in no particular order. Her utterances still sounded like sentences; they had her cadence and tone, and they had the rhythm of normal speech. But they didn't mean anything.

And when she could speak in coherent sentences, they were more agitated and confused than before. She'd call me in New York to ask where she was and whose house she was in. She'd call my sister in Phoenix to tell her to have Dad come pick her up—while he was sitting on the couch next to her.

When it was time for her annual Mini-Mental State Examination at the neurologist's office, which measured her mental decline, we weren't sure what to expect. The previous year her decline hadn't made much of a dent in her score. This year, however, the doctor stopped the test midway and came out to tell my father that there was no need to continue; her deterioration was tremendous and undeniable.

This news confirmed what my father had witnessed—that her decline really had gotten much worse recently, and he wasn't imagining it. So on that level, he felt validated. But at the same time, the results were also something of a reality check: From this point forward, this disease wasn't going to be easy, or gentle, or gradual. It was going to get bad, and then worse, and then unbearable—and soon.

I returned to Maryland with Mark in March. My mother greeted us at the door and seemed to recognize us, even if she couldn't remember our names. "My son," she said, giving me a hug. Then she turned to Mark and gave him a hug. "And you're—you're—like my son," she said. It was clear she was confused; she recognized Mark, whom she'd known for more than twenty-five years, but couldn't recall exactly who he was.

"He's your son-in-law," I said.

"That's one way to think of it," said my father.

"No, that's literally who he is," I said.

By the next morning, she didn't recognize either of us, and had no interest in interacting. When I tried to talk to her while I ate breakfast, I was met with silence; she was busy waiting by the window for her mother to take her home. When she got home from Kensington Club that afternoon, she still didn't know who we were. We all went out to dinner at a Greek restaurant up the road. We took two cars, and when my mother saw me in the parking lot, her mouth dropped open with excitement and she ran over to give me a big hug. I was the same person she hadn't recognized less than five minutes earlier, but in the parking lot, for some unknown reason, the correct neuron fired.

The day after that, I got word that my childhood friend Will, who had come to visit my parents' house over Christmas, was critically ill with cirrhosis and had days to live. Before I left my parents' house in Maryland and flew to Chicago to see him, I tried to explain to my mother what was happening. I reminded her who Will was again—the "Will-protectors," the broken-down Pinto, the time Killer bit him—but this time those stories didn't seem to register, even temporarily. I tried explaining where I was going: to Chicago. "Remember when you and Dad used to live there?" I asked. "Remember your chip-and-dip bowl that got invited to a party that you weren't invited to?" She laughed, but I sensed that it was because I'd said something funny—a story that had taken place before I was even born but that I'd presented as if I remembered it first-hand—rather than something familiar, a story that was actually her own.

The next day, while I sat alone in a café in Chicago's Boystown, waiting for a ride to meet my oldest friend Billy at Will's hospice, my mother called me in tears on my cell phone: "I don't know where I am!" At one time, her calls were mostly confused. By now, they were distressed. She was trapped in a strange house with a man she didn't recognize, and she was terrified. I tried to be soothing and clear—*Yes, you do know where you are; you're in your own house*—without being patronizing, but I'm sure the waiter and the people at the next table heard my tone and thought I was talking to a very dim child. In reality, I was just trying not to cry in public.

This was the first time I remember thinking—attempting to calm my crying mother while I waited to say goodbye to my best friend, who would die the following morning—that this was all too much to handle emotionally. This, I realized, is how my father must have felt for years, and probably every minute of every day for the past several months as she got worse. I couldn't begin to imagine how my mother felt, in a constant state of confusion where even the rare moments of clarity and certainty vanished immediately without a trace.

In the spring of 2015, the director of Kensington Club emailed my father to say that my mother was withdrawing from social interaction and having trouble participating in activities, and couldn't seem to comprehend what was happening anymore. "She is no longer initiating conversation with her peers, she is responding to their conversation to a lesser degree, she is not comprehending the discussion topics that once interested her, and requiring more assistance with the location of things in the club (bathroom, etc.)," she wrote. "These are triggers that she is ready to move from a social day program to a medical day program."

The director suggested a move to a place called the Misler Center, which is overseen by the Jewish Council for the Aging and oriented toward people with more severe dementia. And she also intimated that more changes would be coming as my mother's condition deteriorated: "I would really consider using this time while Susan is at Misler to start exploring all your options," she wrote to my father, giving him the name of a social worker he could contact. "You and your family can start to explore the 'next step' for Susan."

This was not an unusual pattern: Clients started at Kensington Club, and then switched to the Misler Center as their condition worsened, before ultimately moving into a full-time care facility. My parents' friend Helen had moved her husband Howie to Misler a couple of years earlier—before he later moved into a residential home and died at the end of 2013.

After Passover in 2015, my father decided to switch my mother to the Misler Center. There wouldn't be field trips and museum visits with this group. And she'd be there five days a week, with her home aide Genete watching her after the group, and one morning on weekends.

As my father needed more help, he hired Genete to work even more hours. Beyond keeping her company and making sure she stayed out of the kitchen, Genete was now helping with things that were becoming tougher for my mother—everything from shower-ing to getting dressed.

But even with all these people watching her, it was still difficult to keep my mother safe. She walked out the door at the Misler Center; one of the staffers found her in front of the building. Then, in the summer, she walked out the door at home, and this time she kept going. She'd put on her winter coat, even though it was ninety degrees outside—inability to choose clothing appropriate to the weather is common for people with "moderate" Alzheimer's—and walked down their hilly street, turning the corner to the next street, which went up a steep incline. She started walking faster and faster until she collapsed on the street, face-first—much as she'd done on the marble floor of our vacation apartment in Tel Aviv a few years earlier. My father jumped in the car and drove around the development until he found her. Strangers had already come out to help her and, since she didn't know who she was or where she lived—another hallmark of the "moderate" phase—they'd called an ambulance.

She was now officially a danger to herself. (In the words of one Alzheimer's resource website I read, in this stage, the disease was now preventing her from leading a "catastrophe-free, independent" life.) My father changed the locks, removing locks from interior doors and putting extra locks on exterior doors—locks that re-quired keys. He could no longer leave her unattended at all. He couldn't play tennis on weekends, or go shopping for groceries, or attend synagogue without her. He couldn't even leave her alone downstairs while he ducked upstairs to do work.

There were still things my father could do to entertain my moth-er—or at least keep her occupied. They'd go to the movies frequent-ly; she had lost the ability to retain what she was watching long ago, and much later lost the ability to comprehend what was hap-pening while it was happening, but at least she could sit still in one place, quietly, while my father got a breather. Finally this, too, unraveled. She couldn't make it through a movie—and if she couldn't, neither could he.

Dining out was another respite, something they could do togeth-er to break up their routine. By 2015 this was already getting more complicated: Eating at their favorite Italian restaurant near their house, I watched my mother sprinkle Splenda on her bread, and then, after fumbling with the menu (she'd open it, choose a dish at random, close it, forget what she'd picked, open it again, pick something else at random, close it, and start over again), she ultimately ordered lasagna—entirely non-kosher lasagna, with pork and beef and cheese, something she would never have even thought of eating before, and a dish that would have physically nauseated her with its meat-and-cheese combination. (I had seen her eat *treyf*—non-kosher food—exactly twice as an adult: Both times it was shellfish, which is technically just as taboo as pork but carries none of the cheese-on-meat "ick" factor for observant Jews, and both those times we were in foreign countries, at restaurants where our non-Jewish hosts had ordered for the table and it would have seemed impertinent to object and complicated to explain.)

Shopping was overwhelming for her. Going for a walk exhausted her. Television baffled her. She would still flip through the *Washington Post*, but eventually this was just a reflexive physical exercise: She couldn't understand the stories anymore.

When my parents came to the Catskills for the Fourth of July in 2015, Mark and I once again invited "the F's," their old friends from New Jersey, whom they'd known for more than fifty years.

At first, Phil and Bibi and Carole and Arnie were surprised by just how much worse my mother seemed. It had only been several months since they'd seen her. They had grown accustomed to her gradual decline, but this time it seemed much more notable. When they walked in the door, she had trouble formulating complete sentences to greet them.

By the next day, however, it seemed more like old times. The three couples sat on our front porch in rocking chairs, laughing and reminiscing. I looked out the window, and it appeared as though my mother was part of the conversation, or at least following along.

Smiling broadly, Carole and Bibi came inside to tell me how well my mother seemed to be doing. While they had initially been taken aback when they arrived the previous day, now they were reevaluating the situation: My mother was not back to her old self, of course, but back to where she had been the last time they'd seen her.

As we stood in the living room, talking about how well she was doing, my mother came inside. She looked at Carole and Bibi—

two women she'd known for decades, with whom she'd been having a conversation minutes earlier—and extended her hand to them. "Hi," she said with a blank smile. "I'm Susan."

The following week, my third novel came out. I had told my mother about it many times, but she couldn't remember. The book release party was in Provincetown, Massachusetts, where the book is set, and then I had my big New York reading the next week.

When it was time for my reading in Washington, my mother wasn't up to going; my father would need to stay home with her. This was fine with me, since I wasn't sure I wanted them in the audience while I read a fairly X-rated excerpt at a gay literary event.

My mother hadn't come to my reading in Washington for my first novel, which was also sexually explicit, when it came out nearly a decade earlier. She'd never read that first novel—upon the advice of my father, who had read it; but she had taken a peek at the acknowledgments, where I thanked my parents "for offering more than anyone could reasonably expect from his mother and father." That alone made her proud. On Mother's Day in 2006—years before my mother's decline began—my parents came to our house in the Catskills for the first time, and that Sunday, I did a non-explicit reading at the bookstore in our little town. It was the only reading for that book that she attended, and Mark captured it on video. At the start, I introduced my parents, and my mother called out to the rest of the audience from her seat: "When you buy the book, read the acknowledgments on the last page!"

She wouldn't make it to any readings for this third novel in 2015. But before my event took place in the city, we gathered some of my parents' friends at their house in Silver Spring, to hear me read a brief, PG-rated section from the new book. I also told their friends— some for the first time, others for the third or fourth time—about my great-grandmother's murder in Winnipeg.

Ever since I had wrapped up my research two years earlier, it had become one of my favorite stories to share. I told relatives, co-workers, and friends what I'd discovered—the bogus tale my mother had passed down, and the real story I'd dug up in old newspapers. At parties, or barbecues, or any social situation where I met new people, it was a yarn that was guaranteed to entertain; I'd learned from my mother how to tell stories for maximum effect, with the right tone and facial expressions and hand gestures. A raised eyebrow here, a shrug there, every phrase parsed out with proper emphasis to telegraph my own doubts about what I was saying: "on the *front porch*...in *Winnipeg*...in *winter*."

My mother used to tell the story herself. It was a well-rehearsed part of her repertoire, and it always began the same way: "When I was growing up in Jersey City, I found a photograph in my parents' drawer."

She could no longer tell that story herself. Her storytelling days were over.

But I could tell it in her place; even if I couldn't precisely replicate my mother's delivery or perfect cadence, I could preserve the memory of the story itself. My version was longer, because it included not only what she was told as a child, but what I had since discovered about what really happened. But my story, now a fixture in my own repertoire, began the same way: "When my mother was growing up in Jersey City, she found a photograph in her parents' drawer."

Years before, my mother would have told me, "That's what your next book should be about." But not this time. She was done making suggestions.

That fall, my father invited my brother's youngest son Ethan—named in memory of my mother's mother Ethel, his great-grandmother—to move in, while he started community college nearby. Having Ethan around to help meant that my father could leave the house, go shopping, or even go swimming at the local pool, without worrying about leaving my mother alone on the days when her aide Genete was not around. Even more than that, he could get some alone time without leaving the house at all: If my father needed to work or watch a basketball game or just have a moment of peace and quiet, he could go upstairs while my mother was downstairs in the living room, or he'd go downstairs to the kitchen while she was upstairs in the bedroom.

"Having Ethan there definitely gave Dad time and space to figure out what to do," my brother said. "It didn't change the outcome, but it did push it back."

My father had assembled a whole team of loving and supportive people helping to keep my mother safe: my nephew, Genete, the staff at the Misler Center, the driver who took her back and forth every day, good friends like Doris who'd come and take my mother out to lunch. But there was only so long that this complex arrangement could last. My nephew, in particular, was in Maryland for just one semester, and as my brother said, "When Ethan leaves, it's not going to be manageable."

This became evident almost immediately. In January, right after Ethan left, my sister went home to accompany my parents to a cousin's bat mitzvah. And while my father slept upstairs, with his hearing aids on the nightstand, my mother woke up early, placed the blouse she'd intended to wear to the bat mitzvah in a Tupperware, unlocked the front door, and stepped outside into twenty-degree weather without a proper coat, or hat, or gloves. She fetched the newspaper from the curb and then forgot what to do. She stood outside for a half hour, shivering and on the verge of tears, before she rang the doorbell and woke up my sister. The rest of the day got worse: She had trouble walking, needed my sister's help in the bathroom, and couldn't stay awake during the service; it's possible that she'd taken too many pills, or taken them at the wrong time, because sometimes after my father handed her what she needed to take, she'd forget that she'd taken anything and help herself to more. "It was like *Weekend at Bernie's*," Stacey told me. "She couldn't even keep herself up in the chair. Finally after a little while, I'm thinking I'm sitting here watching my mother die." They rushed her, almost catatonic, to the emergency room, where doctors couldn't find a specific problem and sent her home when she'd become more alert after a few hours.

On a visit to Maryland soon after that incident, I had a talk with my father about what the next step might be. In the end, the two main options seemed to be either moving Mom into a home, or moving both of them into a senior community where she might have a smoother segue from home care to a facility on the same campus. "If you had to choose between staying in the house without Mom, or staying with Mom but giving up this house," I asked him, "which would you choose?"

This was an easy one, he said: He wanted to stay with my mother. The house was just a house.

We started researching places where they might move together, and fortunately, there was an excellent option barely a mile up the road. It was a sprawling complex of apartment buildings in a senior community that had restaurants, entertainment, and convenient transportation options, as well as home aides and a separate memory care facility. It seemed like the kind of place where Mom could transition easily as needed, and a place where my father wouldn't have to change his routine: He could still go to his usual tennis courts, the same supermarket, his longtime barber, and his synagogue. The price was within reach. And he had a couple of glowing references from people who lived there.

My father went to take a look, and thought it seemed like a lovely place to live. But now that he'd seen the actual apartment and tried to visualize their life there, he had changed his mind—not just about this particular complex, but about his broader statement that he wanted to stay with my mother no matter where they lived. Not normally a man to make hasty decisions or issue intemperate pronouncements, this time my father made up his mind quickly and unambiguously.

"If I have to live in an apartment with your mother," he told me on the phone, "I'm going to kill her."

It was an unusually strident way for my father to talk; even when he was having a difficult day with her, he typically tried to keep an upbeat long view. But after visiting the senior complex he understood that such a move was not merely undesirable, but impossible. They lived in a three-story, four-bedroom house. As long as someone else was there to watch her, he could go to a different room or different floor, and close a door. But in a small apartment, he realized, there was no escaping from my mother—and her repetitive questions, her mood swings, her nonsensical chatter. He needed to be able to get away from her sometimes, even if only for a few minutes, and that wouldn't be an option in a one-bedroom apartment.

Now, my father decided, when the time came, we'd need to find a place for her to move, while he stayed in the house alone.

26: MOVING OUT

In 2016, for the first time, my mother didn't make it through the Passover Seder.

She started off well enough, sitting between her sister Marilyn and her best friend, Doris. She didn't talk much, but she hummed along with the songs, chuckled at the corny jokes we make every year, and sipped the Manischewitz wine. "She was, for the most part, an observer," Doris said later, reflecting on that evening, "but with a smile on her face." Before we finished the first half—which usually runs under an hour at our house, leading up to the big "festive meal" that splits the Seder in two—she ran out of gas. She got flush, perhaps overheated from the oven and the stove heating up the meal near her table, or over-chilled from the door to the deck open behind her seat. Her smile faded, her eyes got glassy, and she seemed suddenly disoriented and panicked. Doris and Marilyn got her away from the table, but there was no way she could rejoin us—she was too confused and irritable. My father took her upstairs and put her to bed.

Three years earlier, when she'd had a meltdown over something she believed a guest had said at the Seder, we had wondered how many Passovers my mother had left. The year after that had gone smoothly, though, without any outbursts or unusual emotional problems. The one after that was difficult, since everyone knew my mother's situation was deteriorating quickly: We celebrated her seventy-fifth birthday and tried to stay upbeat, but we suspected that it might be her last Seder, and out of my mother's earshot and away from the children at the table, some of us cried over this real-ization. We had rallied one more time in 2016, assuring ourselves that she could make it through one more gathering.

We were wrong. After she went upstairs to sleep, we ate the fes-tive meal—matzo ball soup and brisket and a whole turkey (just one, no spare "just in case") prepared by the butcher, cakes ordered by mail—without her, opened the door for Elijah without her, sang *Chad Gadya* without her. Nobody cried this time.

While the family was gathered together, we went one afternoon to look (without my mother) at a few facilities near my parents' house—specifically memory care facilities for people with dementia—so that whenever the time might come when a move would be necessary, we'd have a place in mind. Fortunately, my father, my sister, my aunt Marilyn, and I all agreed which one was the best. It was a fif-teen-minute drive from the house, and it had a full slate of activities, an attractive physical facility, and a seemingly attentive staff.

We took business cards and agreed that when the time came, we'd discuss the next steps. My mother was already having trouble sitting through a meal or a movie, or speaking on the phone. We figured we might need to make a move relatively soon, maybe a few months down the road.

"How will we know when it's time?" I asked my father.

He had dealt with so many things he never thought he'd have to do. But he still had two red lines, things he knew he couldn't deal with at home. One was bathroom-related; he had handled a couple of incidents involving incontinence, but he couldn't go further than that—and the next stage of the disease, "moderately severe" Alz-heimer's, is typically marked by "toileting" issues.

My father's other red line was about her physical safety. "If I can't keep her safe at home," he said, "then we'll know it's time."

My mother was in better spirits for a couple of days after the Seder, having no recollection at all that she hadn't made it through the whole thing. But within the week, she would have a series of terrible days. Difficulty with bathroom habits. Fits of rage at my father and her home aide, which also fit the "moderately severe" phase of Alzheimer's. And one truly terrifying incident.

My mother had started rolling out of bed in the middle of the night. It wasn't that she slipped while turning over or fell while trying to stand up; she'd simply roll off the mattress onto the floor. She wouldn't try to break her fall, either. She'd face-plant on the carpet. So my father had started putting her to sleep in the middle of their queen-size bed, where she'd be less likely to roll over the edge, and he'd sleep down the hall in my sister's old bedroom. This routine had been altered for a few days while the house was full of guests for Passover, but once we all went home, my father went back to his separate bed.

One night, my mother woke up at two or three in the morning and started going from room to room, seeing who was there. She turned on his light and woke him. He walked her back to her bed and he went back to his.

But she didn't stay asleep for long. She went downstairs to the kitchen and decided, after months of avoiding cooking, that she'd make some eggs. Trouble was, the eggs she put on the burner weren't actually eggs, but pieces of white plastic, which soon started to melt, setting off the smoke alarm, while my father was asleep upstairs with his hearing aids on the nightstand.

Within one week of my discussion with my father, the red lines he'd laid out had been crossed. I was in frequent contact with my brother and sister about what was happening, and we all agreed: The time had come for her to move.

"He held out a lot longer than I ever thought he would as a caregiver," my brother told me. "But he can't put the Superman cape on anymore."

My father was more succinct in an email he sent me: "I'm beat."

He started the ball rolling with the memory care facility we'd visited. It would take almost two more months before the paperwork was ready and a room was available. Actually, it took exactly the length of the counting of the Omer, a solemn stretch of seven weeks on the Hebrew calendar beginning on Passover and ending on Shavuot, a holiday when Jews commemorate receiving the Torah at Mount Sinai. While they're counting the Omer, Jews are supposed to refrain from certain joyous activities—dancing, weddings, parties. None of us was in the mood.

As the Omer ended on this particular Shavuot, in June 2016, my mother moved out of the house she'd lived in since 1971.

I came home to help. The night before the move, I drove my father to the facility with a suitcase of Mom's clothes and a few family photos. We set up her closet, and put the framed pictures of the family around her room. Her last night at home was otherwise ordinary. She ate dinner, took her pills, and went to bed early.

The next morning, when my mother would normally have waited for the driver to take her to her day group at the Misler Center, she got in the car with the two of us instead. My father had a whole shpiel prepared to explain what was happening, with enough detail to calm any anxiety but not so much detail as to stress her out. Fortunately, she was in a docile mood and didn't seem to notice anything was amiss.

The staff met us at the front desk.

"Susan!" one woman announced cheerfully. "We've been waiting for you!" My mother had never seen this woman before, but she mirrored her warm enthusiasm and gave her a smile and a hug.

"You look so pretty today!" the woman said. "Can I take your picture?"

My mother smiled for the camera, unaware that this would be the identification photo for her records.

"Do you like coffee?" another woman asked. My mother nodded, perhaps because she understood the question, or perhaps she was simply nodding along to be agreeable. "Well, they're making some inside right now," said the woman, taking my mother by the elbow. She opened the door, and in they went without a look back or a goodbye. The door closed behind them, and the transition was over in about two minutes.

My father had been particularly anxious about the big move, for more than the usual reasons.

His mother, my grandma Rose, had Alzheimer's. We had watched her decline for years starting when I was in junior high, when she'd come to visit.

There were the early stages, when she'd written down the names of her three grandchildren to keep in her pocket, so she wouldn't forget who we were.

There were the middle stages, when she'd sit at the table across from my mother—her only daughter-in-law—complaining about "my rotten daughter-in-law." Then she'd tell my mother, whom she believed to be a stranger, "You look familiar—are you from Jersey?" My mother would nod her head. "That must be where I know you from," Rose would say, before asking a question most people would never think to ask a stranger: "Have you always had a weight problem?" (Her fixation on my mother's weight stretched back to the days when my parents were first dating. "I'd go to your father's house for dinner, and your grandma Rose would put the chicken on the table," my mother recounted to me many times. "And she'd say to me, 'Susan, let the men have the meat. You and I will have an egg.' I'd go home after dinner and rip the door off the refrigerator, I was so hungry. And my mother would ask me, 'Didn't they feed you over there?'")

Then there were the later stages, when Rose forgot whether panty hose went over or under pants, and walked around the house carrying a roll of toilet paper, completely befuddled about what it was or where it belonged. By the time I had my bar mitzvah—with my grandma Ethel enduring her final, confused weeks in a nearby nursing home—Grandma Rose was in bad shape.

Fortunately, she had a devoted caregiver in my grandpa Harry. This wasn't my father's father—Willie had died before I was born, and I was named in his memory. This was my grandmother's second husband, a gentle and loving man who had already lost his first wife; Harry and Rose got married when I was a toddler, and he was always Grandpa to me.

When the time came when Harry could no longer take care of Rose—a tiny woman who was once a huge presence in any room, a "Hadassah lady" known for her skill in cajoling friends and neighbors into donating money to charity, a dynamo with boundless energy and a perfect memory—he moved her into the Daughters of Israel nursing home in West Orange, New Jersey, near their house in Maplewood. And as they pulled up to the home, Grandma Rose, who hadn't seemed to recognize anyone or speak a coherent sentence for months, turned to Grandpa Harry and said: "I know what you're doing, you son of a bitch."

This moment burned into my father's memory, and explained why he had such trepidations about moving my mother. "It was like Dad was watching a bad movie for the second time," my brother Scott told me. "First it was Grandma Rose, and now Mom." So the two-minute handoff my father ultimately experienced with her move, without any farewell or acknowledgment at all, was a relief.

My mother's adjustment to the home was smooth. She seemed less distraught, ironically, over her new surroundings than she had been in her own home. And she had a whole staff to keep her occupied and engaged.

My father had been so wrapped up with her care for so long that he hadn't fully appreciated the degree to which she had declined. On his very first visit, the day after she moved in, he made a realization.

"I sat down with her on a bench so we could talk," he told me afterward. "She really couldn't carry on a conversation."

"She hasn't been able to have a conversation for months," I told him. But in his mind, he had created conversations where none had existed: She'd come home from her day program and her aide Genete would sit with her on the porch. "What did you have for lunch today?" my father would ask, and Genete would answer, "Tuna." My father would ask, "Was it good?" And my mother would make some kind of indistinct gesture or shrug, which he took as a yes. And between the aide's interjections and my mother's vague responses—including her silences, which he imbued with whatever meaning made sense as a response—a conversation appeared to have occurred. Now, in the home, one on one, it was suddenly clear to him that meaningful conversations would be unlikely.

Instead, the staff at the home recommended that he show up during a scheduled group activity. If my mother wanted to split off to spend time with my father, they could go for a walk or go to her room; otherwise, my father could join the activity alongside my mother, so they could have time together without the pressure of direct conversation.

This approach seemed to work, making his visits more pleasant for both of them, so I tried the same thing when I went to visit on my trips to Maryland. Some activities were clearly beyond my mother's abilities, leaving her withdrawn and quiet. Bingo, for example, was too complicated for her to understand and each round was too long for her to follow. The noise from the other residents didn't help. Once, I sat by her side during a game. There were three other women at her table. One sat in a wheelchair, largely oblivious to the proceedings, but babbling loudly at her young, male attendant.

Another was nearly catatonic, quiet and withdrawn. And the last, a talkative woman with a French accent who had better cognitive skills than the rest, aimed a steady stream of relatively coherent chatter at my mother, who responded with bewildered smiles and nods; this woman was quite intent on playing the game, but she'd forgotten how to do it. "Bingo!" she'd call every time a number was called, only to have the attendant show her that she did not, in fact, have bingo; a woman at a nearby table was exasperated with this routine, turning around and telling her to shut up every time she called out. For my mother, this was too much stimulation and too much noise, without any understanding of the game itself.

But other activities—singing, in particular—brought her to life; even when she couldn't get a coherent sentence out, she still re-membered the lyrics to old show tunes from *Oklahoma!* or *Carou-sel*, just as she had when we sang around the piano in our house in the Catskills, or at least enough of the melody to hum along with the discs the staff played on a karaoke machine. Musical memories often endure far longer than other memories in people with Alzhei-mer's; they're stored in a different part of the brain.

It seemed like we'd made the right choice that Passover, choos-ing a facility that had a good staff and a wide slate of activities. Because it was specifically a memory care facility, many of the residents didn't have apparent physical issues, so sometimes the home looked more like senior apartments than a nursing home. The home where my grandma Ethel had lived when I was in ju-nior high was much more medicalized: people being pushed down the hallways in wheelchairs and sleeping in hospital beds, with portable commodes and curtains separating roommates in double rooms. My mother's memory care unit, in contrast, was a far less daunting place to visit.

I hadn't anticipated, however, how dramatically my communica-tion with my mother would be reduced after the move. Even though she hadn't been able to have a real conversation of any length for many months, I had still spoken to her on the telephone regularly when she was living in the house; she'd pick up and get in a few sentences before handing the phone to my father or Genete, or I'd hear her in the background when I spoke to Dad. But after the move, she didn't have a telephone, and she was no longer around when I called my father at home. So I went from hearing her voice almost every day to only hearing it when I visited her in Maryland.

I began to miss her immediately. It wasn't that our actual conversations had been particularly profound or intimate for a long time, but I'd always been able to hear her voice. After years of feeling her gradually fade away, now I felt like I was suddenly losing entire pieces of her.

I started reading books about Alzheimer's, or by authors who'd witnessed their parents' decline. I had avoided such things for years; when the movie *Still Alice* came out in 2015, I told Mark I didn't want to go: "I don't need to go to the movies to see what Alzheimer's looks like," I said. "I already know exactly what it looks like." But now that my mother wasn't part of my daily life, I found comfort in other people's stories that reminded me of her. Weeks after my mother moved out of the house in 2016, I picked up cartoonist Roz Chast's graphic (and comic) memoir about her parents' deaths, *Can't We Talk About Something More Pleasant?* Her Jewish family's dynamics were familiar to me, as was her ability to turn difficult events into funny stories; Chast is a great storyteller, like my mother. Mark found me reading the book in bed, laughing out loud, and asked me to read him a funny section. As I launched into a section about Chast's mother's horrible and lengthy decline, though, I burst into tears, thinking of my own mother. "You don't have to keep going," Mark said. But I shook my head; I still wanted to share a good story. "Just wait," I said, wiping my nose, "this next part is hilarious."

The first time I visited my mother, I don't think she recognized me. She hadn't always recognized me—at least not specifically as her son—for the last several months she'd lived in my parents' house, either. But at least at the house, there had been some contextual clues: I might be just one of three people in the whole house, and someone who acted like I knew her. Or my father might refer to me by name, which sometimes seemed to trigger some recognition. Or the fact that I called her Mom. Once she moved into the home, however, she had dozens of people around her at all times, including residents and staff and other visitors, and I suppose I must have been lost in the commotion. Still, if I could catch her eye and open my arms with a cheerful "Hi, Ma," I could sometimes get a smile and open arms in return—much as the staff had done on the day she moved in.

A few months later, I came to visit with Mark. We were pointed toward the main activity room. But standing in the doorway, we didn't see her in the crowd of perhaps two dozen people. We both scanned the faces, and couldn't find Susan. I suggested walking down the hall to see if she was in her room, when Mark realized that we had looked right past my mother without even seeing her.

"How can that be?" I asked, scanning the room again. But sure enough, there she was. What kind of son doesn't recognize his own mother? I was ashamed. Maybe, I thought, I haven't visited her often enough.

Much of our confusion stemmed from the fact that she had stopped having her hair colored, so my mother—who'd dyed her hair a range of shades from blonde to red over the years—had pure white hair. It's not that I didn't know, intellectually, that my mother's hair had gone gray decades before; I was a man in my forties with salt-and-pepper hair and a gray beard, so I knew roughly when people in my family go gray. It's just that I had never seen my mother with gray hair, so it hadn't occurred to me that it was her.

But the main thing that prevented me from recognizing my mother, I realized, is that she didn't recognize me. When you're looking for a familiar face in a crowd—at a party, at an airport gate—you expect that familiar face to be looking back, making eye contact, saying hello. When my mother looked at me in the doorway, nothing registered on her face. When I looked at her, I didn't see the usual recognition on her face. So we had both quickly looked past each other, like total strangers.

Firsts are much easier to identify than lasts. The first time something happens, you're often conscious of that milestone—however large or small—in real-time; you know your first kiss is your first kiss even as it's happening, and the same goes for your first date, or first day at school, or first trip to a new destination. For years, my mother told stories about her own firsts—first job, first house, first child.

But lasts are often evident only in retrospect. The last time I spoke with my mother on the telephone, I had no way of knowing it was the last time; when was it, and what did we say? When was the last time she recognized me, or knew my name? Was there a specific date when that information vanished from her brain, never to return?

These are questions I can try to answer, however poorly, through recollection, or going through old emails, or talking to my father. I know the last trip we took together, the last Passover we spent together, the last time she came to the Catskills.

But for my mother, who had lost the ability to recollect her own life, life experiences simply ended without notice, even in hindsight. What was the last meal she cooked, the last movie she saw, the last thing she bought in a store? When was the last time she knew where she was? Or who she was?

PART 5

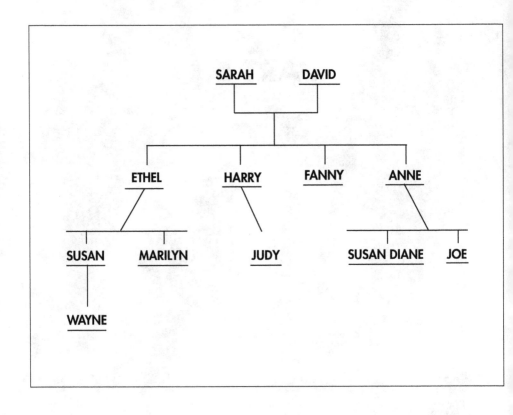

27:

REOPENING THE INVESTIGATION

I hadn't done any more research into my great-grandmother's murder since 2013—the hundredth anniversary of her death. By then, I had already learned the basic story about what really happened to Sarah Feinstein. I had subsequently made the whole saga into an anecdote I regularly told on my own. There were still a lot of questions I would have liked to answer, but there didn't seem to be any way to do it; I'd amassed all the newspaper clippings and official records I could find.

Besides, my mother couldn't follow the twists and turns of the story anymore. For a while, my research had brought us together, and given us something to talk about—a shared story about our shared history. But she'd since forgotten everything I'd discovered, and everything she'd originally heard as a child, too.

And yet, soon after my mother moved into a memory care facility, she gave me an unexpected clue to solving the Winnipeg murder mystery—a clue that led me to restart my investigation, in a new direction, three years after I'd brought it to a halt.

In the fall of 2016, I found myself missing the sound of my mother's voice. We had spoken on the phone almost every day for years. But now that she'd moved out of the house, that connection was severed: She had no landline in her new facility, and she'd never learned how to use a cell phone.

As I was longing to hear the sound of her voice—not even a conversation; I'd settle for the sound alone—I realized I could hear it once again. Looking through the files on my computer, I found the video I'd made in 2010, when I recorded her telling stories soon after she was diagnosed with dementia. I hadn't been able to bring myself to watch this video since shortly after I'd made it: All I could think about at the time was how much she had forgotten already, and how obvious her illness was becoming.

But now, in 2016, I watched the whole thing again for the first time in years. And all I could see now was how much of her had still been present back in 2010, and how relatively clear-headed she was, compared to what she had become since then. She still remembered names and events, even if she sometimes needed prompting. She still made eye contact, cracked jokes, and turned scraps of family lore into neatly packaged anecdotes with punch lines, even if she sometimes lost her train of thought. She even looked like the mother I remembered: with reddish hair that had been neatly brushed, gesticulating hands, and an enormous range of animated expressions. I was reminded how vibrant and engaging she had been, even after her diagnosis. And like a before-and-after photo, it underlined just how much she had lost in those six years.

In the recording, she told the story of her grandmother's murder in Winnipeg—the old sniper story that I had finally debunked. But in addition to rehashing the usual details that I had remembered, she brought up, in one brief aside, a tidbit about the family that had never properly registered in my mind.

Six years after I recorded the video, this bit of information—a single sentence—would get me started on a new round of research into my great-grandmother's murder.

When my mother was born in Jersey City in 1940, she was named in memory of Sarah Feinstein, her maternal grandmother. In accordance with a common Ashkenazi Jewish tradition, she was given the same Hebrew name as the deceased—Shifra—and an English name starting with the same letter: Susan.

But she was not the only person to be named for Sarah.

In the video from 2010, my mother went through her aunts and uncles one at a time, trying to recall the names of their children—her first cousins. That's when she got to her mother's sister Anne: "Anne has Susan and—I've forgotten Susan's brother's name," my mother said. (My father called from off-screen: "Joey.") "We were two Susans, because we were both named for Sarah."

This other Susan—who was also given Sarah's Hebrew name Shifra—was born clear across the country in Yreka, California, in 1942. These two Susans, both named after the same person, were first cousins. I never met this other Susan, but she was always known in our family as Susan Diane, to distinguish her from my mother.

My previous efforts to dig into family history had focused on one person alone: my mother's cousin Judy, daughter of Ethel's older brother Harry, because I wanted to know what story she'd heard as a child about their grandmother's murder. My search for Judy had hit a dead end, and I'd given up.

But what about Susan Diane? She, too, was one of Sarah's grandchildren, and perhaps her mother Anne had told her about Sarah's murder—either the truth, or the sniper story, or something else entirely. Susan Diane was also named for Sarah, so I thought she might have learned more about her grandmother; maybe her parents told her about Sarah when they explained that she'd been named in her memory.

But how could I find Susan Diane now? I'd had no luck finding Judy a few years earlier, and I was in the same situation now, knowing neither Susan Diane's full name nor where she lived.

By this point, my mother wasn't able to offer any leads. But my aunt Marilyn, who had been in touch with Susan Diane when she lived in California in the sixties, remembered her last name, and her husband's first name. Between those two bits of information, I was able to track her down online and find a phone number for her in northern California.

When I called, I quickly explained who I was. And almost immediately, the fact that we had never spoken, and this call came unexpectedly, didn't matter. I caught her up on decades of family life, including my mother's condition; I also told her about my aunt Marilyn, whom she did remember from California in the sixties.

Then I told her about the research I'd been doing into Sarah's

murder in Winnipeg. "I don't know much about it," she said. I
asked if I could interview her about what she did know, and we set
up an appointment for later that week. In the meantime, I emailed
her one of the stories from the *Winnipeg Tribune*.

After many years as a journalist, I wasn't usually nervous about
doing interviews, but this wasn't an ordinary interview. I wasn't
merely a cousin casually trying to connect with a long-lost relative;
I was looking for specific information about Sarah's murder, and
family history more broadly. But I also wasn't a disinterested journalist hunting for facts from a random source; she was my cousin.
I wrote up a list of questions, and then called her from my apartment, sitting in front of my computer typing notes while we talked
on my hands-free headset.

First, I was curious about her name. All I really knew about her
was what my mother told me when I made the video: "We were two
Susans, because we were both named for Sarah." But how, I asked,
did my mother get to be simply Susan while her cousin became
known within the family as Susan Diane? She told me how her
two-name moniker arose on a childhood trip to Vancouver—a trip
her family took every year from California, but my mother took
just once from the East Coast in 1954, the time she and my Aunt
Marilyn and their mother Ethel (known as Auntie Et to Susan Diane) flew first class. "We were going to Vancouver, all of us, and we
arrived before the East Coast contingent," Susan Diane told me.
"When they got off the plane and got to the house, I said to Susan,
'I got here first so I get to be Susan, and you can use your middle
name.' And she said, 'Not with my middle name: Gertrude!' And
I said, 'Okay, I'll be Susan Diane.' And I was Susan Diane to the
whole family."

This made sense to me. "My mother always hated her middle
name," I told Susan Diane.

While Susan Diane got to know her grandparents David and Bella on her annual trips to Vancouver, where they'd moved in 1947,
she didn't know much about Sarah Feinstein—the woman she'd
been named after. She had never even seen a photograph of her
until I emailed her the *Tribune* story with her picture on the front
page. "I recognized Zayde, because I knew him really well," she
told me. "But I never saw a picture of my mom's mom."

Susan Diane's mother Anne never told her any stories about

Sarah. "I just knew that I was named after my mother's real mom. And that was it, for years, even after I knew I was named after her," she told me.

She did learn, when she was a child, that Sarah had been murdered—but she didn't hear about it from her mother. "It was somebody on my dad's side" who told her about the murder, she said, although she couldn't remember exactly who. "They would have known. They lived in that Hebrew colony."

Susan Diane's mother was Anne, whose mother was Sarah. But Susan Diane was connected to the family on her father's side, too: Her father was Sam Friedman, whose aunt was Bella. "My dad's dad is Bubbe's brother," she said. "The two families are intertwined."

Anne and Sam, Susan Diane's parents, were married in July 1938 in David and Bella's house at 452 Mountain Avenue in Winnipeg's North End—the house my grandmother called her childhood home. Anne was a saleslady in a dress shop, Sam was a law student already living in Yreka. The wedding was performed by Rabbi Israel Isaac Kahanovitch, one of the two rabbis who had presided over the funeral of Sarah Feinstein, Anne's mother, twenty-five years earlier. (In his own book of marriage ceremonies he'd performed, for Anne and Sam's wedding, Kahanovitch listed the bride's mother's maiden name as Sarah Brooks. However she was known while she was alive, this was apparently the name—not Awerbruch or Auerboock—that stayed with her in people's memories after she was killed.)

Susan Diane had never heard the details of the murder—neither the actual details, nor the tall tale about a drive-by sniper that my mother was told as a child. All she knew was that Sarah had been murdered when Anne, Susan Diane's mother, was a baby. "That's all I ever heard and I never asked," she told me. "My mom was very closed-mouthed about things like that. I think my dad knew, too, and he never commented."

Anne didn't talk about Winnipeg or her childhood when her daughter was growing up—something Susan Diane believes may be connected to the murder, and its psychological aftermath. "People say that when something traumatic happens, it affects you the rest of your life," she said.

Susan Diane told me that her brother Joe—the one my father

had remembered as "Joey" in the 2010 video—also lived in the Bay Area. She gave me his number, and I called him the following night. Like his sister, he told me he hadn't heard much about Sarah's murder when he was growing up.

He agreed that their mother Anne carried some kind of fear within her even as an adult. "Growing up, we could never have a door closed at night," he told me. "She was absolutely adamant that when we were sleeping, doors had to be open. I didn't know for the longest time why." But when Joe found out about the murder, as a teenager, from his father, he realized there was probably a connection.

By now, I had spoken to four of Sarah Feinstein's five grandchildren: Anne's children Susan Diane and Joe, and Ethel's children—my mother Susan and my aunt Marilyn. And Susan Diane gave me a clue that helped me find the fifth, Harry's daughter Judy, the one I'd tried unsuccessfully to contact three years earlier. She knew her last name and where she lived. And more importantly, as it turned out, she knew her kids' names.

Judy's son and daughter, roughly my contemporaries, were on Facebook, easy enough to track down. I sent a note to both, explaining how we were related. Then I told them I was looking for their mother: "I wanted to talk to your mom to see what she remembers," I wrote, "even if the answer is nothing at all."

Within a few hours, her daughter Stacey—the same name and spelling as my sister—had given me Judy's phone number in Vancouver. "She is excited to talk to you!" Stacey wrote. "She's always been interested in the story around her grandmother."

It had been more than three years since I'd come to believe, mistakenly, that cousin Judy didn't wasn't "interested/willing to dredge up old family stuff." Now I realized that may have been a misunderstanding, or a problem of communication.

"I've been digging for years," I replied. "Feels like I just struck oil."

I called my mother's cousin Judy the same week I spoke with Susan Diane and Joe; I had gotten back my momentum on the Winnipeg story, and I didn't want to wait between interviews.

Just like Susan Diane and Joe, Judy at first said she didn't know much about the murder. Her parents—in particular, her father

Harry—hadn't told her the truth, but they hadn't made up an improbable story, either, the way my own grandmother did. Instead they said nothing. "Everything was very hush-hush," Judy told me. "Our family didn't share so much."

I had hoped that Judy might be the cousin who knew the most about Sarah's murder, because her father Harry was Sarah's oldest child. He was nearly six when his mother was killed, and he was the one who'd found her body. He was old enough to understand what he'd seen, I figured, and old enough to remember it. I thought he might have shared a story about the murder with his daughter—either the true story he remembered first-hand, or perhaps the invented sniper story that his little sister, my Grandma Ethel, passed down to her children. But that was not the case. Harry never shared any details of Sarah's death.

"I never asked," said Judy, "and he never brought it up."

She knew her grandmother, Bella, wasn't her father's mother, but she didn't know what had happened to Sarah. "I was told that she died," Judy told me. "But not how. I assumed she was sick."

She didn't even learn that Sarah had been murdered until fifteen years earlier. The person who finally told her was a more distant cousin I hadn't heard about named Danny, who'd done research into family history.

"Sarah's death must have been traumatic, and the kids had to deal with that on their own, and pretty quickly thereafter David married Bella and immediately there were three more kids," Judy said. "So things probably got shoved under the rug."

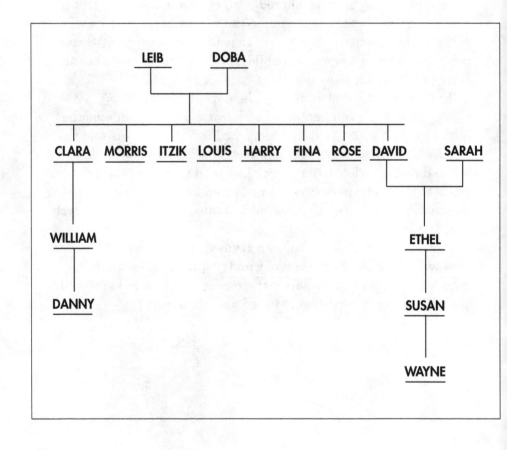

LEIB   DOBA

CLARA   MORRIS   ITZIK   LOUIS   HARRY   FINA   ROSE   DAVID   SARAH

WILLIAM

DANNY

ETHEL

SUSAN

WAYNE

28: FINDING FANNY

Just as I started digging into the Winnipeg saga again, a piece of the mystery I thought I'd already solved started to unravel.

In the fall of 2016, I contacted Lynn Roseman, who helped coordinate Winnipeg's cemetery photography project, taking pictures of all the Jewish gravesites in the city and cataloging them. I was looking for information about the history of the Children of Israel cemetery where Sarah was buried. Roseman had been quoted in a story about the cemetery that summer in the *Winnipeg Free Press*: "Most people think of cemeteries as somber places, but Children of Israel has some delightful stories to go with it," she told the paper.

One of those stories, apparently, was mine. The *Free Press* story quoted maintenance supervisor Bill Croydon, who recounted a story about my 2013 visit: "While it's not easily accessible, those who do come here are often people looking for their roots, Croydon said. 'It's interesting to hear the stories.' Last year, Croydon took a visitor from New York inside the locked gates to look for the gravestone of his great-grandmother, whose murder was never solved."

Roseman provided the information I'd asked for, and did additional research to make sure she was giving me accurate information.

Knowing her connection to the cemetery project, I asked Roseman a second question—about Fanny, Sarah's daughter who'd been in bed with her at the time of the murder, my grandma Ethel's little sister who'd disappeared from family history and official records. I'd already concluded from my research three years earlier—when an archivist in Winnipeg had handed me a snapshot of a gravestone—that Fanny had died in 1919, most probably from that year's influenza epidemic, and was buried in the Hebrew Sick Benefit Cemetery. I asked Roseman if she could get a clearer photo of Fanny's grave, since the one I'd gotten in 2013 was a bit blurry.

Roseman emailed me a better photograph, and now I could read it clearly: Fannie M. Fainstein, Died July 19, 1929. A full decade after the flu epidemic.

I was disappointed, because I'd created an entirely plausible narrative about Fanny's death that this information undercut. Still, even though she hadn't died in the year I'd anticipated, and probably not for the reason I had hypothesized, I still believed I had found her. Then I cross-referenced the date with Manitoba's death records online, and found that this Fannie Fainstein had been forty-five when she died; my Fanny would only have been eighteen in 1929. I had, in fact, found the wrong Fanny.

When I connected with my mother's cousins just a couple of weeks later, however, I was back on Fanny's trail.

"I knew Mom had a sister who died," Susan Diane told me, "and she only said that she was...retarded." She paused before using that word. "She died young."

Judy, too, had heard vague rumors about Fanny. "She was very sickly as a child," Judy told me. "At first I thought she was retarded," she said, also hesitating to use that word, unaware that Susan Diane had told me the same thing, with the same hesitation. "My mom said no, she was just very sickly."

Then Judy gave me the phone number of her second cousin Danny, the one who'd been researching family history. "He'll know what happened," she told me.

Danny is connected to David and Sarah Feinstein in two ways. His grandfather Joe Gelmon had married David's sister Clara—Kreintzi, as he called her in Yiddish. So Danny's grandmother and my mother's grandfather were siblings. That makes them second cousins. But there was an additional link: Danny's great uncle Louis Gelmon—Joe's brother—was married to Sarah's sister Gertrude, known in Yiddish as Greena. So his great-uncle and my mother's great-aunt were husband and wife.

Being related to both David and Sarah, Danny was familiar with relatives on both sides. He had become the keeper of the family's past—photographs, articles, documents. With his assistance, I could create a family tree dating back nearly two hundred years.

Since Danny lived in Vancouver, he had known many of these relatives personally. He remembered the house where David and Bella lived on Twentieth Avenue in Vancouver, the old Chevy pick-up truck David used to drive, and the letters David's sisters used to write to him in Yiddish. He even remembered meeting David's sister Rose, who'd settled in Portsmouth, New Hampshire; "Auntie Rose" came to Danny's bar mitzvah in Vancouver in 1953.

But most importantly, with Danny's help, I was finally able to piece together—with a great degree of certainty—what had happened to Fanny.

When David and Bella were newly married and living in Canora, Saskatchewan, Danny told me, Fanny was "sickly, very sickly." It wasn't clear what her ailment was, but it was too much for David and Bella to handle—securing appropriate medical care would have required frequent train trips back to Winnipeg. Even though the Hugh Waddell Memorial Hospital had opened in Canora in 1914, it was small, with just twenty-six beds, far fewer than the hospitals in Winnipeg.

David's eldest sister Fina—who had been visiting with Sarah the night before her murder, writing letters for her—and her husband Harry Dorfman adopted Fanny, whom they called Feigl, meaning little bird in Yiddish.

With this information, I could finally trace Fanny's life through official documents.

In the 1916 Saskatchewan census, taken in June, Fanny is listed as living in Canora with David and Bella, when she was four years old; the whole family, including David and Bella's new baby Bernice, had moved from Winnipeg that spring. But later the same year—sometime after Fanny's birthday in September—she appears in the Manitoba census as a five-year-old living in Winnipeg's North End, with Fina and Harry on Selkirk Avenue. She moved back to Winnipeg sometime that year, after spending just a few months in Canora.

So the story my mother heard about Fanny being "given away"

wasn't entirely off base.

"The Dorfmans never had kids of their own," Danny told me. While no formal adoption took place, Fina and Harry gave little Fanny their last name. Fina, whom Danny remembers as otherwise domineering and "a terror," babied her and cared for her, but she could not make her well.

The Dorfmans moved four blocks north to 506 Burrows Avenue—into David's old house, where Fanny had lived before David and Bella moved the family to Saskatchewan. She was back in her old home, with her old doctors.

Fanny was living with Fina and Harry in Winnipeg when David and Bella had their last two children, Rae and Herbie, in Canora. She surely met them and knew who they were, but they didn't grow up as siblings. And when David and Bella eventually returned to Winnipeg, moving into their new house on Mountain Avenue, they didn't take Fanny back. Once she became a Dorfman, she remained a Dorfman.

Fanny took ill on September 1, 1927, her sixteenth birthday, and was treated by Dr. Isaac Pearlman, a Russian-born physician who also lived on Burrows Avenue. He was a partner in the First Old Country Clinic on Selkirk Avenue, which had been opened by Dr. George Hirsh Kalichmann, the doctor who in 1913 had pronounced Sarah Feinstein—Fanny's biological mother—dead, after she'd been shot while sleeping with two-year-old Fanny by her side. After treating Fanny for several days, Pearlman had her admitted to Winnipeg General Hospital, where she remained for a week before dying on the morning of September 13, 1927. The immediate cause of death was acute pneumonia.

Fanny's death certificate lists her name as Fanny Dorfman. That's why Fanny Fainstein seemed to disappear from official records when I'd searched by her last name. Her parents are listed not as David and Sarah, but as Harry and Fina Dorfman.

Fina, Danny told me, was devastated by the loss of the niece she'd adopted, and "mourned her the rest of her life." While the precise details of Fanny's lifelong illness were never made clear in official records, the impact of her death on the family was profound. My aunt Marilyn, whose middle name is Fay, wasn't the only person named for Fanny. Danny's sister Reesa was also named in her memory; her middle name is Fay, too.

The September 16, 1927, edition of Winnipeg's Yiddish daily newspaper *Dos Yidishe Vort/The Israelite Press* carried a Yizkor ("In Memoriam") notice for young Fanny, placed by Mr. and Mrs. H. Y. Wilder and addressed to her adoptive parents: "To you, Mr. and Mrs. H. Dorfman, we express our deepest sympathy for your great loss. The darling bud that you so tenderly embraced for sixteen years and raised in angst—she so untimely torn away by an angry wind—has disappeared forever. Your pain is too great for us to be able to comfort you. But we wish you to be strong enough to overcome this tremendous grief."

Once I'd pieced together all the details of Fanny's death, I sent a note to Lynn Roseman. She sent me photos of Fanny's gravestone: reddish-brown with rough edges, neatly engraved in Hebrew and English, with her adoptive family name spelled out in large capital letters across the bottom: Dorfman.

Fanny was buried in Winnipeg's Hebrew Sick Benefit Cemetery—the same place as the other Fannie Fainstein I'd found years earlier—in the section reserved for members of the Orthodox synagogue Chevra Mishnayes. Her tombstone notes that she was the daughter of David Feinstein, but raised by Harry (called by his Yiddish name, Yeruchem) Dorfman. When Harry died in 1959, and Fina died in 1968, they were buried in the Dorfman family plot, right behind Fanny.

My first attempt to find my mother's cousin Judy had hit a dead end; but I'd found her years later after making a second try with a different approach. My first attempt to figure out what happened to Fanny had led me down the wrong path; but my second try found the truth.

I started to wonder if I should take another look at all the material I'd gathered about Sarah's murder. When I'd last delved into my files, I had suspicions and hunches, but no clear notion about who'd committed the crime. Perhaps, I thought, after a break of a few years, I could try to find some new sources of information to give me additional insights, and see with fresh eyes the old newspaper articles and official documents I'd already looked at. Maybe a second trip to Winnipeg would reveal things I'd missed the first time.

A second look had solved the Fanny mystery. Maybe the same could be true about Sarah.

איקאָר טען-מאָן
זונטאָג, דעם 2-טן אָקטאָבער

טאַלמוד תורה גראַדואירונגס פיטרונג
דעם 9-טן אָקטאָבער

די סעמיניקים פון דער אינדאַרסי-
רונג ביורא

Royal Shoe Store
836 MAIN STREET PHONE 54 760

מצבות
WHEELDON & SONS
1055 Main St., Cor Burrows Ave.
Winnipeg

J. H. Brooke
& Sons
Granite and Marble Monuments
366 Main St. Phone 26 629
Winnipeg, Man.

IDEAL CLEANSER

אײדעל קלעאנער
כשר

10 סענט אַ שאַכטל

IDEAL PRODUCTS CO.
78-80 Higgins Ave. Phone 22-219
WINNIPEG

Fanny's Yizkor notice in
Dos Yidishe Vort

THE ISRAELITE PRESS

אין אפגרונט פון לעבן

$1.25
50¢

247

29: FALLING

Our Passover Seder in 2017 was the first without my mother.

The following day, I visited her at the memory care facility. That, however, was the last time I saw her there. A few weeks later, while she was outside on the patio, she fell and broke her arm. The aides found her face down on the cement.

What might have been a relatively minor injury meant months of agony for her—and, ultimately, another move.

Part of the problem was the injury itself, a fairly bad break in her upper arm, with terrible bruising across her back. She was in pain, and would take many weeks to heal.

But the treatment—both medical and personal—that she received at every step of the way pushed my family to the breaking point.

When my mother fell, the memory care facility put her in an ambulance, without any staff members, to take her to a hospital—not the one just up the road, but one clear across the county. So my mother, who didn't know her own last name, much less her address, insurance information, or the exact nature of her injury, was shipped off to a strange hospital unattended by anyone who knew her.

The memory care facility called my father at home, but he was downtown with his friend Don—my mother's friend Doris's husband. When he didn't answer, nobody left a message, nor did they try his cell phone. They eventually contacted Doris, who called Don on his cell and told my father what had happened. They headed to the hospital, where my mother had already been checked in. Nobody from the memory care facility was with her, nor did anybody call to check up on her. "They were finished, as far as they were concerned," my father told me.

What might have been a quick procedure for anyone else quickly became an ordeal. My mother was given morphine and Ativan as they set her arm, and she soon fell asleep. The hospital admitted her overnight, with her release set for the next morning. But the orthopedist didn't show up to discharge her, so she stayed another day. Then the memory care facility didn't show up to pick her up, so she stayed another day. Then the nurses were concerned that she had a urinary tract infection because she'd wet the bed; in truth, the nurses wouldn't let her out of bed for fear that she'd fall and hurt herself further. Since she couldn't communicate the fact that she had to use the bathroom, they kept her in bed until she wet the sheets. So she stayed in the hospital yet another day.

Plaster casts have fallen out of favor since I broke my arm as a child; my mother got a removable plastic splint, held in place by a lightweight sling. "Don't take off the splint," the nurses would tell my mother. Then, as soon as they left the room, my mother would rip off the sling and the splint, and toss both across the room with her good arm—quite a feat for a woman confined to a hospital bed. The frustrated nurses would put them back on, scolding her about not following their instructions; she'd nod, and then the nurses would leave the room, and she'd take them off again.

My father told me about this on the phone. I'd ask him why she couldn't get a plaster cast. "Even if plaster isn't the doctors' first choice anymore, it hasn't ceased to exist in the world," I said. "There must be a way to make an exception for her. She can't possibly be the first Alzheimer's patient they've had who can't follow instructions."

My father asked about the plaster cast. There were no exceptions, no matter how impractical this "improved" cast was for my mother.

This was not the first time we'd found doctors who didn't appear to fully grasp what instructions people with Alzheimer's can comprehend: When my sister had taken my mother to a urologist appointment after her bladder mesh implant surgery three years earlier, the doctor didn't understand why my mother couldn't figure out how to pee in a cup for a urine sample, or understand how to do kegel exercises. "You've got to be fucking kidding me—that's beyond her for about ten different reasons," my sister vented to me after the appointment. "This woman doesn't know her last name. I've never been so exasperated with physicians."

When it was time for my mother to be discharged from the hospital, the doctors said that she couldn't go directly back to her memory care facility because she'd need physical therapy as her arm healed. So they sent her to a rehab facility. What was supposed to be a brief stay—maybe a few days—turned into six weeks.

And here, again, it seemed like nobody in this rehab facility had ever met a person with Alzheimer's—even though there was an affiliated memory care unit in the same suburban complex.

For most patients in rehab, the time between physical therapy appointments was filled with typical daily activities: watching television, reading books, talking on the phone, or visiting with friends and family. There were lounges where patients could play checkers, or flip through magazines. But for my mother—who could no longer follow a television show or read a book or talk on the phone—almost her entire day was empty, spent alone in a strange place with nothing to do but wander the carpeted hallways unattended.

On one occasion, she shuffled very slowly past the apparently distracted receptionists at the front desk and out the front door; she only stopped when she fell in the parking lot, unnoticed by the staff.

Another time, when my father went to visit, she was in physical therapy on another floor. "She'll be done in twenty minutes," the nurse at the front desk told him. He waited in her room, but after an hour, she still hadn't returned. Apparently, when her physical therapist sent her back to her room, rather than taking her there himself, he put her in the elevator alone and pushed the button for her floor. When the doors opened, my mother—confused by her surroundings—wandered the hall until she found an empty bed, like a geriatric Goldilocks. Nobody thought to look for her until my father went back to the front desk, and, after a room-by-room search, they finally found her.

Week after week, this dragged on. My father visited every day, and tried to keep her out of harm's way. The nurses seemed to focus little on her progress, and the doctors would drop by perhaps once a week, simply extending her stay each time without letting us know what progress, if any, they noticed.

All this time, we were focusing on how to get my mother out of where she was—out of the hospital, then out of rehab. But a larger question reared its head at the same time: Once she gets out, where will she go?

The memory care facility where she'd been living for almost a year had many things going for it: It was close to my father, so he could visit often. It had a lot of group activities to keep my mother occupied, and a friendly staff and several sociable fellow residents to keep her engaged. But my father had an understandable beef with the place in light of how my mother's accident had been handled.

My father spoke to Helen. In addition to being my mother's longtime friend, she had also become my father's confidant around my mother's care. While her husband Howie had attended the Kensington Club day group with my mother, Helen and my father had attended the affiliated support group for caregivers together. Even after Howie died, Helen continued to meet with my father and other caregivers to share her first-hand experiences. "I know all too well what people are experiencing as they make painful decisions for their loved ones," she told me.

Helen suggested that my mother may simply have progressed past the point where a relatively large home—like the one where she'd been living for a year until her fall—was the right place for her. Perhaps it was time to trade the range of activities and socializing for more personal care in a smaller facility. Maybe a place with more individual attention would be safer—with fewer chances for her to wander away unattended, or hurt herself.

My father wasn't ready to make a quick decision. He had more immediate things to deal with, such as making sure my mother was getting proper care in rehab. Helen was concerned that my father wouldn't make a decision in time, and that when she was released from rehab, my mother would have nowhere to go except the place where she'd been living before—a place nobody thought was appropriate for her anymore. Helen talked to Doris; Doris talked to me; I talked to Helen. They both asked me to visit my mother, and my father. Where my mother would live, we all agreed, was up to my father. But my father needed more support to be able to make that decision, and quickly.

That weekend, Mark and I drove to Maryland. We visited my mother in rehab. She was clearly in pain, her clothes disheveled and her back covered in bruises. It had only been a few weeks since I'd seen her but she had aged years in that time. Now her obvious ailments were physical as well as mental.

Sitting on overstuffed chairs in a somewhat private seating area, we asked about her broken arm and physical therapy, but she didn't fully understand what was happening to her. Mark was finally successful at entertaining and engaging her: He pulled up videos of adorable animals on his phone, and she was rapt.

While we were in Maryland, we went to look at a small residential home that Helen had recommended. It was on the same street where Helen and Howie had once lived—and it's where Howie was living when he died. Helen also worked there from time to time, doing family counseling and community outreach, so it'd be easy for her to visit my mother. And Doris, who lived just a couple of blocks away, was thrilled to be able to stop by more often.

While my mother's memory care facility housed more than sixty residents, this small house held just half a dozen. There were fewer activities, but a higher ratio of staffers to give the residents individual attention. And it was a kosher facility—something my mother no longer understood or cared about, but all other things being equal, it was a plus.

After some brief discussions, my father decided to move my mother into the new home whenever she was released from the rehab facility. It was located in Potomac, the same tony suburb my parents had considered when they first bought their house in 1971, but my father had rejected it because, as he said, "I'm not a country squire." Forty-six years later, my mother would finally get to live in Potomac.

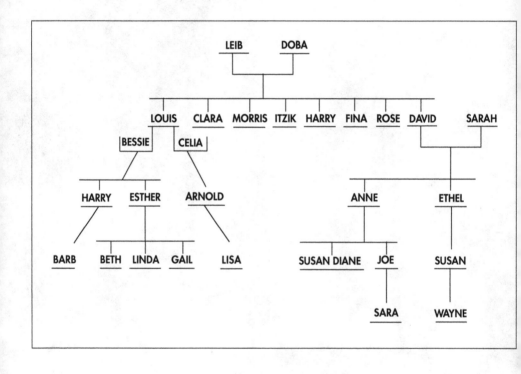

30:
GROWING THE FAMILY TREE

My parents already had two children when my father's father died in January 1970. My mother wanted to have a third child; my father was ready to move past the diapers-and-cribs phase of his life. "Don't you want to have another baby so we can name him after your father?" she asked.

That was the argument that persuaded him, or so the family legend goes. My father was an only child, and if he didn't name a child after his deceased father, there would be nobody to carry on his father's memory. Several weeks later, I was conceived, and when I was born that December, I was named after my father's father.

I was given an English name that began with the same letter as his name: William, or Willie, as he was known. And I was given a Hebrew name that was the same as his—except he didn't exactly have a Hebrew name. He had a Yiddish name, Velvel, meaning wolf. So I was given the Hebrew name Zev, also meaning wolf.

My father, Martin, was named after his father's father, Morris; they shared the Hebrew name Moshe.

It's a family tradition that I love: I'm named for my father's father; my father is named for his father's father. When I was a child, I heard that this tradition stretched back generations on that side of the family. I don't know if that's true, because like many

American Jews, my father has a family history that only stretches back a century with much certainty, to the time when his relatives immigrated to North America from Eastern Europe.

But for Ashkenazi Jews, there's a bittersweetness to being named after someone: It means you carry a piece of the deceased person's soul, if you believe in that kind of thing. But it also means you never got to know that person, who died before you were born. I carry my paternal grandfather's name; I never knew him. My father carries his paternal grandfather's name; he never knew him, either.

I don't have any children. This tradition will end with me.

My great-grandmother Sarah might have been forgotten except for the fact that generations of people were named in her memory.

My mother Susan and her cousin Susan Diane weren't the only ones named after her, I soon discovered. After Anne—my grandma Ethel's younger sister, who'd been in the crib a few feet from the bed when their mother was murdered in 1913—named her daughter Susan Diane after Sarah, Anne's son Joe also honored her memory a generation later, naming his own daughter Sara, after her great-grandmother.

Sara, who was also living in the Bay Area, was born in 1987. She is my second cousin: Our grandmothers Anne and Ethel were sisters.

"I've never liked the name. I've never felt it was mine," Sara told me when I reached her by phone. "But I've also felt like I had a duty to carry the name. I'm doing this for someone else: for Sarah, and also for my grandmother."

Anne, who had been so tight-lipped about her mother's death when she was raising Susan Diane and Joe, started to open up by the time she became a grandmother. When Sara was born, Joe's wife Toni asked Anne questions about family history, so she could put the information in a baby book; Anne finally shared a little about her mother's murder.

Anne would eventually share even more with her granddaughter, who'd been named after her mother. When Sara was in middle school, she did a report on her family history, including her great-grandmother's murder. She took a photo of Sarah Feinstein to class to show the other students—a photo Anne gave her. "The way we heard it was she was murdered at night," Sara told me, "a guy came in through the window, and my grandmother Anne was in the bed with her."

This version of events that Anne told Sara—more than she had ever told her children, Susan Diane and Joe, when they were younger—was far closer to the truth than the drive-by-sniper story my mother learned as a child, and more than I'd ever learned from my grandmother, Ethel.

In discussions of family history, Sara said, her great-grandmother "always was there in this noble sense." She explained: "This woman who got murdered, the person gets mythologized." In fact, she said, being the child of Sarah, who'd been murdered, "conferred a superiority" on her grandmother Anne over Anne's younger half-siblings, who were Bella's children, because her family history included "something older, kind of mysterious."

And all of this history was passed down, in part, because of her name. "I don't know that I would have been told about it if I hadn't been named for her," Sara said. "Carrying someone's name feels like a connection."

Now that I'd connected with several cousins who could share stories about Sarah, I wanted to go further. I started planning a second research trip to Canada, where I hoped to find even more cousins.

I knew my first stop would be Winnipeg, since that's where the family's story in North America began. I had found a few of my mother's first cousins—Susan Diane, Joe, and Judy—but none of them lived there, so I needed to search further back on the family tree. My great-grandfather David had been one of eight siblings, seven of whom once lived in Winnipeg. David had moved to Vancouver in the forties, but I figured that some of his siblings must have stayed in Winnipeg. Perhaps their grandchildren and great-grandchildren were still there, I thought, with personal memories and family stories to share.

Even though these cousins would be one step further removed from my mother's side of the family—these would be her second cousins, rather than her first cousins—I thought they might be able to fill in more blanks about the family's history in general. After all, my mother met her grandfather David just a couple of times, and visited Winnipeg only once, as a small child; whatever stories she'd heard were mostly forgotten, because she didn't have any point of reference. But cousins who grew up in Winnipeg and knew their parents and grandparents well would have heard many more stories; more importantly, since they would have recognized the people and places these stories were about, they would be more likely to remember them and what they meant.

In the spring of 2017, I wrote a note to Bernie Bellan, editor of *The Jewish Post & News* in Winnipeg, which he published in his newspaper. It asked if any of my distant relatives were still there. A local reader—who was not a relative, but knew the family—sent the note to her friend Barb in Los Angeles, who emailed me. Barb is my mother's second cousin, the granddaughter of Louis, my great-grandfather David's youngest brother—the one who had lived with David's family when he first immigrated to Canada, when my grandmother Ethel was a baby.

Barb never lived in Winnipeg, although she'd visited a few times when she was young. She'd never met my great-grandfather David, and had never heard about my great-grandmother Sarah's murder. So Barb wasn't going to be the person to open the door to my family's wider history. She was, however, the one who ended up providing the key.

She dug up an old bat mitzvah invitation from one of her cousins in Winnipeg. I found the bat mitzvah girl, now about thirty, on Facebook, and she connected me to her mother, who still lived in Winnipeg. She was my mother's second cousin. She, in turn, connected me to several other relatives. All of them were the grandchildren of Louis, David's youngest brother; they were my mother's second cousins, none of whom had ever met her or even heard of her. They had grown up in Winnipeg, and while some had moved away—one was in San Diego, another in Toronto—a handful were still there. I made arrangements by phone and email to get together with them when I came to Canada at the end of May.

The first time I visited Winnipeg, in 2013, I thought I knew who my great-grandfather was. He was the immigrant who wore a stiff collar when he posed for his wedding photo. He was the young husband and father who collapsed at the funeral of his wife, who was murdered while she slept. He was the generous grandfather who bought my mother her first—and last—first-class airline ticket. But it turned out that although all that was true, I didn't really know David at all.

Starting over Memorial Day weekend in 2017, I spent a week tracing his life across western Canada—starting in Winnipeg, where he lived when he first arrived in North America, and continuing through Canora, the town in Saskatchewan where he worked as a cattle dealer, and ending in Vancouver, where he moved in the forties. This trip would change how I thought about him forever. And it would renew family connections that had been severed decades earlier.

In Winnipeg I met three cousins, all grandchildren of Louis, my great-grandfather David's youngest brother. And as I'd hoped, I found out stories about my family that I'd never heard before—including one particularly curious tale hidden in a teapot.

I started with Beth, the oldest child of Louis's daughter Esther, from his first wife, Bessie; Beth was named in memory of her late grandmother. Born in 1946 in Winnipeg's North End, she now lives in the South End, where most of the city's Jews are today, on quiet side streets lined with mid-century bungalows in residential neighborhoods like Tuxedo and River Heights.

"I may be the only one of the family who remembers your late great-grandfather, of blessed memory," she told me. In the fifties, "Uncle Dave" came back to Winnipeg, she said, to visit her grandfather Louis. "Very genial"—even "mild-mannered"—is how she described him.

David and Bella had appeared occasionally in *The Jewish Post*—as Winnipeg's Jewish newspaper was then known, before it purchased its longtime rival weekly *The Western Jewish News* in 1986 and became *The Jewish Post & News*—attending social events or donating to a good cause, but that stopped almost entirely once they moved away in 1947. However, David made the newspaper's "Social and Personal" page once more in 1954—above the ads for tuxedo rentals, hair removal, and a *mohel* performing circumcisions—when he visited from Vancouver with his sister Clara to attend the August 25 wedding of their brother Louis's youngest daughter Dorothy. (The wedding was held at Rosh Pina synagogue, which according to Beth, "all the Fainstein men were instrumental in setting up"; the ceremony was performed by Rabbi Arthur A. Chiel, whose 1961 book *The Jews in Manitoba* I would later use to research Winnipeg's Jewish history.) This, I realized, must have been the visit Beth recalled as the one time she met "Uncle Dave" when she was a child.

When David had visited Winnipeg in the fifties, Beth didn't know that his first wife Sarah had been killed many years earlier; I didn't expect as much—if Sarah's own grandchildren weren't told much about the murder, why would her brother-in-law Louis's grandchildren have known more? But Beth did eventually learn about Sarah's murder years later. "When my mother died, she left me a packet of papers," Beth said, "including a few newspaper clippings about the murder."

Louis must have collected articles about his sister-in-law's killing, and passed them down when he died. He must have followed the story in the newspapers, just as I had done a century later.

I shared a hypothesis with Beth: that for much of their lives, Louis and David were the closest of their siblings. I explained that I'd based this on two things. First, that when Louis was a teenager, newly arrived in North America, he'd lived with David and Sarah and the kids, including my grandmother Ethel, on Flora Avenue in Winnipeg's North End. ("I never knew that," she said.) And second, that when the time came for David (and Bella, and the kids) to live in Canora, Saskatchewan, full-time, Louis and his new wife Bessie moved at the same time, living just around the corner. Beth hadn't heard about that either, but she did have another piece of information that buttressed my case.

"I have a tea set that Louis and Bessie used when they lived there," Beth told me. "Well, actually, it's half a tea set."

It had belonged to her grandparents Louis and Bessie, Beth explained, and she and her sister had split it up when they inherited it. "There are notes in the teapot," she told me.

Beth took me to the small room near the kitchen where she kept the set and took the teapot—mostly black, with two silver stripes and a small silver flourish at the base of the spout—out of the cabinet where it was stored. It was engraved with a silver "B" ("for Bessie, I guess," she said). She pulled open the hinged lid to reveal a silver interior that maintained a perfect shine, as well as two small sheets of paper; these were notes that Beth herself had handwritten in cursive decades earlier, recording a story that her mother Esther had dictated to her. Recorded in choppy, incomplete sentences, the story hadn't meant much to Beth at the time, so it had been largely forgotten until we read the notes together and learned about a piece of family history that I'd never known and Beth had never fully appreciated.

"Tea & coffee sets were weddings gifts 1915," the notes began.

In 1923 or 1924, when Louis and Bessie were raising their children in Canora, Bessie had surgery. While she was in the hospital, the notes explained, "children returned home—house cold—slept at Auntie Bella & Uncle Dave's next door." After Louis came home alone and turned up the furnace, "during night house burned down." Louis's wooden house was destroyed. "Had children slept in house, would have been burned," the notes read. When Bessie got out of the hospital, "family moved to Auntie Bella and Uncle Dave's house" for the next year—until Bessie needed more surgery, which required her to go back to Winnipeg, where she died at Winnipeg General Hospital in 1925. ("Young Mother of Three Children Died," ran the September 4, 1925, headline in *Dos Yidishe Vort/The Israelite Press*, in a brief obituary that noted "an operation which failed to save her life.")

The tea set was the only thing that Louis and Bessie owned that survived the fire, the notes explained, because it had been "loaned to Lertzman family"—neighbors who owned a store in Canora—"for an event." (The families would remain friendly for many years: When Clara Lertzman came to Winnipeg in July 1929 for her daughter Sara's wedding, Bella and Frances hosted a luncheon in their honor at Eaton's Grill Room, *The Jewish Post* reported.)

So my great-grandfather David lived with his little brother Louis not once, but twice: around 1911 in Winnipeg's North End when Louis was a teenager, and again in the twenties in Canora after the house fire. They both moved from Winnipeg to Canora around the same time, and they both moved back to Winnipeg around the same time as well. Soon after that, they'd have another important thing in common: Both men lost their first wives when they were still quite young.

My notion that these two siblings were the closest seemed likely to be correct.

When I asked about David's other siblings, Beth showered me with details. In return, I shared a thing or two that she hadn't known.

Beth never met David and Louis's brother Morris ("he died before I was born") or his wife Pearl, who had died many years earlier; she could name their children and their spouses, however, and tell me where they were living, spread out as far as Texas and California. She remembered Isidor—the shortest of the brothers, not even five-foot-one. She remembered meeting David and Louis's sister Fina and her husband Harry Dorfman—known to her by their Yiddish names Freydl and Yeruchem, or "Uncle Richem." "My mother told me that they had a daughter who had died," she told me. Until I told her the details, however, she never knew that this daughter was actually their niece Fanny, whom they'd adopted from my great-grandfather David.

Beth had the most vivid memories of David and Louis's brother Harry—who used to play cards with Louis when she was little—and Harry's wife, Pauline. "We used to go visit them in the fifties," she told me. "They lived downtown on Broadway."

Harry had been a prominent member of Winnipeg's Jewish community. I'd found a detailed story about him that appeared in 1946 in *The Western Jewish News*, written by Joe Gelmon—not the Joe Gelmon who married David's sister Clara, but his nephew of the same name. The article focused on Harry's decades of work in Winnipeg's Jewish community, as an officer with the Jewish Old Folks' Home, the Talmud Torah school, and the Jewish Children's Home. But it also talked about the extended family's roots and his early years in the cattle business with David, which he said began with "a horse and wagon—which we bought on Dave's money." Harry credited Canada for allowing him to rise from a "penniless" immigrant to the "highest positions in the community."

Beth and I met two more cousins for dinner at Rae and Jerry's, an iconic Winnipeg steakhouse dating to 1957. Linda is Beth's younger sister, the one who inherited the other half of Louis and Bessie's tea set. Lisa is also Louis's granddaughter, but from his second wife, Celia, whom he married in 1930, five years after Bessie died. (Like David, Louis also remarried after losing his first wife, and raised a blended family of children from both women.) Lisa's father was Louis and Celia's son Arnold.

"The Fainsteins were true cowboys," Lisa said. "Louis and his brothers used to train wild horses and sell them to the Royal Canadian Mounted Police. In fact, Louis got a job offer from the RCMP to be their in-house horse-breaker, but his brothers got him out so they could keep their outside business with the RCMP."

When Louis co-owned an abattoir in Winnipeg, she said, "he would get on horseback and drive the cattle into the abattoir himself." Louis continued to ride horseback, even on horses that hadn't been ridden before, well into his seventies. This dovetailed with information I'd heard from the other cousins: David and Louis were expert horsemen, and kept horses as well as cattle on their land outside Canora when they lived there.

Louis wasn't always on horseback, of course. Lisa remembered him owning a Model A Ford—already an antique by the sixties—and an Indian motorcycle.

He was, said Lisa, "a very commanding presence, a man's man," physically strong, and particularly keen on wrestling.

The Fainstein brothers were also gamblers. Naturally, being horse-lovers, they went to the horse races. But there was more, too: Those card games that Beth remembered between Louis and his brother Harry? Poker, for money.

"Louis would hide his money in the snow outside the house before coming inside," said Lisa, so his wife Celia wouldn't know if he had won or lost. "He was a liar and a thief," Lisa said of her grandfather, "but lovable."

"Thief" was a strong word, but it was true: A front-page story in the *Winnipeg Tribune* on April 5, 1955, explained that Louis and his brother Harry, as well as three other men who were partners in the St. Boniface Abattoir, had pleaded guilty to a combined 160 charges and been fined a total of $100,000 in Canada's largest tax evasion case to date. The magistrate who ordered the fine warned that in the case of default, each man would be sentenced to three months in prison for each charge, served consecutively; in the case of Louis, who personally pleaded guilty to twenty-six charges, that would have added up to six-and-a-half years in prison.

The brothers were also involved with liquor: "Louis made his own wine," Linda recalled. "He made crabapple wine, in the basement." And Lisa remembered hearing that the brothers had been asked to join an illegal bootlegging operation.

My cousins didn't indicate exactly which Fainstein brothers were involved (David had moved away in the forties, so he didn't figure in many of these cousins' stories), nor whether the brothers actually accepted the offer to get involved in illegal bootlegging—

although Lisa said, "Louis wanted to do it." But these memories meshed with similar stories I'd previously heard from other cousins, intimating that David and Louis kept something besides animals in their barn during their years in Canora—which happened to line up almost perfectly with prohibition.

While the exact dates varied by province, Canadian prohibition began before its American counterpart and ended sooner. Starting in the 1910s, the liquor business in Canada operated mostly illegally. And even after Canadian prohibition ended in the early twenties, liquor remained a lucrative business as legally produced Canadian alcohol was illegally smuggled across the border once American prohibition began in 1920.

I told my cousins that I had one reason, beyond simple speculation, to believe that David and Louis might have been involved with illegal bootlegging: While David and Louis were living with their families in Canora, it's likely that they still occasionally went back and forth to Winnipeg to do business, just as the brothers who lived in Winnipeg probably came to Canora on occasion. But cattle might not have been the only business on their minds: At the same time the two brothers were listed in the 1916 census as living in Canora and working as cattle dealers, they were also working—according to a 1916 Winnipeg business directory I'd found—for their brother Harry in a business called the Manitoba Vinegar Manufacturing Company, at 488 Aberdeen Avenue, three blocks north of Magnus Avenue in Winnipeg's North End. (Harry is listed in the directory as the company's president, David as vice president, and Louis as "vinegar maker.") David's sister Fina and her husband Harry Dorfman were living at that time on Selkirk Avenue in Winnipeg's North End—where they were raising Fanny, David's biological daughter. Harry Dorfman was a cattle dealer like his brothers-in-law, but at that time he was also listed as working for the vinegar company.

"Maybe they weren't making vinegar at all," I suggested.

Perhaps this mysterious vinegar company was a cover for the brothers' illegal liquor business. And perhaps, I said, Sarah's murder was connected to all this—as punishment to David for having gotten involved in illegal activity, or as a warning to David to remain uninvolved. Sarah was murdered a few years before prohibition came into effect—although it's possible that the brothers had an existing connection to organized crime that later led them into the liquor business, rather than the other way around.

"It's just a theory," I told my cousins. "But it's possible."

Linda was the quietest of the cousins at dinner. "I don't remember a lot of stories about people," she told me. But she remembered places, especially places with family history in the North End.

She remembered the house where Louis and Celia lived in the fifties, on Seven Oaks Place, "a fancy street in the neighborhood." She remembered the Sharon Home, a Jewish nursing home where Louis and David's sister Fina had lived; "I remember Freydl," she said, using Fina's Yiddish name, "as an old woman with a babushka." (The nursing home was on Magnus Avenue. "I know where that is," I told Linda. "That's the same street where my great-grandmother was murdered." But that was a piece of family history she had never learned.)

Linda also knew where all the Jewish cemeteries were, and which relatives were buried in each one. "If you'd like, I can take you there tomorrow," she offered over dinner, "and show you the old North End."

The next morning, Linda picked me up in her sedan and drove me around the North End. She showed me the Machray Apartments, where she and her sister Beth were born, and told me stories about their other sister, Gail, who was diagnosed with familial dysautonomia, a Jewish genetic disease. Sick from birth, she wasn't expected to survive childhood, but she completed high school and moved out on her own, before she died in 1982 at age twenty-seven. ("We're better people for having lived through this—it makes you more empathetic," Beth had told me the previous afternoon in her living room. "It enriches your life. But it was hard." She then showed me a photo of Gail as a young girl—a photo that stopped me in my tracks. "She looked exactly like my mother," I told Beth.)

Learning that the genes for familial dysautonomia ran in the Fainstein family, I wondered if that's what Fanny had. What little I knew about her health lined up with the descriptions of the disease I looked up online that night: Fanny reportedly had problems with her mental development, which can be associated with the disease—although not always, as Gail's story proves. Fanny's death at sixteen from pneumonia also seemed to track with what I read about familial dysautonomia, whose patients often die young from pulmonary complications. There was no way to know for sure, but for the first time, I had a possible explanation about what it meant that Fanny was "sickly."

We also drove past the house on Seven Oaks Place, and the Sharon Home. In addition to Fina, Linda and Beth's mother Esther also spent her final years at the Sharon Home before dying of Alzheimer's. I already knew that Esther's brother Harry—the father of Barb, the cousin in Los Angeles who'd found the bat mitzvah invitation that led me to the Winnipeg cousins in the first place—had also died of the disease. "I'm starting to realize this is a common thread in our family," I told Linda.

I was pleased that during our drive, I could show Linda a couple of things in the North End that she didn't know about—in particular, places from David's life in Winnipeg. I showed her the block on Magnus Avenue where David and Sarah had lived when she was murdered. I pointed out the house on Mountain Avenue where David and Bella lived many years later, the house my grandmother Ethel would remember as the place she grew up. And I showed her the house on Flora Avenue where Louis and David had lived together when Ethel was a baby.

As much as I'd learned from my cousins in Winnipeg about David's siblings and their children and grandchildren, I also wanted them to learn a few things from me about David—to understand that this was his city, too, even if he didn't have any direct descendants left to tell stories there. Winnipeg was where he started a new life in a new country—where he learned a new language and a new trade. This was where he started a family, and this is where he buried his wife. This was where he started a new family with a different wife, and raised his children to adulthood. This was where he worked, and prayed, and helped build a community that survived long after he left.

And I wanted Sarah—a woman my cousins never knew personally, and scarcely knew anything about—to become part of their family history in Winnipeg, part of the story of their North End. She lived here, too, on Flora Avenue, with their grandfather Louis, when he first arrived in Canada as a teenager. Magnus Avenue is the street where she was murdered, where throngs waited outside hours later as police officers and journalists tried to investigate, and where even larger crowds gathered days later for her massive funeral. And across the river, in that tiny cemetery in Transcona that hasn't been in use for eighty years, a member of their family, and mine, is buried. She lived in Winnipeg for just seven years, but her name was known throughout the North End's Hebrew Colony, and her tragic end was front-page news.

Linda took me to a couple of North End institutions that dated back to David's years in Winnipeg: the Ashkenazi Synagogue from 1922, and Gunn's Bakery, a kosher store opened by Polish immigrants in 1937 that still sells everything from bagels to marble rye to macaroons. (I bought some kichel and a prune hamantaschen "for later" and then proceeded to eat them in the passenger seat of Linda's car before we'd driven two blocks.)

And then, of course, we visited the cemetery—not Children of Israel, where Sarah is buried, but the Hebrew Sick Benefit Cemetery, where most of our other relatives are. It's located down a rutted asphalt access road that runs behind a development of houses with fenced yards, its gated parking lot leading to the flat, unshaded, grassy graveyard with neat rows of headstones.

We found Morris, and his wife Pearl. We found Isidor; his gravestone was dedicated to "our dear brother," since his wife Bertha had died seven years before him and they had no children. We found Leib and Doba, David and Louis' parents—the ones who'd brought the whole family over from Russia; they'd both lived well into their eighties. Following Jewish tradition, we left small stones on their graves.

We found more Fainsteins, most likely second and third cousins, whose names neither of us recognized. "I live here, and even I can't keep track of who everyone is," Linda said. One of them was Fannie Fainstein, the woman I had once mistakenly thought was my grandmother Ethel's sister. "This Fainstein isn't a relative," I told Linda, "but I've got a story about her anyway." I explained how I'd searched for Fanny, and thought I'd found her, only to discover that I had the wrong person.

"So where's the real Fanny?" Linda asked.

We walked around until we found her: Fanny Dorfman, buried right in front of her adoptive parents, Fina and Harry.

My cousins in Winnipeg already knew who Fina and Harry were; Linda remembered her great aunt's babushka, and Beth recalled how quiet her bearded "Uncle Richem" had been. But until my visit to Winnipeg, they hadn't known that their daughter Fanny—whose grave they had surely walked past many times on previous visits to this cemetery—was actually the biological child of their Uncle Dave and his first wife, Sarah.

Now they knew the whole story. I placed one more stone on her grave, and we headed back to the car.

Top: Fanny's gravestone; Bottom: the teapot

31: GOOD SPIRIT COUNTRY

As I entered Canora, Saskatchewan, I was greeted by Lesia, a fifteen-foot-high statue of a woman in traditional Ukrainian dress standing at the side of Route 10, holding a loaf of braided bread and a shaker of salt on a tray draped in fabric.

My great-grandfather David would never have seen Lesia. She was only erected in 1980 as a tribute to the town's Ukrainian community, who counted among the region's first settlers and remain a major demographic group today among Canora's two-thousand residents. But she was my welcome to this small prairie town a three-hour drive from Regina, the provincial capital of Saskatchewan, in the heart of what is now known as "Good Spirit Country."

I turned up Main Street, which was decorated with maple leaf flags in honor of the summer's upcoming celebration of one hundred and fifty years of Canadian independence: Here, in a month's time, a festival would feature jugglers, magicians, a petting zoo, and bands playing everything from rock to country to Ukrainian music. I saw just one familiar chain store: Tim Hortons, Canada's ubiquitous doughnut shop. Otherwise, Canora still looked like a small town untouched by the outside world; in some ways, it reminded me of Livingston Manor, the even smaller but less remote Catskills town where Mark and I have our house. There was a pizza parlor, a dollar store, a local bank, just like we have in the Catskills. But I also saw places that only made sense in

Canora: the outdoor ice cream stand that serves poutine, the Chinese restaurant that advertises its chili and pierogies in the window, the Ukrainian Heritage Museum.

At the end of Main Street, I parked in front of the Canora Hotel, which is more than a century old, and looks every minute of its age. This was a prominent building—a three-story brick block that today comprises eight guest rooms over a bar and restaurant—that my relatives would surely have known well. They would have arrived in Canora not by road, but by train, and as they exited the station, the first building they would have seen was this hotel, just across Railway Avenue. A hundred years ago, after a long day buying cattle on the ranches outside town, my great-grandfather and his brothers might have stopped for a drink in the street-level bar. My grandmother Ethel must have walked past it dozens of times in her childhood. Now, this was where I'd be spending the night.

When I was growing up, Winnipeg wasn't a place anyone in the family spoke of with warm nostalgia. But at least it was a place I knew was part of my family's history, a city I could potentially visit someday and find a personal connection. Canora, on the other hand—a town I never knew was connected to me, a town I'd never even heard of—was never part of the narrative. I could never have imagined I'd end up here.

I bet my grandmother Ethel felt the same way when she first arrived in 1916, a six-year-old girl in a five-year-old town. When she was little, Canora had been a place she'd only heard about, somewhere her father David used to go on long business trips— where he built a lucrative business with his brothers—while she stayed at home with her mother Sarah. Then, within a few years, her mother was killed, her father remarried, and the whole family uprooted itself and settled in Canora, where she'd spend half her childhood—the half she never discussed with her children and grandchildren decades later.

In Winnipeg, I had cousins to show me around and a list of places to visit; in Canora, I was on my own. I didn't have a list of houses to see, or even graves to leave a stone on. I had no relatives left there, not even distant ones; there aren't any Jews left in Canora at all, according to the most recent census. Soon after I arrived, however, I found people to help me discover my connection to this place.

Canora has a museum of local history, housed in its small train station. But I knew that when I arrived on the last day of May, the CN Station House Museum wouldn't yet be open for the season. That's why I had contacted Canora's community development officer Brandi Zavislak several weeks before my trip, to see if she could let me in when I arrived in town. "Tourism is one of my departments," she'd emailed me. "I will gladly meet you. Please call me when you arrive, or stop by the town office on Main Street. You won't have a hard time finding the town office."

She was right. The office was easy to find, three blocks from my hotel. The building takes up nearly a full block, with a big sign and small fountain out front.

Inside, I met Zavislak, a young woman with a warm smile. I explained my family's Canora connection. "My great-grandfather was a cattle dealer, and he used to come here for business more than a hundred years ago," I told her. "But one day, in 1913, while he was here for work, he got a telegram telling him that his wife, my great-grandmother, had been killed back in Winnipeg." I took a brief detour to tell Zavislak my standard story: the photo my mother found, the sniper story my grandmother told, the real story I'd discovered about the murder, the funeral, the police investigation. "But then he remarried, and the whole family moved to Canora full-time, and this is where my grandmother spent much of her childhood."

Zavislak seemed intrigued, particularly by the murder; this wasn't the kind of story she heard on a typical day, about this sleepy town's connection to a crime that made headlines across Canada.

Before we walked back up Main Street to the train station, she called Joy Stusek, the volunteer who runs the museum, and told her we were on our way. Then she called reporter Rocky Neufeld at the *Canora Courier*, and told him to meet us there.

In any small town, outsiders stand out. So as Zavislak and I walked the few blocks from the town office up to the train station, where the museum is located, cars would stop, and drivers would roll down their windows to ask her, "Hey, Brandi, who's that?" Everyone knew her, and nobody had ever seen me before. "He's a writer, from New York," she'd say. "He's here investigating a murder."

Neufeld was waiting for us when we arrived. Standing in the dirt lot in front of the station, he asked me about the murder and my family's history in Canora, scribbling notes in his reporter's notebook. Then he took my photo, with Main Street stretching out behind me in the background.

After my brief interview, Stusek unlocked the door to the museum and visitor information center and showed me around. Canora has the country's oldest Class 3 railway station still in operation, built in 1904 for five-thousand dollars. These days the VIA Rail trains only run twice a week to Winnipeg; the trip takes eight-and-a-half hours each way—a long ride, but shorter than the twelve-and-a-half hours it took my great-grandfather back in 1913 when he'd come here on business.

As I walked through the museum, I saw several exhibits on display: an eight-foot-tall Orange Crush bottle that was used to promote the brand's new clear soda bottles in the fifties, souvenir golf shirts and DVDs, and a poster touting Canora for winning a competition for the best-tasting municipal water in Canada. More along the lines of what I'd expected, there were train-related artifacts from the past hundred years. A quilt made during World War I commemorated the area's early homesteaders, and historical photos, where the Canora Hotel is readily recognizable, hung on the wall.

Looking at the black-and-white photos, I tried to figure out which house might have belonged to my family, but it was difficult to pinpoint exactly. "The 1916 census lists David and Bella as living on Third Street, but without a specific address," I told Stusek. "Louis and Bessie are listed at Second Avenue and Third Street." I explained that this was where they presumably lived until Louis burned the house down several years later; I told her about the notes I'd found in my cousin's teapot a couple of days earlier in Winnipeg. (The Lertzmans, who borrowed and thus saved Louis and Bessie's wedding tea set, lived on Railway Avenue, around the corner from David and Bella.) Stusek and I looked at the pictures, but we couldn't be sure which houses might have belonged to my relatives. Adding to the uncertainty, she explained, Canora's streets had been renumbered decades ago, so what is now Third Street was not where Third Street used to be. Nonetheless, even if I couldn't be sure of the exact buildings where anybody lived, I could see the style of houses that they likely lived in: two-story wooden homes. The kind a fire might easily destroy.

The museum was filled with curiosities that helped me understand Canora in a broad sense, but there wasn't much that connected me to my family's specific history—not the quilt, or the giant soda bottle, or the delicious tap water. And then I saw a small item on display that seemed quite old. "This is the train station's original telegraph," Stusek said.

I'd found a piece of my story. It was this very machine that transmitted the message to my great-grandfather back in 1913, telling him that his wife was dead, and he needed to return to Winnipeg at once.

It was just past noon on a Friday when he got the message. I imagine he was returning to town after spending the morning on the family farm a few miles away. Distraught, he probably packed a suitcase as quickly as he could before heading back up Main Street, past the Canora Hotel, to the train station. The next train to Winnipeg wasn't leaving until four fifty-five in the afternoon, so he had time for the news to sink in. Maybe he had a drink at the bar across the street. Maybe he sat silently for hours on a bench on the train platform, or asked the telegraph operator to send a message back to Winnipeg to say he was on his way. Or maybe, while he waited to begin his twelve-and-a-half-hour journey home, he stood in the sun in the dirt lot where I'd just had my photograph taken, staring down Main Street at this remote prairie town where one chapter of his life had just come to an abrupt end—and, a few years later, another chapter of his life would begin.

Canora's original telegraph

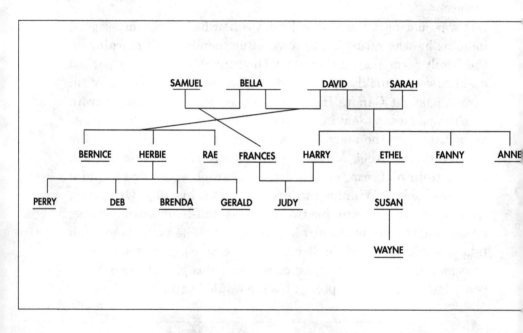

32: 'ZAYDE DIDN'T TELL STORIES'

My great-grandfather David was probably not a bootlegger—but his brothers almost certainly were. That's what my mother's cousin Judy told me over hot-and-sour soup.

I had tried unsuccessfully to reach Judy—whose father was Harry, my grandma Ethel's older brother—for a long time, before finally connecting by phone the previous autumn. But I only met her for the first time over dinner during my visit to Vancouver, right after I left Canora.

She was sharing her memories of David, her grandfather. When I mentioned the possibility that David and his brothers had been involved in illegal bootlegging—something that had come up in Winnipeg a few days earlier—Judy suggested that this rumor was partially true, and partially not. "My grandfather's brothers were in the liquor business and they were doing things that weren't legal," she said. "Their cattle business was legal, but they also set up the liquor business in the barns where they kept the cattle. They made a fortune."

This wasn't exactly a family secret at the time. "I asked my mom how come David's brothers were so wealthy," Judy said. "She said because they had done stuff that was illegal."

But the liquor business only involved David's brothers, she said: "David, my grandfather, who was as honest as can be, wouldn't get in with them."

That didn't exactly sound definitive to me. Of course, Judy wouldn't want to believe that her grandfather was a criminal; she'd been particularly close to him, living with him when she and her parents moved to Vancouver from Detroit when Judy was a little girl.

I told her about the vinegar company David ran with his brothers in Winnipeg, but she wasn't convinced he played any illicit role in it. His brothers may have been shady, but he'd left them behind when he moved from Winnipeg to Vancouver.

"From what I hear," Judy said, with the implicit reminder that she knew him better than anyone else I'd spoken to, "David wasn't involved."

I'd learn much more about my great-grandfather in Vancouver, on the last leg of my trip across western Canada. I had been there once before, some twenty-four years earlier. The skyline had changed since then: Gleaming residential and office towers crowded the waterfront, and several new skyscrapers had sprouted; the five tallest buildings in the city had all been constructed since my last visit. But this trip was novel for a more personal reason, too. Last time, I hadn't made any effort to dig into family history or meet relatives. This time would prove very different.

As soon as I arrived, I called my cousin Danny, who'd been so helpful in my research. We had never met, but Danny greeted me as if we'd always known each other. We were family.

He took me to his apartment, which has a marvelous view of the city's skyline. There he showed me family photos and official documents that he'd collected in binders over the years: birth certificates, death certificates. And as he showed me things, he told what he remembered about my great-grandfather. Danny is the grandson of David's sister Clara, so David—whom he referred to as Dave, just as the cousins in Winnipeg had done a few days earlier—was Danny's great-uncle.

David and Bella moved here from Winnipeg in 1947; Danny knew them when he grew up in Vancouver.

"He was a rough guy," Danny said of my great-grandfather, prone to temperamental outbursts. "I remember hearing Dave have a screaming argument over the phone, in Yiddish."

"Who was he arguing with?" I asked.

"His sister, Freydl," Danny said, using Fina's Yiddish name.

"What were they fighting about?"

"About who stole his false teeth," he said. "Then he stuck his hand in his bathrobe pocket and there they were."

That afternoon, Danny took me for a drive around the city, just as my cousin Linda had done in Winnipeg, so I could see where David and Bella used to live.

And, of course, we visited the Jewish cemeteries. David and Bella are buried side-by-side in Schara Zedek, with matching tombstones—broad and black, with gently rounded tops. ("In memory of a beloved wife and mother," says hers; "In memory of a beloved father and grandfather," says his.) Danny quickly found the grave for his grandmother, David's sister Clara. Two of David and Bella's kids are there, too: my grandmother Ethel's younger siblings Bernice and Herbie. Two more of her siblings, Harry and Frances, are buried at Beth Israel, which we also visited. I left stones on the graves, just as I had done in Winnipeg earlier that week.

But in Vancouver, I found as many living relatives as dead ones. When Danny drove me to a Chinese restaurant that night to meet Judy, I thought we'd have a small dinner for the three of us; I didn't realize they had invited more cousins for me to meet. So instead of a little gathering, we had something bigger. And better.

There were nine of us in all: Danny had asked his brother Tommy; they were both my mother's second cousins. Judy, my mother's first cousin, brought her husband. My grandmother Ethel's baby brother Herbie had four children—also my mother's first cousins; three of them lived in Vancouver, and all three of them joined us: Deb, Brenda (with her husband), and Gerald.

We sat around a large round table with a white tablecloth. As we ate family-style, sharing soup and noodles and stir-fried vegetables on a glass lazy susan, I told everyone about my trip to Canora and Winnipeg, and the cousins I'd met; the Winnipeg cousins and these Vancouver cousins didn't know each other.

As had been the case in Winnipeg, I wasn't the only one learning things: I had stories to share with them as well. Herbie's kids didn't know much about my grandma Ethel, whom they called Aunt Ettie. So I told them about Ethel, and my aunt Marilyn's family, and my own parents and brother and sister. I also told them about Fanny, their father's sister; they'd never heard about her, which didn't surprise me since she had already been adopted by her aunt and uncle by the time Herbie was born, and she died when Herbie was just four years old. And I told them the story of Sarah's murder—both the sniper legend my grandmother and mother had told, and the true story I'd since discovered in my research. This was also not a family story they'd learned from David, their grandfather.

In return, they shared stories about the family, most of which centered on David. Even though Herbie's kids and Judy are all my mother's first cousins, they're a generation apart: Herbie was my grandmother's baby brother, while Judy's father Harry was my grandmother's older brother—sixteen years Herbie's senior. They all know each other and see each other for family occasions, but their memories sometimes differ because of this generational difference; the grandfather Judy remembered as "stern" and "not lovey dovey" ("He was never an affectionate man as far as I could see," she told me) had mellowed into a slightly warmer grandfather by the time Herbie's kids were born.

Deb, Brenda, and Gerald had vivid memories of their grandfather—they all called him Zayde, just as my mother always had. When they were children, they'd visit David at his house—or later, at the Louis Brier Home, a Jewish nursing home in Vancouver. "I remember him as a grumpy old guy," Deb told me, "but then my dad was a grumpy old guy, a glass-half-empty kind of person."

Deb had some fond memories of David nonetheless: "I remember him giving us chocolate. My dad explained that chocolate was rationed during the war, so Zayde felt it was a very big treat to give the children every week." Other times, David would come to Herbie's house to see the kids. He'd ask them to play piano, even though they couldn't manage much beyond "Twinkle Twinkle Little Star." ("None of us were in any way talented," Deb told me.) He wouldn't eat at their house, because it wasn't a kosher home, but he'd drink tea—in a glass mug, with sugar cubes.

They all remarked on his accent, and the fact that he always felt more comfortable in Yiddish than in English, even after spending most of his life in Canada. "My Zayde talked to my dad in Yiddish," Gerald said, adding that David spoke to his grandchildren in English—but "not very good English."

Brenda remembered one physical detail: "He had huge hands and a cane," she told me.

None of them remembered Bella, who died when Deb was an infant, before Brenda and Gerald were born. But Brenda, who was named in Bella's memory, heard many stories about how her grandmother was the "center of the family," and "a fantastic cook" in particular. "It's a tradition in the family that was very important to my parents," she said about being named for a relative who'd died. "It's a way of remembering people who are gone."

Sarah's murder wasn't something the family discussed when they were growing up. "I imagine it was painful to talk about," said Brenda.

Even when things weren't painful, David wasn't big on sharing his memories: "Zayde didn't tell stories," said Deb. "The family was kind of secretive. Looking back, they probably were worried that people would judge."

Dinner stretched on for hours, as we swapped stories. Before we all went our separate ways afterward, we took a family photo in front of the Chinese restaurant. Everyone in the picture is smiling. But the one with the biggest smile is me, standing in the middle of a line of newfound family members.

33: THE CULPRITS

After I returned to New York, I flipped through my notes again, to see how the things I'd discovered in Winnipeg, Canora, and Vancouver fit into what I'd already known about my great-grandmother's murder. By this point, I knew the basics quite well; I'd been researching the case, and telling stories about it, for years.

In the early hours of Friday, August 1, 1913, someone came into my great-grandparents' house, most likely unlocking the front door with a key. After entering the rear bedroom, where my great-grandmother Sarah lay sleeping—her two-year-old daughter Fanny by her side in bed, baby Anne in the crib nearby—the killer put a .32 caliber pistol to her right temple and pulled the trigger. She died instantly, making no noise or struggle to awaken the children. Without taking any of the valuables off the bedroom bureau, the murderer left through the front door and vanished into the night, leaving nothing but a pack of Russian matches and a series of unanswered questions. When the police arrived, they found the keys to the front door missing; they mysteriously reappeared a few days later, after police allowed the house to be opened to visitors on the day of Sarah's funeral.

These were the facts. I'd gone over them for years.

But this time, as I reviewed my notes and all the newspaper articles I'd collected, I saw things I hadn't noticed before. And this time, I came up with a new hypothesis about who killed Sarah Feinstein. And whereas the first time I'd gone through the evidence, I thought the most suspicious character was Abram Schurman—the young man who was waiting for an uncle who never arrived, and happened to be staying next door at the exact moment the murder happened—this time my suspicions fell elsewhere.

Within hours of the murder, investigators had a working theory. Sarah's former hired girl Mary Manastaka and her boyfriend Stefan Kushowsky were the leading suspects, and Sarah's current hired girl Victoria Komanowska was also a person of interest. Police arrested Mary and Victoria on the spot, and put out a warrant for Stefan, who turned himself in two days later.

Their theory was that Sarah had fired Mary because she didn't approve of Stefan, a railway worker. Police believed that Mary, disgruntled after being rudely dismissed, had come back to the house to urge Victoria to quit as well. Her motive wasn't strictly personal; Mary, they believed, was an anti-Semite. Canada should get rid of its Jews, she told Victoria—and at the very least, gentiles shouldn't lower themselves to working for Jews.

Hearing that, Sarah pushed Mary off the veranda. Insulted and embarrassed, Mary swore revenge. And it was Stefan, police believed, who carried out Mary's plan, sneaking into the house in the middle of the night and putting a bullet through Sarah's head.

There was ample motive to back up this theory: Mary, who already held anti-Semitic beliefs, was furious that Sarah had fired her, and even more livid after being physically pushed off the veranda. And there was opportunity: Mary, who had worked in the Feinstein home, knew where the spare keys were kept. Stefan could have used that key to enter the house and carry out the crime. Victoria's role was more ambiguous, but police guessed that she may have played some role in the murder itself, perhaps slipping a key to Mary or leaving the front door unlocked.

The entire theory collapsed shortly after Stefan turned himself in. It turned out that Mary Manastaka had never worked for the Feinsteins; she worked for a neighbor a few doors down on Magnus Avenue. As for Stefan, he was at work in the rail yards at the time of the murder; he had an alibi.

Rather than questioning their grand theory of the crime, however, police stuck with the theory that the Feinsteins' neighbors had proposed to them—a former employee named Mary had been fired and sworn revenge—and looked for a different suspect: Mary Platak, a different young woman who had, in fact, once worked for the Feinsteins. Police found her, but after questioning they concluded that Mary Platak bore no malice toward her former employer, and hence had no motive to kill her. Both Marys were released, as was Stefan. Victoria was held for a few more weeks while police followed leads around other suspects: a mysterious man whom she claimed to have seen scraping at the window, an unnamed youth being held on other charges in the boys' ward of the jail, and Abram Schurman, the unemployed young man who'd been staying at the neighbors' house the night of the murder. But she was ultimately also let go without being charged.

Rumors about secret societies and jilted lovers in the Old Country made for good copy once the newspapers had run out of specific suspects. But none of these stories seemed to go anywhere.

As I pored over newspaper reports about the case, particularly the inquest, I started to think that the police had been right from the very start, and had only gotten thrown off the trail because of a case of mistaken identity.

From the outset, police believed that there was a single person named Mary who fit the entire profile they were looking for: a former employee with anti-Semitic beliefs who swore revenge on Sarah. Mary Manastaka turned out not to be a former employee; Mary Platak had never sworn revenge. Since neither fit the complete profile, police seemed stumped.

But what if rather than trying and failing to fit each Mary into a single overarching narrative, the police had understood from the beginning that they were two different women? They might have understood that neighbors, journalists, and detectives had conflated two stories—only one of which was relevant to the crime—and thus led police to look for a woman who didn't really exist.

Mary Platak, who actually was Sarah's former servant, is clearly innocent; she left on good terms, bore no grudge against Sarah, and had gone to work at a restaurant in a different neighborhood. Her only offense, it seemed, was that she was named Mary.

Mary Manastaka is another matter. It's true; she never worked for the Feinsteins. But the rest of the case against her still stands. And if police had only understood that the suspect was not necessarily a former employee, as they initially believed, they might have realized that Mary Manastaka was almost certainly at the center of the crime. And Stefan and Victoria were her likely accomplices.

Going back over the newspaper reports, I tried to separate gossip from information that seemed more credible.

Mary Manastaka worked three doors down from the Feinsteins, for the Hershfields, at 526 Magnus Avenue. But she certainly knew Sarah Feinstein.

One week before the murder, Mary Manastaka quarreled with Sarah at the Feinsteins' house; she admitted as much herself at the inquest. The nature of the quarrel is uncertain: Some neighbors said that Mary was trying to convince Victoria to stop working for Jews—which may sound odd, considering that Mary worked for a Jewish family, too, but perhaps she wanted to leave her employers as well, and wanted to enlist Victoria to take a stand with her. She had argued further that Canada should get rid of its Jews just as Russia had done; that's why the newspapers cited "anti-Semitic feeling" as a likely motive in their initial reports. Regardless of what exactly the argument was about, according to people who claimed to have witnessed the exchange, Sarah shoved Mary off the veranda, at which point Mary swore revenge.

After such a violent interaction, it might seem surprising that Mary had been back in the house since that fight, and more than once. But she came to take Sarah's baby, Anne, out for a walk, as she testified at the inquest—although it's unclear whether Sarah or Victoria had invited her to do so, or if Mary had volunteered. And she also came by the house again two days before the murder, as she also testified, to chat with Victoria.

On the night of the murder, Mary testified, she came home alone to the Hershfields' house at nine in the evening. But a couple of hours later, she went out again: As the Feinsteins' neighbor Lucy Kesler testified, Mary and Stefan walked by while Lucy and Sarah were sitting out front on the veranda around eleven o'clock. After Mary and Stefan had passed, Sarah confided in Lucy that Mary had looked at her funny, "as if she'd never seen me before."

That was one of the last things Sarah would ever say. A few hours later, she'd be dead.

What had Sarah meant when she said Mary looked at her "as if she'd never seen me before"? Had she been expecting a nasty glare, residual resentment from the previous week's fight, and instead found blank neutrality in Mary's eyes? Or had she been expecting a more congenial kind of recognition since they'd moved past that argument—after Mary paid two more visits without apparent acrimony—and instead found a distant coolness? What was Mary thinking, and was it written on her face for Sarah to see?

Mary Manastaka, as far as I could tell, had two good motives for hating Sarah: One was general—anti-Semitism. This wasn't unique to her; attacks against Jews, even physically violent ones, were commonplace at the time, even in the North End's "New Jerusalem." And the other was personal, since Sarah had argued with her and shoved her off her veranda, whether the argument itself was about Jews or Mary's boyfriend or simply the fact that Mary was keeping Victoria from doing her work.

Mary certainly had the opportunity to commit the crime, since she lived just a few doors down, and apparently—unlike Victoria, who claimed she never left the house alone—was sometimes out of the house late at night. (The Hershfields didn't have any children yet, I learned by checking census reports, so she would have been freer in her downtime.) She may not have known where the Feinsteins' house keys were kept, but she certainly could have found out from Victoria when she came over two days before the murder, or she may have spotted them herself when she came to pick up Anne, whose crib was in the rear bedroom, where the spare keys lay in plain sight.

She may also have been the one to return the missing key. At first I'd discounted this possibility: Police assumed the key had been returned to its usual place—on the bureau in the rear bedroom—before the funeral on Sunday morning, when hordes of people came into the house to pay respects. Mary was still in jail, so she couldn't have returned the key at that time, and since detectives believed the person who had the key had committed the crime, that would seem to absolve Mary. But police may have been wrong in their assumptions. The murder took place early on Friday morning, and when police arrived, the keys were gone. They were still missing on Saturday, when David returned to Winnipeg from Canora and police questioned him about them.

Then came the funeral on Sunday morning, when the cordon was lifted and many people filled the house—including David, who may well have noticed if the keys had reappeared on his bureau; Sunday afternoon, the cordon resumed. But after that, it was only on Tuesday afternoon that the police found the keys on the bureau, so they might have been returned any time between Sunday afternoon and Tuesday afternoon, a time when the house was empty, because David and the children were staying down the street with David's brother Harry and his wife Pauline. Victoria was in jail this whole time, so she couldn't have returned the keys. But Mary was released from police custody at five o'clock Sunday afternoon, and sent home to the house where she worked, three doors down from the crime scene. Since Mary was often free to go out on her own late at night, she could well have sneaked past the cordon and back into Sarah's house, using the key to gain entry. This would have been possible Sunday night or Monday night, at any hour when the house was empty and police were not on the scene.

Mary was also certainly aware of another vital piece of information: that Sarah's husband David was hundreds of miles away on business. He'd already been gone when she'd had her quarrel with Sarah a week before the murder, and he was still gone when she'd come to take Anne for a walk, and when she stopped by to chat with Victoria (who surely knew when David planned to return to Winnipeg), and when she walked by the night of the murder itself. For anyone hoping to kill Sarah, knowing when David was out of town would be crucial to planning the right time to do it.

As for Stefan, he told police that Mary wasn't really his girl-friend, that they were mere acquaintances. But that also didn't bear much scrutiny.

The proprietress at Feinman's confectionery store, around the corner from the Feinsteins' house, had seen them together enough times to know that Stefan and Mary were connected. When Stefan stopped in the store the afternoon after the murder, and asked what the commotion was about on Magnus Avenue, she told him that Sarah had been killed. When Stefan asked if anyone had been arrested, she told him: "Mrs. Feinstein's girl, and the one that used to come here with you." Meaning: Victoria and Mary Manastaka.

When he turned himself in to police two days later, Stefan said he had only been out with Mary a few times. But he doesn't seem to have mentioned that one of those "few times" had been just hours before the murder, when the couple walked past the Feinsteins' house around eleven o'clock and Mary gave Sarah a strange look. (That wasn't just a casual late-night stroll, either; a neighbor told reporters she'd seen Mary with a man—presumably Stefan—behaving amorously a block away on Magnus Avenue an hour later, around midnight.) Mary and Stefan had clearly done more than go for a walk or share a soda from the confectionery shop. They'd gone to a professional photo studio together, where they'd had a picture taken; Stefan had dressed up as a cowboy, borrowing a costume the photographer set aside for gag photos. Mary had kept the photo in her room.

None of the detectives had ever suggested that a woman had actually pulled the trigger when Sarah was killed; such things were extraordinarily rare. But it's entirely possible that a woman had convinced her boyfriend to pull the trigger. Had Mary convinced Stefan to do her dirty work?

He certainly had more access to a gun than Mary or Victoria did, whether he bought it, borrowed it, or stole it. As a single man living alone in a room in a boarding house, he had more privacy than either of the women, who lived in their employers' homes, so it would have been easier for him to hide the gun prior to the crime. And after the crime, his job in the rail yards provided even more potential places to dispose of the gun, which was never found.

If Stefan was the murderer, it could also explain the missing key—the period between its disappearance and its reappearance. Police searched Mary Manastaka's room on Friday before they took her into custody, and didn't find the key there. But they never searched Stefan's home. It's entirely possible that Stefan, after getting the key from Mary and using it to enter the house and commit the murder, stashed the key in his own home, or somewhere else, and gave it back to Mary after they were both exonerated on Sunday. That would explain why the key wasn't found during a search of Mary's room on Friday—and yet she might have had the key back in her possession again after being freed from jail on Sunday, so that she could return it to the bureau before Tuesday's inquest, throwing the entire investigation into disarray.

Stefan had been released from custody after providing an alibi—that he'd been working at the rail yards that night. But it's easy enough to believe that Stefan could have slipped away unnoticed long enough to commit the crime in the middle of an overnight shift; Magnus Avenue was just seven blocks away. Or that he could have convinced a co-worker to cover for him.

What about Victoria? I also wasn't convinced that she played no role in my great-grandmother's death. Police had incarcerated her for a solid month—they even held her for two weeks after the inquest ended—so they must have also had serious suspicions. I didn't believe that she committed the murder herself: The idea that a seventeen-year-old girl would murder a woman in front of her children seemed far-fetched. And then there's the matter of the gun: Where would Victoria, who was never out of Sarah's sight, have obtained a gun, and where could she have hidden it in the few minutes between the shooting and the arrival of the Feinstein children, and the neighbors, and then two doctors and more than twenty police officers, on the scene?

It seemed more plausible to me that Victoria may have passed a spare key to someone else, and may have provided the killer information about when David would be out of town. And who else could Victoria—who, again, was rarely out of Sarah's sight—have passed the keys to? The only likely suspect is Mary Manastaka, who'd visited with Victoria at least twice in the week leading up to the murder.

Why would Victoria consent? It remains unclear to me. Perhaps she shared Mary's anti-Semitic feelings. Maybe Mary threatened to harm her if she didn't cooperate, or bribed her with promises of money if she did. Or perhaps Victoria had her own personal animus toward her employer. She never had a day off, and never left the house without her, so she was basically on duty twenty-four hours a day. She didn't have the opportunity to go on dates with men, the way her friend Mary Manastaka did. (Victoria was far freer to go on dates after her employer had been killed; she was married the following July, ten months after being released from jail.) Sarah even tried to limit the time she spent with other hired girls—pushing her friend Mary off the veranda, for instance.

Victoria, it seemed to me, may have been lying about one important detail. She was the only one who'd ever claimed to see the mysterious man scratching at the window—and even she said she hadn't ever seen his face, so she couldn't identify him. David testified that he had heard about the man at the window—but he'd heard from his wife Sarah, who'd heard from Victoria. Nobody else claimed to have actually seen him, and Victoria offered no concrete details of her own, and the newspapers didn't hear about this development until the inquest, more than two weeks after the murder. Perhaps he was fabricated by Victoria as she and Mary hatched their plot, to throw police off the trail. Or perhaps the man at the window was Stefan, and Victoria was fearful of identifying him and thus implicating herself.

Soon after Sarah Feinstein's murder, the police took three people into custody: Mary Manastaka, who had motive; Victoria, who could assist from the inside; and Stefan, who was more likely than either woman to actually pull the trigger.

All of them had been released. But now, more than a century later, I came to believe that the police had been right from the very start of the investigation. All three of them, I concluded, were involved. Only Victoria could help the killer gain access to the house—by providing a key, or leaving a door unlocked—and assist in planning the perfect time, when David would be out of town. Mary, who had the strongest reason to plan the crime in the first place, is the only one who would plausibly have returned the key. And Stefan is the only one of the three who could have readily obtained a gun, hidden it, and disposed of it.

The three of them, I now believe, were in cahoots. It was Mary's plan, which Victoria helped facilitate, and Stefan actually carried out.

Years earlier, I would have phoned my mother to share my theory: Finally, I could explain what probably happened to her grandmother. But my mother was beyond phone calls and murder mysteries by this point. She was even beyond family itself.

34: GRANDMA

When my Grandma Ethel died in 1983, my mother inherited dozens of old family photos. But my grandmother had never put them
in an album. Instead, the loose snapshots were stuffed, mostly un-
labeled, into a plastic shopping bag, which ended up on a shelf in
our linen closet.

At some point, during my mother's years struggling with Alzheimer's, that bag disappeared. She may have moved it somewhere
else—either intentionally, or because she forgot where it belonged.
She probably packed it into a suitcase one morning, on one of the
days when she was certain her mother was coming to pick her up;
perhaps in the unpacking, my father moved it. Or maybe someone—my mother, my father, the housekeeper who comes every
other week—threw the unremarkable plastic bag in the garbage
by mistake.

I still had the photo of David and Sarah, my great-grandparents,
taken on their wedding day in 1906—the photo my mother found
as a child, which said "Sarah Brooks" on the back. Most of the rest
of my grandmother's old family photos had gone missing before I
ever took that trip to meet my cousins—people who might have
finally been able to identify the people and places in grandma Ethel's pictures. But my cousins gave me photos of their own, dating
all the way back to a family portrait taken in a photo studio in
1922, the girls wearing dresses with bows in their hair; my aunt

Marilyn gave me more from her collection.

Together with the few I already had, I could start to piece togeth-er a family photo album—the kind my Grandma Ethel had never managed to organize out of her plastic bag of loose snapshots.

My cousins Joe and Susan Diane didn't have many old family pho-tos, because their mother Anne had burned most of them years before she died, telling her kids, "You don't know these people any-way." But one very important photo survived.

I'd learned about it from Joe's daughter Sara, who'd been named in memory of our great-grandmother. When we'd spoken on the phone, Sara told me about bringing a photograph of Sarah Fein-stein to class when she was in middle school, doing a report on family history. Anne, her grandmother, had given it to her.

"There was this picture, on a piece of white card paper," Sara told me. "It looked like a bookmark. I took it to school once and brought it back very carefully, because I was told all hell would break loose."

When I went to San Francisco to meet these cousins, they showed me the original. It is just as Sara described it, a sepia-tone print on a vertical strip of card stock. An embossed stamp indicates that it was produced by CBW Photographers in Winnipeg, likely as a me-morial memento after she was killed. A note on the back, in Anne's cursive handwriting, reads: "My mother. Sarah Brooks."

The image is a cropped version of the original wedding photo, which photographer William A. Martel had taken shortly before closing his North End shop in 1906: David has been cut out of the picture, which only includes Sarah's face and upper body, fading into whiteness just below her shoulders. Her hair is pulled up and back, revealing an oval face that—more than I ever noticed years before—definitely resembles my mother.

In August 2017, two months after my trip across Canada, Mark and I drove down to Maryland to visit my mother on a Saturday morning. It was the first time we'd seen her since she moved that summer into her new home in Potomac.

She didn't seem to recognize me. By this point, I didn't expect her to. She hadn't really recognized me for a couple of years. She had entered the final phase of Alzheimer's, the "severe" phase, which can still last several years; she had trouble sitting up without assistance, she wore an adult diaper at all times, and her verbal communication had been largely reduced to the occasional word or phrase.

We sat and talked with her. Or perhaps it's more accurate to say that we said things to her; she occasionally responded with wide eyes or a nod, and other times looked around the room as if she didn't know we were there at all. Only rarely did she utter any words in response. More often, if there was a moment of silence, she'd say, "Okay, let's go," and start moving toward the front door. Whether she thought we'd take her home with us, or whether she intended to leave us there while she walked out the front door alone, we weren't sure.

But photos often brought a glimmer of light to her eyes. I showed her a black-and-white photo my cousin Deb had sent, of my grandmother Ethel with my great-grandfather David at Vancouver International Airport in 1954.

David was in his mid-seventies, nearly fifty years older than he was in the wedding photo my mother had once found in a drawer, where he posed with his wife Sarah. In the older photo, from 1906, David had a starched collar and a tie, a trimmed moustache, and a full head of dark hair. In the later photo from Vancouver, he was dressed more casually: wearing a loose sport coat over an open-collared white oxford, one hand in his pants pocket pulling back the jacket enough to reveal his suspenders. A white fedora, a bit askew, covered his balding head, and glasses with hexagonal frames sat atop his nose. He was smiling slightly.

"Do you know who that is?" I asked my mother, pointing to the man.

"Dovid," she answered, using the Yiddish name she had always used for her grandfather. She recognized him immediately, just as she had nearly seventy years earlier when she'd found the photo of him with an unfamiliar woman in a drawer.

In the photo from 1906, David's new bride Sarah stood by his side. In the photo from 1954, David stood next to Ethel, his oldest daughter, who was forty-four at the time. One of Ethel's hands was hooked through her father's elbow, while the other held the pocketbook that surely contained a pack of chewing gum, the one treat she had permitted her daughters—my mother and my aunt Marilyn—on that day's first-class transcontinental flight to Vancouver.

She wore glasses, which I remembered from her later years when she lived in our house. But her hair in the photo was dark; I had only ever seen her with gray hair.

"And who's this?" I asked my mother, pointing to Ethel.

"Grandma," she said.

I was caught off-guard by the fact that she answered at all. It was the longest conversation we'd had, back and forth, all afternoon. Even just a few words were remarkable.

Then I was impressed that she could identify the people in the photo, a picture from more than sixty years ago—including her grandfather, whom she'd only met a few times. Such moments of lucidity were rare by this point.

It was only after I left that I grasped the most significant thing about her answer.

"Grandma."

It wasn't a name my mother had ever used for anyone. She called her own grandmother Bubbe. And she called her mother Mommy. Or Mom. ("Where's Mom?" had been the question she first asked me on Yom Kippur years earlier, at the moment where I finally understood the grip Alzheimer's had on her; "Where's Mom?" was the question she would ask over and over in the years that followed, as she waited by the front door for her mother to pick her up.) She also might refer to her occasionally as "my mother" or, if it seemed more appropriate to use her name, Ethel.

But Grandma isn't a name she ever called her mother, Ethel; Grandma is what *I* called Ethel. By referring to Ethel as Grandma, my mother had indicated not only that she recognized the woman in the photo, but that she also recognized me. It was an implicit acknowledgment that she knew who I was, even if she couldn't express it, or remember my name. I had not lost her completely—or, rather, she had not lost me. Not yet.

Alzheimer's had pushed us inexorably apart for years, and yet we had come together for one more moment—a moment that echoed so many others from my childhood, sitting side-by-side on a couch, looking at old photos, as my mother told me stories about our family history. Only now, the photos were mine. And so, too, at last, were the stories.

David and Ethel at the Vancouver airport in 1954

A family portrait from 1922. From the left: Ethel, Harry, Rae, Bernice, Frances, Anne. (Fanny has already gone to live with her aunt and uncle, and Herbie has not been born yet.) A dressmaker before getting married, Bella was a skilled seamstress. She would go to Winnipeg's department stores to see the latest ladies' fashions, and then replicate them for her daughters.

Winnipeg, June 1938. In the back, from the left: Anne, David,
Bernice, Frances. In front: Herbie and Rae.
A few weeks later, Anne got married—at the house on Mountain
Avenue where my grandmother Ethel grew up;
Rabbi Israel Isaac Kahanovitch, who had officiated at Anne's moth-
er Sarah's funeral in 1913, conducted the ceremony.

David and Bella in Winnipeg in the mid-1940s, right around
the time my mother went for a childhood visit, before they
left the city's winters behind and moved to Vancouver.

Posing in front of Bernice's new Pontiac Firebird convertible,
outside Herbie's house in Vancouver, 1969.
From left: Bernice, David, Ethel, Frances.
This is the last photo I have of David, who died in 1971.

At my brother's bar mitzvah in Maryland in April 1977.
From left: Ethel, Rae, Anne, Frances, Bernice.
It was the last time the sisters would all be together.

Sarah's memorial card

A NOTE ON SOURCES

This is a work of non-fiction; every detail I have included has a source to back it up, as much as possible.

But that does not mean it is without potential inaccuracies, however unintentional.

In the sections set a century ago, I have relied on official documents and newspaper reports for every quote and fact I cite. But as I've explained, these sources are not infallible, or even entirely consistent. When details in certain documents and newspaper reports conflict with details in other sources, I've used my best judgment as a journalist to determine which is most likely the more accurate source. Which is to say: There may be sources that contain certain facts that differ from the ones I've presented here, but I haven't presented any facts that don't have reasonably reliable sources to back them up.

In the sections from the more recent past, my sources fall into three main categories: There are interviews, dozens of them, that I've conducted in the course of writing this book, and those interviews are quoted verbatim; the same goes for facts I've discovered first-hand during my research—they're all backed up with supporting evidence. Then there are conversations and events that I've reconstructed from my personal memory—incidents that occurred in my childhood, or even in more recent years; these I've reconstructed to the best of my ability, with the knowledge that my own memory is not perfect, nor without its own biases. Lastly, there are my memories of other people's memories: me remembering a story my mother told me about what she remembered. These are the least reliably accurate and the most subjective: I'm confident, for instance, that my father has different recollections about many things I describe—both incidents he experienced first-hand, often before I was born, and stories he also heard second-hand from my mother but remembers differently. He may have a more direct experience of what his trip to Paris with my mother was like, or what their friends in Chicago said to them, or how my mother told her friend Honey about meeting him on a blind date, and he may remember it differently than I've presented it; but what matters to me, here, is how I remember my mother describing it. This is, after all, a book about memory—my mother's, and my own.

My mother and me, at my nephew David's bar mitzvah, 2006

ACKNOWLEDGMENTS

First, thanks to those who helped turn this story into a book: my publisher Naomi Rosenblatt and my agent Mitchell Waters. And thanks to Susan Shapiro and Don Cummings for their advice.

My family has listened to these stories for many years, and helped me recall many details along the way: my parents Susan and Martin Hoffman, and my siblings Stacey and Scott Hoffman. My aunt, Marilyn Liebling, was also a key to recalling things that my mother had since forgotten.

This book expanded my family in many ways, and introduced me to many cousins I'd never met or known, and they've all broadened my family knowledge, with unexpected generosity and openness. In Vancouver, my thanks to Judy Weiss, Danny Gelmon, Tommy Gelmon, Deb Collins, Brenda Greczimel, Gerald Fainstein, Perry (and Judy) Fainstein, Rita Taylor, and Neil Parker. In Winnipeg, thanks to Beth Goldenberg, Lisa Fainstein, Linda (and Elliott) Katz, and Jeff Shector. And elsewhere—from California to Ontario to Nairobi—thanks to Barb Fain, Betty Fain, Susan (and Ron) Rau, Joe (and Toni) Friedman, Sara Friedman, Tara Fainstein, Bob Brooks, and Larry Gelmon.

Then there are my mother's friends, who have always been part of her family—and mine—and who shared so many stories and showed my mother so much kindness, before and after her diagnosis: Doris Herman, Helen Abrahams, Carole and Arnie

Felberbaum, and Phil and Bibi Feintuch.

And many, many others who helped with my research, often going above and beyond what I'd asked for: Allan Levine, Bernie Bellan, Stan Carbone, Ava Block-Super, Andrew Morrison, Louis Kessler, Lynn Roseman, Bill Croydon, Ross Read, James Ham, Jack Templeman, Leif Larsen, Ismaila Alfa, and Sari Fields in Winnipeg; Brandi Savislak, Joy Stusek, Rocky Neufeld, Sharon Gerein, and Garth Materie in Saskatchewan; Anna Zanardo in Toronto; Lewis Rendell in Halifax; Elinor Ginzler, Colleen Kemp, and Jim Brigl in Maryland; and Chana Pollack in New York.

And finally, thanks to my husband, Mark Sullivan, who has been with me on this journey the whole time.

Photo © 2021 Frank Mullaney

ABOUT THE AUTHOR

Wayne Hoffman's cultural reporting has appeared in the *Wall Street Journal, Washington Post, The Forward, Village Voice, The Nation, Billboard,* Slate, and dozens of other publications; he is currently executive editor of Tablet magazine. His novels include *Hard, An Older Man,* and *Sweet Like Sugar*—winner of the American Library Association's Stonewall Book Award. He lives in New York City and the Catskills. **www.waynehoffmanwriter.com**